Medium format photography

Medium Format Photography

Ernst Wildi

Focal Press
Boston   London

Focal Press is an imprint of Butterworth Publishers.

Library of Congress Cataloging-in-Publication Data

Wildi, Ernst.
  Medium format photography.

  Includes index.
  1. Medium format cameras. 2. Photography—Handbooks, manuals, etc. I. Title.
TR257.W55 1987   770'.28'22   86–4852
ISBN 0–240–51719–9

Butterworth Publishers
80 Montvale Avenue
Stoneham, MA 02180

10 9 8 7 6 5 4 3

Printed in the United States of America

Contents

Preface   xi

1   The History of Medium Format   **1**

2   The Medium Format Advantage   **13**

Image sharpness   13 | Image evaluation   15 |
Ground-glass screen   17 | Cropping   19 | Film
changing   20 | Instant photography   21 |
Shutters   21 | Camera size and operation   22

3   Sizes   **25**

Selecting the format   25 | Comparing formats   38 |
Image sharpness   38 | Other medium formats   39 |
35 mm in the medium format camera   41

4   Camera Types   **43**

Single lens reflex   43 | Twin lens reflex   49 |
Rangefinders   53 | Wide angle cameras   54 |
Panoramic cameras   56 | Press cameras   58 |
View cameras   58 | Studio cameras   59 |
Manufacturers   59

5   Shutters   **69**

Focal plane shutters   69 | Lens shutters   73 |
Operating considerations   75

6 Films   77

*Black-and-white film 77 | Color negative film 80 |
Color transparency film 82 | Film roll 83 |
Sheetfilm 87 | Instant film 88 | Loading
film 95 | Operating signals 99*

7 Lenses   101

*Lens cost 101 | Focal length 103 | Angle of
view 103 | Area coverage 106 | Covering
power 108 | Long telephotos at close range 108 |
Maximum aperture 108 | True telephoto 109 |
Retrofocus lenses 109 | Floating lens
element 110 | Lens names 111 |
Teleconverters (extenders) 111 | Lens aberrations 113 |
Partial close-up lenses 287 | Extension tubes and
Multicoating 118 | Lens shades 119 | Relative
illuminance 122 | Color rendition 122 |
Distortion 123 | Zoom lenses 126 | Fish-eye
lenses 128 | Filters and sunshades 128*

8 Lenses and the Image   129

*Perspective 130 | Viewing distance 131 |
Foreshortening 135 | Selective backgrounds 135 |
Verticals 137 | Lens control 140 | Creating
images with zoom lenses 140 | Fish-eye lens
photography 143 | Depth of field 144 | Hyperfocal
distance 147 | Creative use of lens aperture 147 |
Manual diaphragm stop-down 149 | Action and
shutter speed 149*

9 Seeing the Image   155

*Parallax 155 | Rangefinder focusing 156 | Twin
lens versus single reflex 156 | Screens 158 |
Viewfinders 163 | The image 171 | Leveling the
camera 174 | Composing the image 175*

10 Exposure   179

*Aperture 179 | Shutter speed 180 | Exposure
values 180 | Film sensitivity 182 | Estimating lens*

settings   183 | Exposure meters   184 | Gray
card   195 | Palm readings   197 | Flesh tone
readings   197 | What to expose for   198 |
Bracketing   200 | Special effects accessories   201 |
Other uses of meters and gray cards   201 | Subject
brightness range   202 | Typical subjects and measuring
methods   203 | Double and multiple exposures   204

11   Electronic Flash   **213**

Flash synchronization   213 | Portable flash
units   214 | Flash firing failures   215 | Ready
light   215 | Flash unit size   216 | Batteries   216 |
Light output and guide numbers   216 | Covering
power   217 | Determining aperture   218 | Power
ratio   218 | Filters   219 | Shutter speed   219 |
Ghost images   221 | Modeling lights   222 |
Automatic flash   222 | Energy-saving circuits   225 |
Flash exposure   226 | Indirect and bounced
flash   228 | Automatic flash units in indirect
light   229 | Combining flash and daylight   231 |
Fill-in automatic flash   232 | Changing the lighting
ratio with automatic flash   233 | Fill-in manual
flash   233 | Changing exposure   234 | Flash as an
accent light   236

12   Filters and the Image   **239**

Filters as lens protection   239 | Neutral density
filters   239 | Filters for black-and-white
photography   241 | Combining filters   242 |
Exposure increase   242 | Haze penetration: Haze,
UV, and skylight filters   243 | Color quality of
light   244 | Light balance and conversion
filters   245 | Decamired filter system   246 | Color-
compensating filters   246 | Fluorescent lights   247 |
Polarizing filters   247 | Filters for infrared
photography   249 | Partial filtering   249 | Diffusion
filters   251 | Lens attachments for special
effects   252 | Quality of filters   253 | Filter
position   254 | Coating and multicoating   254 |
Filter maintenance   254

13 Motor Drives   255

Motors versus winders 255 | Motor-drive benefits and applications 256 | The intervalometer 259 | Multiple camera operation 259 | Batteries 260 | AC operation 262

14 Image Quality   263

Hand held or tripod 263 | Camera steadiness 267 | Mirror lockup 268 | Tripod use 269 | Other camera supports 272

15 Special Medium Format Capabilities   275

Built-in bellows 275 | Extended depth-of-field control 276 | Medium format view camera 277 | Perspective control lens 280

16 Close-up Photography   283

Lenses 283 | Reversing lenses 284 | Magnification 284 | Proxar or close-up lenses 285 | Partial close-up lenses 287 | Extension tubes and bellows 288 | Photographing subjects life sized 290 | Depth of field 290 | Exposure 292 | The camera 293 | Focusing 294 | Slide copying 294

17 Copying   299

Camera alignment 299 | Focusing 300 | Films 300 | Lenses 300 | Filters 301 | Lighting 301 | Exposure 304 | Copy stand 304 | Final preparation 304

18 Slides   307

Slide mounting 307 | Slide projectors 310 | Legibility of artwork 314 | Combining sound and slides 315

19   Applications   **321**

*Wildlife and bird photography   321 | Nature
photography   321 | Close-up photography   322 |
High magnification photography   322 | Aerial
photography   325 | Architectural photography   325 |
Press photography   325 | Wedding
photography   326 | Child photography   326 |
Fashion and beauty photography   326 | Portrait
photography   327 | Sports photography   327 |
Medical photography   328 | Commercial
photography   328 | Ultraviolet photography   328 |
Fluorescent photography   328 | Infrared
photography   329 | Video displays   329 |
Underwater photography   330 | Space
photography   330 | Industrial photography   330 |
Outdoor scenery   331 | Creative
experimenting   332 | Copying   333*

20   Maintaining Equipment and Materials   **335**

*Carrying cases   335 | Cleaning the camera   336 |
Cold weather photography   337 | Caring for
film   339 | Color prints   341*

Index   **343**

Preface

As I look over the photographic bookshelf, I see many books dealing specifically with 35 mm photography and even more with 35 mm equipment, and I also see that view camera techniques and studio photography are well covered. But there is not much about medium format equipment and even less about medium format photography, though it is one of the most popular and important film sizes in professional photography and also used extensively by amateurs. There are, perhaps, good reasons for this lack of medium format information. The modern medium format cameras, especially the single reflex types, have similar, in some cases identical, features to their 35 mm counterpart and are operated basically in the same way. Thus one might think that the expert 35 mm photographer does not need much additional help to become a good medium format photographer.

Most medium format cameras are also ideal for professional studio use in fashion and commercial photography, and if one forgets the use of swing and tilts, studio photography in the medium format is little different from that done with the larger view cameras. The success depends mainly on lighting and proper use of lenses. So again, there may not be much point of a special book on the medium format. Although all this is true, I believe that medium format photography is sufficiently different from working in 35 mm or with the larger formats to justify special instructions, and even a special book.

Although the severe competition for a bigger market share in 35 mm has brought the equipment to a level where there are only small differences among cameras, medium format equipment still differs in many major and important aspects. The maximum benefits can be obtained only if the photographer is thoroughly familiar with the equipment and knows how medium format cameras, lenses, and accessories are used to obtain the maximum benefits.

The majority of photographers do not start in the medium format but most often move up from a smaller film size, such as 35 mm. They move up hoping or believing they will produce better pictures or become more successful photographers. This is possible but only if they are aware of the possibilities and the limitations of the format and equipment.

There are equally good reasons for the professional who normally works with larger negative sizes but moves down to the medium format because of its convenience, faster shooting capability, and portability. This photographer will undoubtedly evaluate medium format results with a very critical eye, hoping to find an image quality and result that come close to what he is used to seeing on the large sheetfilm. This can be accomplished only if the equipment is selected carefully and used properly. That is what this book is trying to do: to be a guide for using the medium format camera and its features so that photographers can obtain the best possible image quality regardless of purpose or field of photography.

Since medium format cameras are so universally used for almost all types of photography from candid action with a hand-held camera to critical studio work from a tripod, special chapters are devoted to these different applications and the type of equipment that most likely meets the requirements best.

A move into the medium format can be a costly undertaking if one is looking at a complete system with lenses, finders, and film magazines rather than just a basic camera. This book explains clearly this format's benefits, advantages, and disadvantages and provides a comparison of medium format equipment to other formats so you can decide whether it is right for you and your photography. It details the different camera and lens designs and gives a photographer's view of which features are important for specific applications and in different fields of photography.

Camera equipment is described in very general terms rather than in the form of a product guide or catalog describing specific makes and models of cameras. Cameras change rapidly, with manufacturers bringing out new or modified models every year, and sometimes more often. Thus descriptions of models made today may be outdated tomorrow, and updated information about specific products is readily available from manufacturers. This book is simply a guide to medium format equipment, design, and photography; it does not mention specific pieces of equipment, except to illustrate a general point or consideration. This book describes everything in a neutral way, describing pros and cons of everything, and the where, why, and how of things.

The book is not a camera instruction manual for medium format cameras. The instructions come with the camera and should be studied carefully before you start using the camera. Even expert 35 mm photographers should not assume that they know everything about the camera. Although some medium format cameras look and operate like 35s, some are quite different, especially if they feature interchangeable film magazines and lenses with leaf shutters. This manual goes beyond, but does not duplicate, what the camera manufacturer can supply. It is a camera manual that takes over where the camera manufacturer's data stop.

There is one more objective I tried to accomplish: to inspire you to use your cameras, lenses, and accessories not just to record things as you see them but to experiment and to use photography's unique capability to create a different world of images. This is an important part of the book because medium format cameras are well suited for creating images that are different from the way we see the world; they are, in my mind, the best photographic tools for this purpose.

Medium format photography

CHAPTER 1

The history of medium format

"Medium format" as it is defined today—to categorize the film formats between 35 mm and the larger view camera formats 4 × 5 in. and up—is quite new. It probably goes back to the 1930s, after 35 mm had established itself. Before 35 mm, the 4 × 5 in. film size could well have been called medium format because it was between the roll film formats, the smallest ones generally used at that time, and the large 8 × 10 view camera size. So if we want to look at the history, what does medium format refer to? In my mind, the most logical viewpoint is in reference to the size of the image recorded on the film. Since *medium format* today refers to negative sizes obtained on roll film from 40 × 40 mm up to 6 × 9 cm and panoramic formats, we will review the history from the point of view of image size produced in the camera. We find then that the medium format is not only much older than generally considered today but as old as photography.

Photography actually started with the medium format. The daguerreotype plates used in the 1840s were 6 1/2 × 8 1/2 in. large. But since silver and copper, the components of these plates, were very expensive, the image was not often recorded to cover its full size. They were split into smaller sections (1/2 to 1/16) as follows:

Full, 6 1/2 × 8 1/2 in.

1/2, 4 1/2 × 6 1/2 in.

1/4, 3 1/4 × 4 1/4 in.

1/6, 2 3/4 × 3 1/4 in.

1/8, 2 1/8 × 3 1/4 in.

1/16, 1 5/8 × 2 1/8 in.

Judging from the high number of photographic images to have survived from this time, a good medium format of 2 3/4 × 3 1/4 in. was most popular.

The original Kodak from 1888 made for 100 exposures, 2½ in. diameter on 2¾ in. wide stripping film. There is no viewfinder. The instruction: "You press the button, we do the rest." Courtesy International Museum of Photography at George Eastman House.

A similar division of plate area applied to the Ambro-type plates appeared somewhat later.

These were wet plate processes that required the photographer to carry a darkroom in the field. The dry plate process that appeared in 1880 eliminated the need for laboratory work in the field and also opened the way to new camera designs.

Camera design changed even more with the invention of placing sensitized emulsion on a flexible base; roll film was born. That change led to the development of the first roll film holder.

Roll film, which forms the basis for the design of the modern medium format camera, appeared in 1888 when George Eastman introduced the first camera with the Kodak name. The camera was factory loaded with roll film for one hundred exposures, and the entire camera had to be returned to Eastman for processing the finished roll of film and for reloading. The image size on the negative was a 2 1/2 in. circle. It was circular apparently because that is the image a lens produces. The Kodak camera 2 in 1889 used roll film for sixty exposures with a 3 1/2 in. circular image—another medium format. Although the Kodak camera was still a

In one of the early photographic promotion pieces, the Kodak camera was shown handheld to emphasize its compact size. All these early "handheld" camera were simply aimed at the subject without the help of a finder. Courtesy International Museum of Photography at George Eastman House.

box, its main feature was compact size (3 1/4 × 3 3/4 × 6 1/2 in.). To emphasize its compactness, advertisements showed a woman hand holding the camera, not mounted on a tripod. In a way, the idea of hand-held photography was born.

The early compact cameras had no aiming or focusing devices, so photography was somewhat of a hit-or-miss proposition. The photographer was advised to have subjects at least 5 or 6 ft from the camera.

Until 1891, when the Kodak Daylight camera appeared, the camera had to be loaded in a darkroom. In 1891 the film was placed inside a light-protected cardboard box, and the film moved from one light tight box to another in the camera.

Meanwhile, the Boston Camera Company had developed the concept of roll film spooled together with a black paper leader with numbers and running from one spool to another. Today's 120 roll film is still based on this principle. The numbers on the paper leader, however, are no longer needed since the film in medium format cameras stops automatically at frame 1 and the following frames. In 1892 the Boston Camera Company introduced the Bulls Eye, the first camera to be loaded with a numbered roll film and a red window at the back to guide the film advance. The company and its patents for these innovations were later bought by George Eastman.

Although the first folding cameras with bellows and ground glass

The original Box Brownie made in 1900 with a 105 mm *f*17 lens. The film support box at the rear was removable with a hinged panel in later models. Six 2¼ in. square images were produced on rollfilm. Cameras with the Brownie name were produced until 1965. Courtesy International Museum of Photography at George Eastman House.

were made for larger film sizes, they became the pocket type in 1897, producing a 2 1/4 × 3 1/4 in. image on daylight load roll film. This camera no longer carried a ground glass. The 105 camera and image size were reduced in 1902 with a six-exposure roll of 1 5/8 × 2 1/2 in. negatives on roll film 121. The "modern" folding cameras also included a tiny waist-level finder.

The medium format took a giant step toward becoming the most popular film format for years to come when the Box Brownie appeared on the market in 1900. With the price tag of $1, it hoped to fulfill Eastman's dream to bring photography to every schoolchild. It was also the beginning of today's most popular medium format: the 2 1/4 in. square, which was produced in the Box Brownie on a cartridge of 117 roll film with six exposures. The cost was 15 cents.

Film pack, which is also associated with the medium format, was introduced in 1903 by the Rochester Optical and Camera Company. It made possible the design of cameras without rollers, winding knobs, and window. Another innovation was the Autographic Kodak, which allowed the photographer to write data on the film while it is in the camera.

Brownie and folding cameras of many types and makes using the same type of film remained the amateur camera until the 1930s, to be replaced eventually by the twin lens types, and later by the SLRs (single lens reflex). The 120 roll film, which is the film mostly used in today's medium format photography, dates back to 1902 when it became a popular type for producing 2 1/4 × 3 1/4 in. images in Brownie and folding cameras. Other popular roll film sizes were (or still are) 127, introduced in 1912, and 620, which dates back to 1932.

The 127 roll film size was standard on compact folding cameras during the vest pocket era before World War I. The standard negative size was 1 5/8 × 2 1/4 in. (4.5 × 6 cm), which was already used in Europe. The Hawk Eye models also date from this era.

In the 1920s German camera models appeared featuring the most advanced shutters, especially Compur, and the finest lenses. The Voight-länder cameras, prominent during that time, had their own lenses; camera bodies made by other companies had the Zeiss lenses, which already were considered the symbol of lens perfection. Some of these German cameras were made for 9 × 12 cm, but the majority were medium format models with a 6 × 9 cm negative size. Also from Germany came an innovation that permitted a choice of eight or sixteen pictures on a roll of 120 film: eight in the 2 1/4 × 3 1/4 in. size or sixteen in 1 5/8 × 2 1/4 in. The choice had to be made before loading the film in the camera.

Concerned about the European competition, Kodak decided to join rather than fight and bought the Nagel factory in Stuttgart in 1932, bringing to the United States the first German-made Kodak medium format cameras, including the first Kodak camera to take sixteen pictures on a roll of film originally designed for eight photographs. The numbering system on the

By the early 1900s Kodak promoted photography as a hobby for everybody everywhere. Female models were used, perhaps to emphasize that the camera had become so lightweight and so simple that it could be operated by everyone. The outdoor location emphasized that photography was no longer limited to the studio. Courtesy International Museum of Photography at George Eastman House.

paper backing was changed to accommodate all cameras, whether they took eight, twelve, or sixteen images on a roll. The location of the red window on the camera determined which numbers could be seen.

A 1903 Kodak Model 3A folding pocket camera with Bausch & Lomb 170 mm *f*4 lens with iris diaphragm. The waist level finder was reversible for horizontal and vertical framing. A plate back accessory for groundglass focusing and use of dry plates was available for some models. Courtesy International Museum of Photography at George Eastman House.

The AL-Vista, in 1901, the earliest American-made popular-priced panoramic camera. The 5 in. *f*12 lens pivoted almost 180° making the exposure on rollfilm held in a curved frame within the camera body. Exposure was controlled by varying the speed of the lens sweep. A clockwork at the bottom of the camera moved the lens. Courtesy International Museum of Photography at George Eastman House.

There were twin lens reflex (TLR) cameras before 1900, but the TLR era was really born in 1929 with the appearance of the Rolleiflex. It was fast handling and compact, with a crank to advance the film. They were immediately recognized as excellent tools between the slow-handling larger format models and those using the small 35 mm film, which also established itself in the 1920s. The Rollei advantages were recognized by serious photographers, and the camera became one of the most successful types of all time. Rollei models were changed, improved, and became available with different makes of lenses and in a lower price range known as Rolleicord.

The success also brought competition. Other companies, especially Zeiss and Voightländer, introduced TLR models. The success also brought along a Rolleiflex for the 40 × 40 mm format, today known as superslide.

SLR cameras for large film sizes date back to 1880, dominated later for many years by Graflex, which introduced in the 1930s a small model with interchangeable lenses made for ten pictures on 120 roll film.

Medium format SLR models, however, go back to earlier years. From Germany in 1922, for instance, came the Paff Reflex for 120 roll film selling for $15. The Reflex Korelle using 120 film and the Vest Pocket Exacta for

A first model of the Rolleiflex Twin Lens Reflex camera from 1930, designed by Dr. Reinhold Heidecke and built by Franke and Heidecke in Braunschweig. It was equipped with a Tessar lens and built for a 6-exposure roll of film.

127 film of the 1930s, both featuring interchangeable screw-in lenses, can be considered the forerunners of SLR cameras for the medium format.

Not much happened to the SLR medium format concept during the next few years. The milestone came in 1948 when Victor Hasselblad showed his 1600F model. Not only did it have a new medium format shape but also the concept of film magazine interchangeability, which is the main attraction of the modern medium format SLR camera. Hasselblad's camera concept eventually also resulted in the slow death of the twin lens camera, the model that popularized the medium format and the square image format among serious amateurs and in professional photography.

If we consider medium format as film formats 1 1/2 to 3 1/2 in. in

Single lens reflex cameras already existed in 1899 as can be proven by this Patent Reflex hand model with internal bellows manufactured by the Reflex Camera Company in Yonkers. These cameras were made for 4 × 5 dry plates (shown) as well as for larger plate formats and in a stereo version.

size, medium format photography was unquestionably the most popular during the first eighty or ninety years of photography. And since during this time more medium format cameras were produced than any other type or all other types combined, it should not be surprising that most camera design developments were also first introduced on medium format cameras, including the film numbering system on roll film. Rangefinder focusing appeared in 1916 on a Kodak Autographic camera 3A. The focal plane shutter had shutter speeds of up to 1/1000 sec. The focal plane shutter was unquestionably the basis for photography's most dramatic developments, such as high-speed lenses. High-speed lenses are generally associated with the development of 35 mm. They go back further, however. Lenses with ƒ2 and ƒ1.8 apertures existed already before on medium format cameras—the Ermanox 4 1/2 × 6 cm camera introduced in 1920, for example.

The panoramic image also started in the medium format. In 1899 Kodak introduced the Panoram-Kodak camera 4. It had a swinging lens producing a "large" 3 1/2 × 9 in. image on roll film 103. The panoramic camera design came down to a more normal medium format in 1900 with the Kodak 1 Panoram camera. It produced 2 1/4 × 7 in. images on 105 roll film.

Even the idea of an interchangeable film magazine, which is a most important feature on modern SLR medium format cameras, goes back to 1893. A small all-metal box camera, called Kombi and selling for $3, was a system camera featuring a section that contained the film that could be removed from the camera body so that another preloaded section could be attached.

In almost 150 years of photography, some film formats have disappeared completely or are no longer used in some fields of photography; others have appeared and gained in popularity. But the medium format was in constant use in almost any type of camera and is still today the chosen film size in almost every field of professional photography, as well as for amateurs.

Today the medium format includes everything between the small format (35 mm and smaller) and the larger formats (4 × 5 in. and over) and is somewhat of a compromise between the two. That is the reason it is so popular and so valuable in almost all types of photography. It combines many of the conveniences of 35 mm with the benefits and advantages of larger studio cameras.

CHAPTER 2

The medium format advantage

In the early 1900s, the medium format was the most popular—almost the only—format used by amateur photographers. That was when the Box Brownie was the most cherished photographic gift and when the next step up from the Box Brownie was the folding camera. Both used roll film and created medium formats of various sizes, as did the TLR that appeared somewhat later. Professional photography at that time was limited to view cameras, and newspaper photographers were still carrying 4 × 5 in. press cameras.

Although the medium format became gradually accepted in professional photography, another film size, 35 mm, appeared and took over a dominant role in serious amateur photography, as well as many professional applications, especially news photography. 35 mm did not replace the medium format. New types of sophisticated medium format cameras have been appearing on the market since the 1940s and are used today in almost every field of professional photography, as well as by amateurs.

IMAGE SHARPNESS

For the best image definition, the 4 × 5 and 8 × 10 in. formats still need to be considered. Professionals use these larger formats when detail is necessary and when the client requests it, when it is desirable to produce 8 × 10 in. contact prints instead of enlargements, or when swings and tilts are necessary for perspective control or increased depth of field. Hobbyists and even serious amateurs seldom reach for these larger formats.

35 mm combined with modern high-resolution films and lenses produce an image sharpness that is satisfactory for blowups into the common picture sizes. It will not, however, equal or even approach the sharpness possible on the medium format. Most black-and-white and color emul-

A

B

sions are the same in 35 mm and roll film, but the medium format negative or transparency is anywhere from two and a half to four times larger in area than is the 24 × 36 mm frame. Its sharpness is proportionately better. To look at it in another way, the medium format negative can be blown up proportionately larger (to 30 × 40 in. instead of 16 × 20 in.) with equal quality, assuming everything else is equal.

Salability

Prints made from almost any sized negative are salable for many purposes, but commercial shots and portraits call for the medium format size. 35 mm transparencies are also accepted for many purposes, but the medium format is still preferred or requested in many fields for quality advertisements and editorial purposes. Presenting the medium format rather than 35 mm transparencies will also convey a professional image and impression to clients, who will be better able to see the results and determine how the image will fit into the advertising layout.

Although 35 mm cannot approach the sharpness of the medium format enlargement or the beauty and effectiveness of a medium format slide presentation, image sharpness is not necessarily the major reason for stepping up to the medium format. Other benefits are more helpful and valuable.

IMAGE EVALUATION

It is often said that once you work in the medium format, you'll never go back to 35 mm, probably because the medium format negative or transparency is easier to evaluate. For example, when a 35 mm and a medium format negative or transparency are placed side by side over a light box, the effectiveness, even the quality, of the medium format negative can be determined more easily, usually with the naked eye. There is no need to use a magnifying glass except to determine critical sharpness. Cropping possibilities also can be determined effectively and accurately.

Sorting slides is simplified with medium format transparencies. The same applies when working with contact sheets, a favorite method of proof printing 35 mm and medium format negatives. The twelve 2 1/4 in.

The advantage of the medium format over 35 mm for evaluating the quality and effectiveness of the image is obvious when the two are placed side by side on the lightbox. The 3025 mm² area of the 2¼ in. square (A) is three and a half times larger than the 865 mm² of the 35 mm frame (B). The difference is still more obvious when compared to the 2¼ × 2¾ in. format, which is about four and a half times larger.

A

The images on the 2¼ in. square and 6 × 4.5 cm proofsheet are usually large enough to be evaluated carefully with the naked eye. Final cropping can also be determined easily (A). This is difficult or impossible with 35 mm contact proofsheets (B).

square or sixteen 4.5 × 6 cm images from a 120 roll film fit well on a single sheet of 8 × 10 in. paper, as do 35s. Proofsheets make it easy to compare images taken of the same subject or in the same location in order to select the best and decide the final cropping. This is certainly true on the medium format contact sheet. Differences in pose, lighting, expression, depth of field, composition, and even sharpness can be detected easily and usually without the use of a magnifying glass. The 35 mm contact

B

proof images are frequently too small for this purpose. This is why many 35 mm photographers have the more expensive enlarged proofs made.

Proofsheets also provide a simple way for filing negatives. Negatives in their protective envelopes can easily be stored next to the proofsheet in a ringbinder or filing cabinet.

GROUND-GLASS SCREEN

Few photographers include the ground-glass screen size among the film size considerations.

On any SLR or TLR camera, the ground-glass screen is the size of

The large ground-glass screen is an important feature of the medium format camera. It provides a view camera view on a compact camera.

the negative; consequently, the medium format ground-glass screen is anywhere from two and a half to four and a half times larger than its 35 mm counterpart. The larger screen does not necessarily provide more accurate focusing, but the large screen can be viewed without the use of a magnifying finder.

I was beginning photography when the view camera was still the professional's camera. It was used not only because of the larger negative but because of the large ground-glass screen, which allowed careful, complete, and accurate evaluation of the image while viewing the screen with both eyes open—as one evaluates the final print or projected transparency.

I still believe that viewing the ground-glass screen with both eyes open is the best way to evaluate the effectiveness of the image or decide what might be necessary to make it more effective. Viewing with both eyes gives a different impression from looking with one eye through a prism finder. Indeed this might be the most important step in making you a better photographer. Standard so-called waist-level finders, which allow two-eyed image evaluation, are available for most medium format cameras.

Waist-level finders, unfortunately, have almost completely disappeared from 35 mm cameras. One reason is that it is practical only for horizontal images and unusable when the camera needs to be turned for verticals. One reason the square is such a popular medium format is because such cameras are always held the same way; they never need to be turned and thus are also usable with any type of finder, eye level or waist level.

CROPPING

For maximum image quality from a negative, the photographer must frame the subject or scene so that the entire negative can be used for the enlargement. A cropped negative must be enlarged more; thus, there will be a decrease in quality. Cropping, however, is a great technique for the serious photographer—an important step in putting an image in its final form. Here the medium format can show its advantage and increased possibilities. Even if the photographer used only about 30 percent of the total medium format area, the negative can still be as large as the full 35 mm frame. If the photographer used only 30 percent of the total 35 mm format, the remaining negative would be about 13 × 20 mm.

The medium format's possibilities for creative framing in the darkroom are enhanced if the medium format negative is a square. This size offers wide possibilities to leave it as a square or frame it into a horizontal or vertical or into a long, narrow vertical or horizontal. You will un-

The 2¼ in. square offers extensive cropping possibilities. The negative can be cropped down to less than 30 percent of its total area, and the remaining negative area is still as large as the full 35 mm frame. Even more cropping is possible from a 2¼ × 2¾ in. negative.

doubtedly start to see different compositions and different image shapes that you probably overlooked when evaluating the image on the camera's ground glass. The easy possibility of changing a square into other shapes is also a major reason why art directors in advertising agencies often prefer or insist on receiving square images. It offers them more freedom for fitting the image into their layout.

FILM CHANGING

Various medium format cameras, especially SLR types, are designed with a completely removable film magazine. The film is not loaded into the camera, but rather a magazine that can be attached to the camera or removed from it at any time without fogging the film. Several magazines can be preloaded, so changing from one roll to the next is almost instantaneous; the photographer is not likely to be loading film when the most important action takes place. It is somewhat like carrying two or three loaded cameras, except you need only one camera and lens. You can also change from one type of film to another, from black and white to color, negative to positive, daylight to tungsten, high speed to low speed or instant, at any time. There is no need to finish the roll. Changing can be done mid-roll without wasting a frame and without carrying more than one camera.

Changing mid-roll can be one of the most important advantages in almost any type of photography and could also be a major reason for selecting the medium format. It is, next to the film format, the major advantage of the medium format. It places the medium format one giant

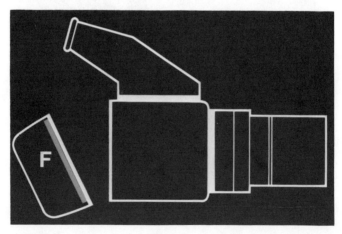

On various medium format cameras, the film is not in the camera body but in a separate film magazine, which can be removed at any time without exposing the film. Thus film can be changed in midroll.

step above 35 mm for serious photography. Since magazine interchangeability must be a major consideration in camera selection, the medium format camera list in chapter 3 specifies which manufacturers make cameras with this magazine interchangeability.

INSTANT PHOTOGRAPHY

Several medium format cameras also let you attach a Polaroid magazine, which might be a major reason for considering the medium format. This possibility exists on some 35 mm cameras, but the magazine is not as practical and the Polaroid image size is too small for careful evaluation. A 35 mm can also be loaded with Polaroid slide film, but the camera must be reloaded, unless a second camera is used, and the film must be removed and developed. On a medium format camera, all that is necessary is to detach the regular magazine, in the middle of a roll, and attach the Polaroid back. You can shoot one or several Polaroids and see the image a minute later.

Polaroid film shows the image exactly as seen through the lens and confirms that everything in the camera works properly (the flash is synchronized to the shutter, for instance). Nothing else can give that peace of mind in important jobs. The photographer can check exposure, lighting, and lighting contrast, especially valuable with multiple flash or when combining flash with daylight. The Polaroid image can also show things that cannot be seen with your eyes or through a finder of any camera. For instance, you cannot see whether a certain shutter speed freezes or blurs moving subjects and how much blur is created. You cannot see what a zoom shot or a camera-produced double exposure looks like or what effect a moving camera produces on the film. All of these effects and others must be recorded on film before they can be seen. So if you do professional work or are interested in creating images, and not just recording things as they exist, the Polaroid magazine is a great help. Other benefits of a Polaroid are that you can show the client what the image will look like and get instant approval and use it as a teaching tool to show photographic students the results instantly.

SHUTTERS

Medium format cameras do not take a back seat to any other format when it comes to shutters. They are right in the front seat giving the serious photographer a wide choice between focal plane and leaf shutter in the lens. Although all 35 mm SLR cameras used for serious photography have focal plane types, some medium format cameras have either. There are even focal plane shutter types that can also be used with shutter lenses, thus offering the advantage of both.

Focal plane shutters offer high shutter speeds, usually up to 1/1000 sec but going as high as 1/2000 sec in the medium format. Not having to worry about a leaf shutter in the lens, the lens designer has also more freedom in the lens design, the focal length, the maximum aperture, and the focusing range.

With focal plane shutters, flash is synchronized only up to a certain shutter speed, and in this respect medium format types take a back seat. While most 35 mm types can be used up to 1/125 sec and some even higher, the best that is possible on the larger format is 1/90 sec. Most go up to 1/60 and some only to 1/30 sec. Keep this in mind when you check camera specifications if flash is important. This limitation is reduced with shutter lenses that are available for some focal plane shutter cameras.

All leaf shutters can be used with flash up to their top speed, which is usually 1/500 sec. Therefore they are a better choice when flash synchronization at 1/500 sec is necessary or desirable, such as when photographing indoor sports. Flash synchronization at all shutter speeds is also valuable when combining flash with daylight.

The medium format twin lens reflex and rangefinder cameras have lens shutters as their counterparts in 35 mm do, and so do the wide angle press and panoramic types. Focal plane or leaf shutters can be completely mechanical or controlled electronically. Even if done electronically, the actual shutter opening and closing is still a mechanical function. Since shutters are an important consideration in camera selection, the shutter type is also mentioned for each camera in the equipment listing in chapter 3.

CAMERA SIZE AND OPERATION

The large negative or slide can be obtained with cameras that carry many of the 35 mm benefits. The cameras are somewhat larger and heavier, but most are still lightweight and suitable for hand-held photography. With most you can also photograph as fast because shutter cocking and film advance is a single operation. Motor drives are available, although they do not operate as fast as 35s and do not shoot several frames per second.

Most cameras are made for roll film for ten, twelve, sixteen, twenty-four, or thirty-two images per roll depending on the format or type of film. It is not quite the thirty-six per roll of 35 mm film but a sufficient number to limit film changing to a reasonable level when film needs to be changed. Roll film does not need to be rewound; thus film changing can be fast. Several medium format cameras can also take 70 mm films with seventy exposures on a daylight loading cassette, and even more—over one hundred—from a darkroom spool load.

The line of lenses is as extensive as for 35s. The lenses, however, tend to be somewhat slower than the 35's equivalent. Medium format cameras have become automated in many ways, especially with built-in exposure devices, and are hardly more difficult to operate. These 35 mm advantages are combined with various benefits of the large sheetfilm cameras—mainly the large negative with its possibilities for retouching and also the possibility of changing from one type of film to another at any time and the use of Polaroid film material.

CHAPTER 3

Sizes

SELECTING THE FORMAT

All 35 mm cameras produce the same 24 × 36 mm image. In the medium format, different cameras produce different formats, so it is worthwhile to determine which format serves which purpose best. In the days of the Box Brownie and folding camera, the rectangular format of about 6 × 9 cm was dominant. Later, when TLR cameras took over, the 2 1/4 in. square became the standard. Today it is still a popular size in most fields of medium format photography. Other rectangular shapes, however, have reentered the medium format and are preferred by some photographers, especially for portraits and weddings.

The format decision is important because the medium format camera is likely to become your most used photographic tool. Professionals use the medium format camera daily or at least a few times each week, so a low price should not overshadow the camera's format and design characteristics.

The format decision for the camera should not even be based on the image shape of the final picture. For example, a user should not choose a camera that shoots rectangular images simply because he or she or a client prefers such images over square ones. A rectangular camera is a fine choice if it has all the features that are important in one's photography, or if shooting rectangular pictures does not carry with it some inconveniences. On the other hand, shooting with a square camera that is ideal for the job and then cropping the negatives later might be a more satisfactory solution. Since the medium format negative is so large and provides excellent cropping possibilities, the shape of the final image is something that can be decided in the darkroom. Rectangulars can be changed into squares, and even more easily, squares can be converted into rectangles. Also, users should not let the usual rectangular shape of enlarging papers be a guide. Instead give serious consideration to the following points:

1. The convenience of viewing and focusing and holding the camera in hand-held photography.

A

B

C

D

Various medium formats compared. The 2¼ in. square with 3020 mm² *(A)*; superslide with 1600 mm² *(B)*; the 2¼ × 2¾ in., which is about 3850 mm² *(C)*; the 6 × 4.5 cm with an area of 2200 mm² *(D)*; the 6 × 9 cm with a 4760 mm² area *(E)*; and the two panoramic formats, 6 × 12 cm *(F)* and 6 × 17 cm *(G)*. All are considerably larger than the 35 mm frame *(H)*.

E

F

G

H

2. Size and weight of equipment, if used on location.
3. The camera features: shutter, flash synchronization, available lenses and accessories.
4. The availability and degree of interchangeability of film magazines and the emulsions that are usable.
5. The possibility of attaching a Polaroid film magazine.
6. The difference in the degree of enlargement of the different cropped and uncropped negative formats.
7. The availability of projection equipment if slides are to be produced.

2 1/4 × 2 1/4 In. Square

Most photographers associate the medium format with the square, probably because the 2 1/4 in. square has been the most popular medium format in the last three decades. (It is also known under the metric measurement of 6 × 6 cm, indicating centimeters.) The actual negative size, however, is not 6 × 6 cm but slightly less, or about 55 × 55 mm. Twelve images fit on 120 roll film, twenty-four on 220, and seventy or more on 70 mm perforated film, which requires a special magazine.

The 2 1/4 in. square format can be found in SLR, TLR, and wide angle medium format cameras, many offering a second choice of a smaller rectangular format. The rectangle is the standard in rangefinder types.

Square cameras are frequently a second choice, or not considered at all by photographers who know that their negatives end up as rectangular prints. They do not want to waste part of the negative. It is, of course, always desirable to fill the negative so the entire area is usable in the enlargement. What is important, however, is not whether some of the negative area needs to be cropped but whether the remaining area needs to be enlarged more. That is not the case when a rectangular print is made from a square negative. The degree of enlargement is determined only by the long side of the negative, not the negative area. The long side remains the same; thus the 2 1/4 in. square cropped to a rectangle has to be blown up exactly the same as the full 6 × 4.5 cm negative. Thus even photographers who may never make rectangular prints should still consider a square camera.

Photography with a Square Camera.   There can be some good reasons for selecting the square. The most valuable may be that there is no need to turn the camera sideways. You hold the camera the same way as it was designed for greatest operating ease and convenience; there is no need to decide whether to photograph verticals or horizontals, an advantage when fast action requires fast shooting.

The real benefit of shooting square, however, is in viewing. A camera that needs to be turned must be equipped with a 90° prism finder. It is the only practical viewing method when the camera is turned for verticals. Thus it becomes an eye-level camera that must always be held in front of

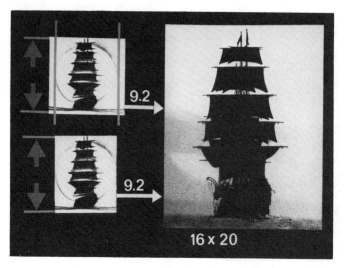

A 2¼ in. square negative cropped along two sides to make a rectangular print requires the same degree of enlargement as the full 6 × 4.5 cm negative: 9.2 times for a 16 × 20 in. print. You are just changing the image shape.

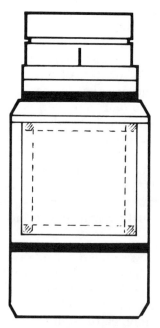

Ground-glass screens with vertical and horizontal cropping lines are available for some square cameras. You can also make the lines on a standard screen with a permanent-ink pen or by pasting thin strips of tape on the screen. The vertical and horizontal formats become even more obvious if the four corners are blacked out with ink or tape. Another method is to make the mask on a separate sheet of acetate or high-contrast film, which is then placed over the ground-glass screen.

Square images provide much freedom in cropping. Subjects can be composed to make good squares *(A)*, verticals *(B)*, or horizontals *(C)*.

the eyes. The square format camera, on the other hand, can be equipped with eye-level finders: a 45° prism finder or a waist-level type for viewing directly from the top. All finders work well because the camera is always held the same way. It gives much more freedom, photographing from practically any angle easily.

Square Prints. Instead of changing square negatives into rectangular prints, why not crop the rectangular paper to make square prints? The final print format must be a personal decision, but square prints can be very effective for just about any purpose. They make beautiful wall decor, are extensively used in advertising, where they can be used as a single image or a layout of multiples as in a multiimage presentation.

5 × 5 in. prints provide an effective way to present wedding proofs. Popular sizes for wedding albums are 8 × 10, 8 × 8, and 10 × 10 in. With square prints, each image fills the entire square page, thus making the best use of the album page without the need to turn the album for viewing.

Square prints make attractive wedding or display albums. Every print fits the square album page with an even border, looking like a framed picture. The bride and groom never need to turn the album, often necessary when horizontals and verticals are mixed.

The square is excellent for public relations pictures. An 8 × 8 in. square image printed on the top part of an 8 × 10 in. piece of paper leaves a 2 in. border at the bottom for caption copy. The picture and copy combination looks like a finished product—like a full page ad in a magazine—and is more effective than a photograph with the copy taped on the bottom or back.

The twelve square images can be contact proofed on one sheet of 8 × 10 in. paper. All images are right side up, so viewers need not turn the sheet.

Square slides make an effective slide presentation, with every image filling the same and the full area of a square projection screen. Audiovisual

The photographs of the soloists and the principal dancers of the American Ballet Theatre which are exhibited at the Andrew Crispo Gallery in New York City varied in size from 20" x 24" prints to 8½' x 10' murals. They have been created by Francesco Scavullo.

A square photograph printed on top of an 8 × 10 in. sheet of paper leaves a 2 in. space at the bottom, which can be used for the caption to the publicity photograph.

A camera with interchangeable magazines may allow shooting superslides *(left)* and 2¼ in. square negatives *(right)* by changing the film magazine. A 60 mm lens covers on a superslide the same area as the 80 mm lens does on the 2¼ in. square.

professionals believe that this is more effective than switching between verticals and horizontals.

6 × 4.5 cm

The true negative size of the 6 × 4.5 cm format is about 40 × 55 mm. Some medium format cameras are made specifically and only for this format. On others it is obtained with a separate magazine, thus giving the choice of shooting squares or rectangles. The 6 × 4.5 cm negative has an aspect ratio that is almost identical to 8 × 10 in. and 16 × 20 in. paper; thus the full negative can be printed. Cropping instructions to the laboratory are unnecessary if the subject is cropped so the full negative can be printed. The degree of enlargement when making a rectangular print is the same as from a 2 1/4 in. square cropped along one side.

There is no benefit as far as image quality is concerned. The real benefit comes from the large number of exposures per roll. Sixteen 6 × 4.5 cm images fit on the same film length as twelve 2 1/4 in. squares if they are equally and properly spaced. Some cameras provide that number of exposures on a roll of 120 film and thirty-two on 220 film. On others there are only fifteen because manufacturers have cut production costs

6 × 4.5 cm format proofsheets. The sixteen images (fifteen in some cameras) fit on an 8 × 10 in. sheet of paper, but vertical images are sideways.

by eliminating the rather complicated mechanism that provides even frame spacing on the unperforated roll films.

The three or four additional exposures per roll are a benefit. The film costs are 20 to 30 percent lower, but now the camera must be turned for verticals. Viewing becomes limited to the 90° eye-level finder. This limitation must be considered carefully. Depending on photographic approach and subject, it may be a big price to pay for the few additional exposures. The cost of film, at least in the professional field, is small compared to most other costs. The fifteen or sixteen rectangular images can be contact proofed on a single 8 × 10 in. sheet. The proofsheet, of course, needs to be turned for viewing if verticals and horizontals are mixed.

6 × 4.5 cm slide mounts are available. For a professional slide presentation, all images should be shot as horizontals and projected on a rectangular movie screen rather than mixing verticals and horizontals. Images can also be composed as squares. The 6 × 4.5 cm slides can be cut into 41 × 41 mm squares and mounted as superslides.

The 6 × 4.5 cm format is frequently referred to as the ideal format, but that does not necessarily mean it is ideal for all photography. It simply means that the format has the same aspect ratio as the 8 × 10 in. enlarging paper. Whether the format or the 6 × 4.5 cm camera is ideal is an individual decision.

40 × 40 mm

Each side of this square format is equal to the short side of a 6 × 4.5 cm format and is known as the superslide. Only one or two medium format cameras offer film magazines made specifically to produce this negative size in the camera. Sixteen superslides are produced on a roll of 120. With others, the long side of the 6 × 4.5 cm format can be cut to make a square. The superslide is more closely associated with 35 mm than the medium format because it is mainly a projection, not a print, format. While the image produced in the camera is about 40 × 40 mm, the slide mounts cut it down to about 37 × 37 mm. Even in the mount, the image area of the superslide is 75 percent larger than the mounted 35 mm slide.

Projecting Superslides. The superslide's close association with the 35 mm comes from the fact that it can be projected on 35 mm machines and does not require a special projector. Some laboratories even place processed superslides into cardboard mounts, ready to drop into standard 35 mm slide trays. The superslide, however, must be associated with the medium format because roll film and a medium format camera are necessary to produce it.

There is much to be said in favor of the superslide compared to 35 mm. Superslides are 70 percent larger on the screen. Each square super-

The 40 × 40 mm superslide as produced in the camera results in an image area almost double the image area of the 24 × 36 mm 35 mm frame. The slide mount cuts the superslide area down to about 37 × 37 mm (A), which is still 75 percent larger than the mounted 35 mm slide (B). A superslide can also be obtained by cutting the long side of the 6 × 4.5 cm image. The short side is the same as the superslide (40 mm).

slide fills the entire square screen without the objectionable switch from verticals to horizontals and vice-versa.

While the outside dimensions of the mounted superslide are identical to those of a mounted 35 mm slide, the image area is much larger and requires an illumination system in the projector that fills the slide without vignetting. This is, unfortunately, not the case in many 35 mm projectors on the market today. A 35 mm projector used for superslides must, therefore, be selected carefully.

Shooting Slides and Negatives.   A medium format camera could be used strictly for producing superslides. More likely, however, most photographers will want to use the same camera for shooting superslides and negatives, and in this case the largest possible negative size is desired. The ideal setup for this dual purpose is a camera with interchangeable magazines: one for the superslide and another for a larger medium format negative. If film magazines can be changed in the middle of the roll of film, the superslide and large negative can be shot right after each other in the same camera.

An alternative is to shoot both in a 6 × 4.5 cm magazine, leave the negative as 6 × 4.5, and cut the slide down to a square. A 60 mm focal length lens covers the same area on a superslide as an 80 mm lens does on the full 2 1/4 in. square. The 60 mm thus becomes the standard superslide lens. Superslides can also be made in the laboratory from 2 1/4 in. squares. These reduction duplicates are usually printed on 46 mm film that is perforated on one side.

2 1/4 × 2 3/4 In. (6 × 7 cm)

This largest of the popular medium formats also has an aspect ratio that closely resembles that of the popular enlarging papers. The actual negative size is about 55 × 70 mm but can vary somewhat from one camera to another. The negative produced in a 6 × 7 cm camera is also about 55 × 70 mm. Ten negatives fit on one roll of 120 film—two fewer than 2 1/4 in. square and five or six fewer than the 6 × 4.5 cm. The film cost is thus 20 to 60 percent higher, and film must be changed more often. More important are the size and weight of the camera. This larger negative can be obtained only on cameras specifically made for this format, which consequently have to be larger and heavier. One 6 × 7 cm camera is in the shape of a 35 mm and thus might appeal to 35 mm users. The size and weight are seldom an objection in studio use but can become a burden in hand-held photography on location when mobility is important.

The 2 1/4 × 2 3/4 in. is seldom used for slide presentation. The full

The film area of a 2¼ × 2¾ in. negative *(right)* is about 50 percent larger than the area of a 6 × 4.5 cm or a cropped-down 2¼ in. square *(left)*, but the recorded image is only about 20 percent larger compared to either. Image size is determined by the long side of the negative, which is 70 mm compared to 55 mm.

image can be projected only in a special slide projector. Other projection possibilities are to cut the rectangle down to a 2 1/4 in. square for use in 2 1/4 in. slide projectors; reduce the 2 1/4 × 2 3/4 in. to 6 × 4.5 cm and project in a 2 1/4 in. projector, or reduce the image to 35 mm and project in a 35 mm machine.

COMPARING FORMATS

Camera size and weight must be measured against the difference in the negative size and the advantages and benefits of the larger format. The 2 1/4 × 2 3/4 in. film area of about 3850 mm^2 is about 25 percent larger than the 3020 mm^2 of the 2 1/4 in. square and 45 percent more than the 2200 mm^2 of the 6 × 4.5 cm. The film area must be considered when comparing the impression of visual observation or comparing the size of a projected image. It is proper to call an image twice as large when the area is twice the size. Area, and on the other hand, cannot be used to compare the size of a subject recorded on the film or the necessary degree of enlargement. The length of the negative side must be used for this comparison. The difference is now reduced to 23 percent when the 55 mm side of the 2 1/4 in. square is considered 100% or only 20% when the 70 mm side of the 2 3/4 in. negative is used as the basis.

In a full-length portrait in which the model covers each negative from top to bottom, the model is only about 20 percent larger on the 2 3/4 in. compared to either the 2 1/4 in. square or the 6 × 4.5 cm. The difference will still make retouching the original negative or transparency somewhat easier, but the difference is not as much as often thought. The same is true of the degree of enlargement. The 6 × 4.5 cm negative, or the 2 1/4 in. square cropped down to the 8 × 10 in. paper proportion, must be enlarged less than 25 percent more than the full 2 3/4 in. to obtain the same size enlargement. The enlarging head needs to be raised less than 25 percent. If the 24 in. easel-to-negative distance is for an enlargement from the 2 1/4 × 2 3/4 in. negative, the same enlargement can be made from a 6 × 4.5 cm or 2 1/4 in. square by raising the enlarging head about 5 in. A square print can be made from a 2 1/4 × 2 3/4 in. negative by cropping the long dimension down to a square. The degree of enlargement is the same as it would be from an original 2 1/4 in. square.

IMAGE SHARPNESS

The difference in the degree of enlargement is another factor in determining image quality. Assuming that everything else in the camera is equal—the performance of the lens, the film flatness, and the accuracy of alignment of mirror and screen—the 2 1/4 × 2 3/4 in. negative should be about 20 percent sharper; or to say it in a different way, the larger negative should allow a 20 percent higher blowup of equal quality. Whether it does is another question and can be determined by an actual film test. Negative size is important, but not as much as many photographers think. Film flatness and lens quality are much more determining factors, especially with high-resolution films.

Both center and corner sharpness should be compared if they are important. In some fields of photography—for instance, portrait or wildlife—corner sharpness is not typically important since the corner seldom contains elements important to the photograph.

The 2 1/4 × 2 3/4 in. requires turning the camera for verticals unless the camera offers a revolving back. With the latter, the film magazine is rotated for verticals or horizontals, the normal method on view cameras. The camera body with viewfinder remains in the same position.

The 2 1/4 × 2 3/4 in. format is not practical for contact proof printing because only nine of the ten images from a 120 roll film fit on an 8 × 10 in. sheet of paper. This is a relatively unimportant consideration since most 2 1/4 × 2 3/4 in. photographers do not contact print their negatives but have individual proofs made.

OTHER MEDIUM FORMATS

6 × 9 cm

One of the original popular medium formats has not disappeared: the 6 × 9 cm (2 1/4 × 3 1/4 in.) size producing eight images on a roll of 120 film. Not counting the panoramic sizes, it is also the largest medium format. It is not found in SLR cameras, perhaps because of its bulkiness and the large-sized mirror that would be required in the camera design. It is available in press cameras, rangefinder and wide angle types, aerial cameras, and special roll film magazines for view and press cameras.

Since standard roll film is used in most cameras, the same wide choice of film is available as in the more popular medium formats. If the 6 × 9 cm camera or film back is made for cut film, there will be a problem finding the necessary film (also the case in a 2 1/4 × 2 1/4 in. sheetfilm adapter). Sheetfilm ready made for either size is no longer available. You must cut your own in the darkroom from 9 × 12 cm, if available, or 4 × 5 in. This process is possible but not convenient.

The 6 × 9 cm format proportions do not match to the 8 × 10 in. paper proportions. The long side is longer, like on the 35 mm frame. The 6 × 9 cm proportions are identical to the 24 × 36 mm frame proportions in 35 mm, perhaps explaining how the 35 mm proportions were chosen because 6 × 9 cm was the popular medium format when 35 mm made its appearance.

For an 8 × 10 or 16 × 20 in. print, the 6 × 9 cm negative needs to be cropped to almost 7 cm, just as the 24 × 36 mm negative is cropped to about 24 × 30 mm. Thus, for making prints in the 8 × 10 in. or 16 × 20 in. proportion, the 6 × 9 cm format has little advantage over 6 × 7 in. The main benefits of the large negative are lost. Those who plan to make 8 × 10 or 16 × 20 in. prints from 6 × 9 cm negatives should keep this cropping requirement in mind when composing the image in the finder or, even better, mask the finder down to the proper proportions.

For other purposes, the large size can be very effective. Projection of the full slide is possible with a special 6 × 9 cm or lantern slide projector. For use in a 2 1/4 in. slide projector, the transparency needs to be cut to the 55 × 55 mm square.

6 × 8 cm

A new medium format 6 × 8 cm appeared in 1986. It is presently used only by one camera company that promotes it as the format that provides the most effective vertical/horizontal ratio. The image size is 56 × 76 mm. Considering the 8 × 10 in. paper proportions as *standard*, the 6 × 8 cm format is closer than 6 × 9 cm but the closest medium format to the paper size is still 6 × 7 cm (2 1/4 × 2 3/4 in.) The 6 × 8 cm format needs some cropping at the long side. You obtain 9 exposures on 120; 18 on 220 film. The 9 exposures can be contact printed on an 8 × 10 in. proofsheet.

Panoramic Formats

Although the usable width of roll film is limited to 56 mm, the image can be stretched along the film as far as the lens is capable of covering. That is what is done in panoramic cameras where the format ranges from 6 × 12 cm (six images on a roll of 120 film) to a format that is almost three times longer than wide: 6 × 17 cm (2 1/4 × 6 3/4 in.) with four images per roll of 120 and eight on 220. The film area of the latter is equivalent to three 2 1/2 × 2 1/2 in. images.

Although the panoramic formats may serve a purpose just to cover a wider area than possible with a wide angle lens on an ordinary format, they are really meant for special uses of the final image. They offer a new way of creating visually dramatic images with excellent overall quality.

Panormaic images also have a lifelike appearance; they are closest to the way we see. Panoramic cameras can take into one picture the wide horizontal sweep that we see with our eyes from the top of a mountain or building, a lake shore, beach, or city street. Since normal viewing is horizontal, this camera is most often used for horizontals, which I believe are usually more effective than verticals. The camera can be used for verticals and can be excellent for this purpose to enhance the height of a waterfall, tall trees, or buildings.

Although panoramic cameras need to be larger than most others, they are still usable for hand-held work and are usually equipped with a spirit level to ensure straight horizontals or verticals. The film gate and pressure plate in such a camera must be well made and be designed to keep the large negative area flat from one side to the other.

Negatives from a panoramic camera cannot be enlarged in an enlarger that goes up only to the typical medium format. The 6 × 12 cm negative requires an enlarger made for 4 × 5 in., and a 5 × 7 in. type is needed for the even larger 6 × 17 cm negative.

35 mm IN THE MEDIUM FORMAT CAMERA

Medium format photography has recently been combined with 35 mm through the introduction of a 35 mm film magazine now available from various manufacturers. Cameras take 35 mm film in standard cassettes of twelve, twenty, twenty-four, or thirty-six exposures. They are listed in the camera section in chapter 4, which also indicates the actual image size recorded on the film. The image size is necessary since the use of 35 mm film on medium format cameras is not limited to the standard 24 × 36 mm image. Some magazines are made for this 24 × 36 mm frame size and some for larger panoramic sizes.

Used with a 24 × 36 mm back, the medium format camera may be used instead of carrying a separate 35 mm model, or for using a film that is made only in 35 mm—such as a color duplicating film, infrared film, high contrast black-and-white film.

Those who believe that producing standard 24 × 36 mm frames on 35 mm is important have two options: buying special 35 mm film magazines for the medium format camera or buying a 35 mm camera for this purpose. With the latter, you have two working cameras, each specifically made for the film and format. Each can consist of a complete system of lenses and accessories, all of them best suited for what the camera was designed for. I would probably choose this option, but the decision must depend on how often the 35 mm option is needed.

35 mm film magazines are also available for various cameras to produce a panoramic format 24 × 56 mm on a 2 1/4 in. square or 4.5 × 6 cm camera with twenty images on a thirty-six-exposure roll, or even wider, 24 × 69 mm on a 2 1/4 × 2 3/4 in. type. This is about the same image proportion as the 6 × 12 cm panoramic type. These wide screen options were easy to obtain because of the size of the medium format film magazine and because the camera lenses were designed for this field coverage. This wide screen format is something that only the medium format 35 mm camera can produce and may be the major reason for using 35 mm in the medium format camera. This double frame can be very helpful for multi-image shows and in printed form.

Since the film in most 2 1/4 in. SLR cameras moves from bottom to top rather than horizontally, the 35 mm film is likely to move in the same direction. This means the camera needs to be turned vertically when producing horizontal 35 mm or panoramic frames.

CHAPTER 4

Camera types

Medium format cameras come in a wide variety of styles. Most are satisfactory for many different jobs, but some are better suited for certain applications than others. The camera selection therefore must be based first on the subject matter of the photograph. Then the final choice of camera can be made by investigating and determining how important the following points are for your application:

- Shape of the camera.
- Size, weight, and portability.
- Type of viewing.
- Degree of electronics and automation.
- Component interchangeability.
- Shutter.
- Special camera features.
- Availability of lenses and accessories.
- Quality and workmanship.

SINGLE LENS REFLEX

The SLR camera has become the most popular type in the medium format, replacing the twin lens reflex that was the standard in the 1930s and 1940s. Medium format SLR cameras existed in those years, but it was not until the Hasselblad came on the market in 1948 that the SLR started to challenge the popularity of the TLR. Now only a few TLR systems are still being made, while the number of SLR systems is constantly increasing.

Shutters and Mirrors

Medium format SLRs are available with a focal plane shutter or a lens shutter. Focal plane shutter types operate like 35 mm SLR cameras. Those

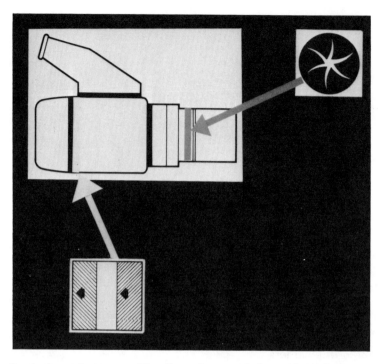

Some focal plane shutter models allow the use of shutter lenses. You can then decide which shutter to use for each shot and switch from one to the other. The focal plane shutter is likely to produce higher shutter speeds, while the lens shutter provides flash synchronization at all speeds.

without focal plane shutters use interchangeable lenses with built-in leaf shutters. Furthermore, some focal plane shutter cameras can be used with leaf shutter lenses—either just one or two special lenses or a complete range. Either the focal plane or lens shutter can be used; use one for one picture, the other for the next, something practically nonexistent in any other format, a medium format exclusive.

In both cases, the reflex mirror swings out of the way so light can expose the film. This blocks out the viewfinder image until the mirror drops back in place after exposure. On some makes, the mirror returns instantly and automatically after the exposure has been made; on others, the mirror returns when the user cranks the shutter and advances the film. At least one camera provides a choice and enables the mirror operation to be changed from instant to noninstant, or vice-versa, at any time.

Those who are used to the instant return mirror operation of the 35 mm may find the blackout of the noninstant return mirror in 2 1/4 in. objectionable, at least at the beginning. Once photographers are used to it, they will see it has no disadvantages. It is often said, but incorrectly, that the instant return mirror lets users see whether they captured the

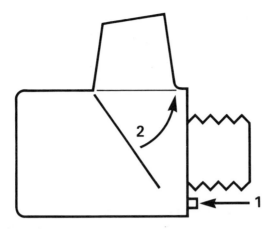

When the camera release (1) is depressed, the mirror (2) swings up, blacking out the view on the ground-glass screen. This happens on all SLR cameras. An instant return mirror swings back to the viewing position immediately after the exposure is made. A noninstant return mirror comes back when the film is advanced.

expression, while the noninstant return type does not. Users cannot see the subject on the ground glass the moment the exposure is made because the mirror is lifted up, blocking out the ground-glass screen. On all SLRs, the subject can be seen right beforehand; with the instant return mirror, it can also be seen right afterwards. To see the subject the moment the exposure is made, a finder is needed that does not view through the taking lens, as on a TLR or rangefinder camera. This can be accomplished on the SLR by attaching a sports or frame finder, part of many 2 1/4 in. SLR systems. Because the mirror must move out of the way before the film can be exposed, all SLRs also have a slight delay between the time the release is depressed and the time exposure is made. The delay is short on most systems and nothing to worry about in most applications. But in action photography, the delay could result in a slightly different action appearing on the film than seen in the finder. The delay can be eliminated on most SLRs by locking up the mirror, prereleasing the camera.

Viewing

Medium format SLRs form an image as a 35 mm SLR does. There is no parallax error. The picture is viewed, focused, and taken through one lens. With a prism finder, the image is right side up and unreversed. With a waist-level finder, the user views from the top; the image on the focusing screen is right side up but laterally reversed.

Most SLRs in the medium format can be purchased with or without the prism finder. Because the viewing image is recorded through the same

Medium format SI R cameras come in the shape of 35s (and are used like 35s) or in the shape of the longer box-type camera, usually with the film loaded in a separate magazine. Pentax courtesy Pentax Corp.

lens that records the image on the film, framing and focusing are accurate, provided that mirror and ground-glass screen are accurately lined up.

When lenses are changed, the viewfinder automatically shows the area covered by that lens. I believe that the most valuable aspect of SLR viewing is that you can see how the image changes as the diaphragm is opened or closed. SLR viewing also simplifies close-up photography. You just focus until the image on the screen is sharp, regardless of what close-up lens or accessory is used. Many SLR cameras offer another benefit: the possibility of light measuring through the lens, combined with more or less exposure automation.

Size and Shape

The shape of the camera is an important consideration, especially for hand-held location work. A medium format SLR can look like an oversized

Box-type SLR models are usually just a little larger than the square film format. A rotatable film magazine made for the 2¼ × 2¾ in. film size eliminates the need to turn the camera but necessitates a considerably larger camera body. Cameras designed for the square format can be used with the foldable waist-level finder, making the camera quite compact. Hasselblad, courtesy Victor Hasselblad, Inc.

35, but most are more of the boxy type, with the largest camera dimension being the distance from the lens to the rear of the camera. The dimension is dictated by the room the mirror needs to move freely up and down and by the design of the film magazine. Width and height are generally kept rather small—usually just a little more than the negative size. The camera type with a rotatable film magazine, on the other hand, needs to be considerably larger. A rotating film magazine allows verticals or horizontals to be photographed without turning the camera; this is an advantage, but the camera's bulkiness is perhaps a great price to pay. Whether bulkiness is a problem depends on whether the camera remains in the studio and used from a tripod or is carried on location and used hand held or from a tripod. Some medium format cameras weigh little more than professional 35s; others may well be twice or even three times as much.

It takes a little time to get used to this boxy type of medium format camera. It is held differently from the 35; the release is likely in a different position; and the viewing method may be different. But one gets used to these differences quickly and soon can hold most medium format cameras as steady as a 35 and shoot as fast as with a 35 mm SLR. Those who find camera holding inconvenient should keep in mind that there are many different ways of holding a medium format SLR. Camera manufacturers make grips for their cameras. These typically mount to the tripod-mounting screw on the camera's base and have a handle at one side of the camera or a grip at the bottom. The most convenient grips have a shutter button on the handle.

Convenience Features

Convenience features are important. Users who do not have to worry too much about technicalities and camera operations while shooting are more likely to produce exciting images. They can instead concentrate on the subject, lighting, and other creative aspects of photography.

Among the convenience features are the signals that show whether the shutter is cocked and whether film is in the camera and is advanced; the interlocks between components that let the release be depressed only when everything is done properly and fire a flash only when synchronized to the shutter; and the positioning of the various knobs and scales, which must be operable without inconvenience when shooting and, it is hoped, without having to switch the camera from one hand to the other. All important scales should be readable, preferably with the camera in the normal shooting position, without having to turn and twist it in all directions.

Until recently, some medium format cameras required separate cocking of the shutter and film advance, a slow, outdated process. In all modern cameras the two operations are combined.

Lenses

Medium format SLRs vary in another respect: the camera body–lens connection. Usually the lens is attached directly to the camera body. A lens attached directly to the camera body results in a rugged camera that can take abuse and is small and mobile. Also, with the lens attached directly, the optical relationship between lens and film plane, so important for image sharpness, is likely to be accurate. Some cameras have a bellows between camera body and lens mounting plate, which allows continuous focusing from infinity down to close distances, somewhat like a view camera. These cameras allow close-up photography without buying additional accessories. The lens board might even tilt to increase field depth.

Bellows are used on some medium format cameras other than SLRs. Several medium format rangefinder types use it to make the front collapsible, so the camera, in the shape of the 35 mm rangefinder type, fits

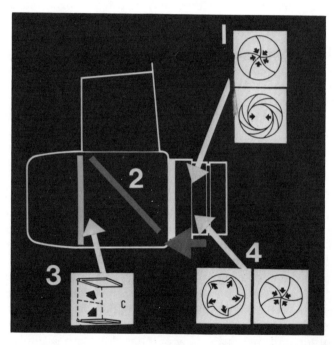

An SLR camera with a lens shutter requires a somewhat elaborate interlocked mechanism. The lens operation must be coordinated with the mirror and rear curtain. When the release is depressed, the lens shutter closes down, and the normally wide-open aperture closes down to the preset aperture (1). At the same time, the mirror lifts up (2). When the lens shutter is fully closed, a rear curtain must open (3). Then the lens shutter opens and closes for the set time to make the exposure (4). The purpose of the rear curtain is to protect the film from light before and after the exposure is made. In a focal plane shutter camera, the shutter serves this purpose.

easily into a pocket or purse. On some medium format press cameras, bellows are used for both focusing and making the front collapsible. This design is rather well known from the Speed Graphic, the press camera of the 1940s and 1950s. View cameras are prime examples of bellows types used not only for focusing but also for swing and tilt control. They can become medium format cameras with a roll film back.

Camera Design

SLR cameras in any format are complex. They contain a mirror that must move in a precise path up and down and must do so quickly and without causing too much camera movement. The mirror must move down so it rests every time in exactly the same position to maintain accurate focusing. Its movement must be synchronized to the shutter in the lens and camera. These features require many components and precision, raising the price of the camera. If lenses are interchangeable, the diaphragm and shutter of every lens must synchronize with the rest of the operation, increasing the price still further. If the film magazines are also removable, still more precision is necessary so that each magazine fits on every camera as if it were part of the camera.

The SLR is the most expensive type of medium format camera. Those looking for a less expensive camera type should choose the rangefinder type or the folding or the TLR type.

TWIN LENS REFLEX

In contrast to the SLR design, the TLR is simple. The mirror is installed permanently and never moves. There is no rear curtain, so the lens shutter need not be synchronized to any other operations. The simplicity means a camera with few problems; little can go wrong from normal operation. And it has another benefit: very quiet operation. The only audible noise when the camera is released is the opening and closing of the lens shutter blades. In contrast, on the SLR, you have the sound of the mirror and focal plane shutter or rear curtain. On an SLR camera with a lens shutter, the sound can be brought down to the TLR level by prereleasing the camera, which lifts up the mirror and opens the rear curtain, the two operations responsible for the sound. When the release is depressed later, only the lens shutter opens and closes, just as on the TLR. Because the leaf shutter is the only moving element during exposure, TLRs have little or no vibration when used on a tripod or camera stand.

Although TLRs are simple in design and operation, they are not snapshooter's cameras. For many years they were the most professional medium format camera available and are still today used in professional work. Experienced photographers have learned to live with the limitations

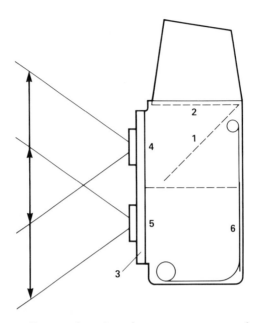

A TLR camera is actually a combination of two separate camera boxes. The viewing box on top contains a fixed mirror (1) and ground glass (2) and is for viewing and focusing only. The picture is made in the box below. The two lenses of equal focal length are mounted on a common plate (3) that moves forward and backward when focusing. Removable lenses come in sets mounted on a common plate. The viewing lens (4) in a TLR camera sees a different area than does the taking lens (5). At long distances, the two coincide. You must compensate for this parallax in close-ups. The film plane (6) is the same size as, although not the exact image of, the ground glass (2).

and make the best with what the camera offers. The limitations do not mean inferior image quality. TLR cameras have always been equipped with top-quality lenses, and some are the same as those on SLR types. Moreover, the simple design, with few moving elements, eliminates some variables like a moving mirror that could be the cause of image quality problems.

Viewing on TLRs

Twin lens reflex refers to the camera's optical system. In a TLR, two lenses of identical focal length are mounted one above the other, with centers 40 to 50 mm apart. The top lens is for viewing and the bottom lens is for taking the picture; the lenses are called, respectively, the viewing lens and the taking lens.

Only the taking lens needs to be of high quality. The viewing lens needs to be just good enough to provide a good image for viewing and focusing. Its focal length must match the focal length of the taking lens.

The image formed by the viewing lens is reflected by a reflex mirror and intercepted by the focusing screen. When the focusing knob is turned, both lenses move together. A focused image on the focusing screen is also in focus on the film plane. The typical viewing lens does not have an adjustable aperture for visually checking the image at the shooting aperture. The image on the screen is always as seen by the lens wide open, perhaps even wider than the taking lens as some viewing lenses have larger apertures to produce a brighter image. But the user cannot see how the image changes by opening or closing the aperture, a great sacrifice for serious photography.

The fixed mirror, on the other hand, has a benefit. When the user trips the leaf shutter, the viewing image is not blacked out. The leaf shutter operates only in the taking lens. The user can see the subject at the moment of exposure, not just before and just after. Thus, if the subject blinks or moves as the photo is being taken, the photo can be retaken right away.

Parallax

The image the user views through a TLR is not exactly the same image made on the film because the centers of the two lenses are separated vertically, giving them slightly different fields of view. The effect is called *parallax error*. It is not a serious problem except with close-up pictures. In these photos, the camera must be moved so the taking lens is in the position the viewing lens was in when the image was composed. Some camera models have an indicator in the viewfinder to help do this precisely.

The TLR's drawback is in the versatility of viewing. It is a great tool for ordinary photography at longer distances, so the range of accessories is thus limited to those necessary for such applications. Viewfinders and screens may be interchangeable. Built-in light measuring also exists.

Camera Shape

The shape of all TLR cameras is identical. With viewing and taking chambers arranged vertically, the longest camera dimension is from bottom to top. This camera is made for the square format, mainly because it would be impractical to turn the camera sideways for verticals. It is not made for interchangeable film magazines but usually offers the possibility of using 120 and 220 roll film. Although the operating cycle is much simpler than the SLR's, shooting speed is about the same. Both require turning a knob or crank to advance the film, which usually also recocks the shutter.

TLR model with interchangeable lenses made for the 2¼ × 2¼ in. format. Mamiya, courtesy Berkey Marketing.

Lenses

TLR cameras come with fixed or removable lenses. When removable, viewing and taking lenses come in sets and are removed and attached together. The number of accessory lenses may be limited and is probably not as complete as the range available for SLR types. But then TLR cameras would not be used anyway in cases where an extensive choice of lenses is required.

TLR camera without interchangeable lenses and equipped with a waist-level finder. Courtesy Yashica, Inc.

RANGEFINDERS

A rangefinder was first incorporated into a medium format camera, and rangefinder medium format cameras were quite common in the types with folding bellows. Just as in 35 mm, they took a back seat when SLRs came in. In the medium format, they practically disappeared completely, just to come back in the last year or so. In a way they are the latest in the medium format.

There are good reasons for their reappearance. Compared to SLRs, they are without the mirror mechanism or complicated lens-camera couplings. They have an optical viewfinder that is as bright and clear as the actual view without a focusing screen between the subject and the viewer. Without a need to worry about a mirror, the camera can be made to fold up, with the lens collapsing into the camera body. The result is an extremely compact camera, the smallest and lightest medium format type. If made for the smaller 4.5 cm × 6 cm format, it can be truly pocket size.

For traveling or casual photography not involving close-up photography or requiring different focal length lenses, they provide all the benefits of the larger medium format without the bulk and weight. The medium format rangefinder type cameras are all designed in the same shape as 35 mm cameras, and operated the same way. All rangefinder cameras have leaf shutters, and some have built-in meters.

Rangefinder devotees can find their favorite type of camera also in the medium format, though the choices and features are somewhat limited. In shape, all look like oversized 35s, with the viewfinder or viewfinder-rangefinder combination on top. Film advance and shutter cocking are identical to the 35 with a rapid crank. Lenses are not interchangeable, but some manufacturers offer two models with the same or similar features but with lenses of different focal lengths. All have shutters in the lens, usually up to 1/500 sec, synchronized for flash at all speeds. All take rectangular pictures—6 × 7, 6 × 9, or 4.5 × 6 cm—without a choice of

Compact 6 × 7 cm folding camera with optical viewfinder and rangefinder focusing. Fujica courtesy Fuji Photo Film.

any other format and no film magazine interchangeability. Most, however, provide the choice of 120 or 220 film.

The major variation in the basic camera design among models is in the lens-camera connection. On some the lens is fixed to the camera body; some are the folding type. The latter are not only more compact but provide complete lens protection while carrying. Although these cameras do not have the range of features and possibilities one might associate with medium format photography, they are not old models. Several have come on the market in the last few years, obviously because camera manufacturers felt that there is a market for these cameras. They are beautiful and modern looking. Some even include built-in light measuring through a separate window rather than the lens.

Those cameras are not intended for sophisticated work but have all the features that the average amateur needs for family and travel shooting.

Rangefinder types have their own advantages, mainly in viewing. The viewfinder is as bright as the view with the naked eye. There is no ground glass between user and subject. Focusing with a full field rangefinder is easy and most accurate, assuming that everything is aligned properly. A rangefinder is a fairly delicate instrument, so its accuracy should be checked once in a while by focusing at a subject at a known distance, infinity or perhaps 10 ft, and checking that the distance on the focused lens corresponds.

Since viewing is not through the lens, on some cameras the finder can be made to show a larger field than covered by the lens. The area covered on the film is indicated by lines within the finder. This wider field can be very helpful when deciding on the composition. Users can easily decide whether going farther away makes a better composition. They can also see subjects that might be coming into the field of view before they actually do. Finally, the rangefinder camera is the other type that lets the user see the subject the moment the exposure is made.

WIDE ANGLE CAMERAS

Some of the viewfinder or viewfinder-rangefinder cameras are equipped with a wide angle lens ranging in focal length from 47 to 65 mm. Although these figures do not look short, keep in mind that these cameras are made for the large 6 × 7 or 6 × 9 cm format. The 47 mm lens has a diagonal angle of view of 93° on the 6 × 9 cm format. A 65 mm lens covers 76° diagonally on the same format. I am mentioning these wide angle cameras separately not just because they have wide angle lenses but because the wide angle lenses are not the retrofocus types found on SLR cameras. They are optically true wide angles, the best quality available. These cameras are made so the medium-format photographer can take advantage and benefit from lenses typically found only on view cameras. Architecture and aerial photography are among the more serious applications for

6 × 9 cm wide angle camera with shift capability. Courtesy Plaubel.

such a camera. For either of these applications, it is not necessary to see the image through the lens. The lens is either set for the distance (in aerials) or to a distance and aperture that has everything from foreground to background within the depth of field (in interiors). A spirit level, built

Special motorized camera with rotary focal plane shutter for aerial photography; produces 6 × 9 cm pictures on 70 mm film. Linhof, courtesy HP Marketing Corp.

Wide angle camera with optical viewing device and nonremovable lens. The film magazine is removable for attaching a Polaroid back or a ground-glass screen for viewing and focusing through the lens. Hasselblad, courtesy Victor Hasselblad, Inc.

in or as an accessory, however, is a great help. It is the only way to be certain that the camera is level to record verticals, straight and parallel.

The Hasselblad SWC/M must be mentioned separately. Like the others, it is a wide angle camera with a built-in, optically true wide angle lens, with 90° diagonal coverage on the 2 1/4 in. square. What separates it from the rest is the magazine interchangeability—the possibility of using 120, 220, 70 mm sheetfilm and Polaroid film.

The second point is the viewing and focusing. Like the others, viewing is normally done with a simple optical finder on top of the camera. For critical work and for visual focusing, a ground-glass back can be attached to the rear of the camera after the film magazine is removed. It now functions like a wide angle view camera.

PANORAMIC CAMERAS

The range of medium format cameras is increased by cameras made for a very long format—5 to 6 3/4 in.—but still using the standard roll film. The images, looking like a wide screen presentation, can be extremely striking, at least as horizontals. The cameras can be turned for verticals, but most of these images lack the spectacular effect of the horizontals, probably because we are not used to looking at high verticals.

The format is appropriate for wraparound book covers, calendars, and annual reports. The panorama can also be used for multiimage slide presentations. To cover that long format with superb corner-to-corner quality, the lens must be made to cover either the 4 × 5 in. or 5 × 7 in.

Panoramic camera for six 6 × 9 cm images on 120 film and twelve on 220 film. The camera features interchangeable lenses and built-in perspective control. Linhof, courtesy HP Marketing Corp.

view camera format. The lenses on those cameras are actually view camera lenses and are by far the most expensive part of such cameras. The full negative requires an enlarger capable of printing from 5 × 7 in. negatives.

The features and operation of panoramic cameras are very much like the viewfinder-rangefinder types. They can be used hand held or on a tripod. A built-in spirit level is helpful because a level camera is important for effective panoramas.

Although they are specifically made for the panoramic image format, the negatives or transparencies could be cropped to a normal format; this, however, is an expensive way to produce normal shots.

There is another way of producing panoramic images with a medium format camera. This second method involves 35 mm film. Several SLR models offer special film magazines for standard 35 mm film in cassettes. The magazine may be made for the standard 24 × 36 mm frame or a panoramic 24 × 56 mm on a 2 1/4 in. square or 4.5 × 6 cm camera or even longer 24 × 69 mm in a 6 × 7 cm model. This panoramic 35 mm format is also a medium format exclusive; it cannot be done with 35 mm

Panoramic camera for the largest medium format, 6 × 17 cm, provides four exposures on 120 film and eight on 220. It has two release buttons and a lens protection frame. Fujica, courtesy Fuji Photo Film.

equipment. The format can be very effective in printed form; it can find use in 35 mm multimedia shows and can also be used in projectors made for the 2 1/4 in. square or 6 × 7 cm format.

PRESS CAMERAS

Press-type cameras—the folding type with bellows or with the lens mounted on the camera body—are another version of medium format viewfinder-rangefinder types. They have a large viewfinder, a permanently attached camera grip, and leaf shutters in the lenses, which can be removed with a choice of focal lengths from wide angle to telephoto. Shutter cocking is a separate operation, not coupled to the film advance. I consider these cameras somewhat outdated, especially for news work.

VIEW CAMERAS

Medium format photography can be done on view cameras by attaching a roll film magazine in place of sheetfilm holders or attaching the camera body with film magazine to the rear of the view camera. Special accessories for this purpose are available from some view camera manufacturers. Combining the two allows the use of roll film instead of sheets in the

Medium format and 4 × 5 in. press cameras were the standard tools of the press photographer in the 1930s and 1940s. They are still available and may come with or without a bellows. They usually provide rangefinder focusing. Pictured here is a press-type medium format camera with interchangeable lenses attached directly to the camera body, used for film formats 4.5 × 6 cm up to 6 × 9 cm. Mamiya, courtesy Berkey Marketing.

Technical or press camera with interchangeable backs for 6 × 6 cm, 6 × 7 cm, and 6 × 9 cm formats and interchangeable leaf shutter lenses. Linhof, courtesy HP Marketing Corp.

view camera and makes it possible to use swings and tilts when photographing in the medium format.

STUDIO CAMERAS

School photographers use motor-driven cameras made specifically for this staged, large production photography. Because studio cameras are made for one specific application, they are mentioned here simply for completeness. The cameras use either 70 mm or 46 mm film and are designed to print information on the negative for identification purposes.

MANUFACTURERS

I recommend that you study the camera types and use the manufacturers' literature and specification sheets when you consider medium format

Press-type camera with swings and tilts made for 4 × 5 in. sheetfilm but usable with 120 and 220 roll film holders for the 6 × 7 cm, 6 x 9 cm, and 6 × 12 cm medium format. Horseman Camera, courtesy Calumet Photographic.

cameras. If possible, try to handle and operate the cameras and their features at a camera store. The greatest, most sophisticated sounding feature on paper may be of little help to you if it does not fit your established method of handling and operating cameras.

Medium format SLR camera with nonfoldable waist-level finder with built-in meter and motor drive built into the handgrip. Bronica, courtesy GMI Photographic.

6 × 7 cm SLR model with interchangeable film magazines for other smaller formats and equipped with accessory 90° prism finder and handgrip. Bronica, courtesy GMI Photographic.

The following list shows what manufacturers make what types of cameras, and it mentions the main characteristics of these cameras, such as shutter type formats, lenses, motor drives, and exposure metering.

Arca Swiss

2 1/4 × 3 1/4 in. yaw free view camera that collapses into a small 5 lb. unit. Screen integrated light measurement with separate exposure meter.

Beattie

Special identification cameras for 70 mm, 46 mm, and 35 mm film.

Bronica

SLR camera (box shape) for 2 1/4 × 2 1/4 in. with interchangeable leaf shutter lenses and 120 and 220 film magazines for 4.5 × 6 cm. Polaroid and 35 mm film producing 24 × 36 mm or 24 × 54 mm images. Motor drive available. TTL metering with prism finder.

SLR camera (box shape) for 6 × 7 cm with interchangeable film magazines for 2 1/4 × 2 1/4 in. and 4.5 × 6 cm on 120 and 220 film. Polaroid and 35 mm film producing a 24 × 36 mm or 24 × 69 mm image. Interchangeable leaf shutter lenses. TTL metering with prism finder.

SLR cameras (box shape) for 4.5 × 6 cm images on 120 or 220 film with interchangeable leaf shutter lenses. Interchangeable magazine for Polaroid and 35 mm producing a 24 × 36 mm or 24 × 54 mm image. TTL metering with prism finder. Motor-drive accessory available.

All of these Bronica models also offer interchangeable screens and finders.

Exacta

SLR camera (in 35 mm shape) with focal plane shutter up to 1/1000 sec for 2 1/4 × 2 1/4 in. on 120 or 220 film. Interchangeable lenses. No interchangeable magazines. Interchangeable screens and finders. TTL metering with prism finder.

Fuji

Rangefinder cameras in the 35 mm shape for 6 × 9 cm with interchangeable lenses firmly attached to body (no bellows). Available with a standard lens or wide angle with leaf shutters. For 120 or 220 film. No metering system.

Rangefinder model in the compact 35 mm shape with foldable bellows for 4.5 × 6 cm format. For 120 or 220 film. Standard, noninterchangeable lens with leaf shutter. Built-in meter.

Panoramic camera for 6 × 17 cm format on 120 or 220 film. Noninterchangeable lens with leaf shutter. Optical type viewfinder.

6 × 8 cm view camera with swing-up mirror for viewing from top as on SLR types. Rotatable, film magazine for 120 or 220 film. Motor-drive, tilt, rise, shift, and swing movements in lens board. Interchangeable lenses with lens shutter up to 1/400 sec. TTL aperture priority metering.

Hasselblad

SLR camera (box shape) with leaf shutter in lenses. Manual film advance. TTL metering with meter prisms. Fully interchangeable lenses, screens, and viewfinders.

SLR camera (box shape) with built-in motor drive and leaf shutter in lenses. Off-the-film-plane TTL metering for flash. TTL metering for existing light with prism finder. Can be used in combination with 70 mm data recording back. Fully interchangeable lenses, screens, and viewfinders.

SLR camera (box shape) with focal plane shutter up to 1/2000 sec, which can also be used with a full line of leaf shutter lenses in addition to faster lenses without shutter. Motor-drive accessory. Fully interchangeable lenses, screens, and viewfinders.

Wide angle camera with optical viewfinder and nonremovable wide angle lens. Visual focusing possible with ground-glass accessory. TTL metering with prism finder attached over ground-glass accessory.

All of these cameras have fully interchangeable film magazines for 120, 220, 70 mm, sheetfilm, and Polaroid; standard magazine for 2 1/4 ×

Camera with standard waist-level finder and motor drive permanently attached to camera body bottom. The rechargeable nickel cadium battery is also in the motor compartment. Hasselblad, courtesy Victor Hasselblad, Inc.

2 1/4 in.; other magazines for 4.5 × 6 cm horizontally on 120 or 220 or vertically on 120, and superslides and 35 mm panoramic (24 × 56 mm). There are two more Hasselblad medium format cameras:

SLR camera basically made for manual film advance but equipped with a motor drive in place of a winding crank. The camera also has a 45° prism viewfinder. Hasselblad, courtesy Victor Hasselblad, Inc.

Special photogrammetric camera with reseau plate and optical finder. Two interchangeable lenses.

Special photogrammetric wide angle camera with reseau plate and optical finder and nonremovable wide angle lens.

Both are made for 2 1/4 × 2 1/4 in. on 70 mm film and have interchangeable magazines but for 70 mm film only.

Calumet

Press camera with bellows for 6 × 9 cm and 6 × 7 cm on 120 film. Also usable for 4 × 5 in. sheetfilm. Interchangeable leaf shutter lenses. Rangefinder focusing. Swing and tilt possibility.

Linhof

Panoramic camera (35 mm shape) for 6 × 12 cm format (2 1/4 × 5 in). Two interchangeable leaf shutter lenses. Optical viewfinder. For 120 and 220 film. Perspective control.

Wide angle camera (press type without bellows) with interchangeable backs for 120 or 220 film for 2 1/4 × 2 1/4 in., 6 × 7 cm, 6 × 9 cm, and Polaroid. Interchangeable leaf shutter lenses. Also for 4 × 5 in. sheets.

View camera with roll film adapters for 120, 220, and 70 mm film. Format choices: 2 1/4 × 2 1/4 in., 2 1/4 × 3 1/4 in., 6 × 7 cm, and 6 × 9 cm. Interchangeable leaf shutter lenses. Swing and tilt controls.

Aerial camera for 70 mm film with rotary focal plane shutter up to 1/1500 sec. Image format 6 × 9 cm. Motor drive for three frames in 2 sec. Interchangeable lenses and film magazines. Data back available.

Mamiya

SLR camera (box shape) for 2 1/4 × 2 3/4 in. with interchangeable leaf shutter lenses and rotatable film magazines so verticals can be made with-

2¼ × 2¾ in. camera with interchangeable, revolving film magazine so verticals and horizontals can be produced without having to turn the entire camera. Mamiya, courtesy Berkey Marketing.

Focal plane shutter box-shape camera made for 6 × 4.5 cm format offers interchangeable lenses, screens, finders, and film inserts but not film magazines. Mamiya, courtesy Berkey Marketing.

out turning the camera. Interchangeable magazines and lenses. Motor
available. For 120 and 220 film. Other film magazines for 4.5 × 6 cm, 70
mm, and Polaroid. TTL metering with prism finder. Interchangeable focusing screens and finders.

SLR cameras (box shape) for 4.5 × 6 cm with focal plane shutter up to
1/1000 sec or up to 1/500 sec, depending on model. One leaf shutter lens
available. Interchangeable lenses. All models offer interchangeable film
inserts. Magazine interchangeability on one model. For 120 and 220, 35
mm and Polaroid film. Motor-drive accessory available for some models.
TTL metering with prism finder. Interchangeable focusing screens and
finders.

TLR cameras with interchangeable leaf shutter lens pairs. For 120 and
220 film. One model with TTL metering in prism finder. Interchangeable
focusing screens. One model with interchangeable finders.

6 × 9 cm press camera without bellows. Interchangeable leaf shutter
lenses. Rangefinder focusing. For 120 and 220 film. Interchangeable film
backs for 4.5 × 6 cm, 70 mm, sheetfilm, and Polaroid.

Rangefinder camera for 6 × 6 cm format on 120 or 220 film. Parallax
compensating viewfinder and interchangeable lenses with flash sync up
to 1/500 sec.

Pentax
SLR camera in 35 mm shape for 6 × 7 cm with focal plane shutter up to
1/1000 sec. For 120 or 220 film. Interchangeable lenses. No interchangeable magazine. Special lenses with leaf shutter available. Interchangeable
screens and finders. TTL metering with prism finder.

SLR (box shape) for 4.5 × 6 cm with built-in motor drive. Interchangeable
lenses but not film magazines. For 120 and 220 and 70 mm. Focal plane

6 × 4.5 cm with attached grip and built-in metering system. The lenses are interchangeable; the film magazines are not. Pentax, courtesy Pentax Corp.

shutter up to 1/1000 sec. Leaf shutter lens available. Interchangeable screens and finders. TTL light measuring for flash and existing light with programmed 35 mm automation.

Plaubel

Rangefinder (RF) cameras in the shape of 35 mm RF type with folding bellows for 6 × 7 cm format on 120 or 220 film. Leaf shutter in noninterchangeable lens. Two models with different focal length lens: one standard and one wide angle. Built-in light meter with aperture and shutter speed coupling. Optical finder with automatic parallax adjustment.

Wide angle camera with built-in horizontal and vertical shift for 6 × 9 cm (56 × 83 mm) format on 120 or 220 film. 35 mm rangefinder shape with leaf shutter lens. Optical viewfinder with parallax connection and sports finder.

Compact 6 × 7 cm folding camera with optical viewfinder and rangefinder focusing. Courtesy Plaubel.

Box-shape camera with interchangeable lens mounted in front of a built-in bellows, which also allows a certain amount of lens tilt for increased depth of field. Rolleiflex, courtesy HP Marketing Corp.

Rolleiflex

SLR camera (box shape) with built-in motor drive. Interchangeable leaf shutter lenses. TTL metering with existing light and flash with programmed 35 mm automation. Available with or without interchangeable film magazine.

Two SLR cameras (box shape) with built-in bellows for close-up photography and 8° swing for increased depth-of-field control. Focal plane shutter up to 1/1000 sec with two leaf shutter lenses available. One model with OTF flash control and TTL metering for regular light; the other model with OTF flash control only.

Both models have interchangeable screens, finders, and magazines. Standard magazines are made for 2 1/4 × 2 1/4 in. on 120 or 220 film. A 4.5 × 6 cm magazine for 120 or 220 and Polaroid film is also available.

TLR camera for 6 × 6 cm format with automatic OTF flash control and TTL metering for regular light.

Sinar

View cameras with adapters for 120 or 220 film. Format choices are 4.5 × 6 cm; 2 1/4 × 2 1/4 in.; 6 × 9 cm; and 6 × 12 cm. Interchangeable leaf shutter lenses. Swing and tilt control.

Toyo

2 1/4 × 3 1/4 in. view camera with rollfilm holder for 6 × 7 cm and 6 × 9 cm formats.

Yashica

Twin lens reflex camera for 2 1/4 × 2 1/4 in. on 120 or 220 film with noninterchangeable leaf shutter lens.

CHAPTER 5

Shutters

Medium format cameras come with focal plane shutters or with lens shutters. One or two also offer both shutters in one camera. Since shutters are an important part of a camera and to a great extent determine what can be done with the camera, a discussion of the function and possibilities of the two shutters is important.

FOCAL PLANE SHUTTERS

The focal plane shutter is part of most 35 mm SLR cameras. It consists of two curtains moving vertically or horizontally in front of the film plane. It scans the film area vertically or horizontally. In the past most curtains were made from cloth. Some are still made from this material, but more often a metal curtain such as titanium is used. Although the titanium curtain may not necessarily be stronger as far as damage is concerned, since it is likely to be very thin, metal allows refinements in performance. Also it is impossible to burn a hole in the curtain, which could happen in the cloth type when photographing directly into the sun.

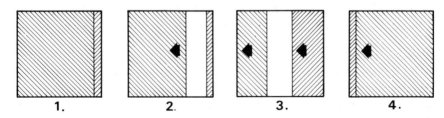

With a focal plane shutter, the film is exposed progressively as the shutter curtain moves across the film area. When the release is depressed, the first curtain starts to move. The second curtain is delayed. The shutter speed determines the delay. At high shutter speeds, the full film area is never exposed at the same time; thus flash synchronization is impossible.

In medium format cameras with interchangeable magazines, the focal plane curtain is at the rear of the camera body and fully exposed to damage when the film magazine is removed from the camera. (The same is also true on 35 mm cameras when the camera back is opened.) To avoid curtain damage, the camera should be stored with the magazine on the camera, and the magazine should be changed with care. Most curtains are damaged when a corner of the magazine accidentally hits the curtain. The problem has been eliminated on one medium format camera in which the focal plane curtain retracts automatically the moment when the film magazine is lifted off. It is no longer there when the magazine is off the camera, a great protection for the delicate focal plane curtain.

Shutter Design

A modern focal plane shutter consists of two curtains. Between pictures, the curtains cover the film completely so that the lens can be changed at any time without fogging the film. At rest, when cocked, the curtains are slightly separated. If the shutter speed is set at the highest speed, both curtains start moving the moment the release is depressed. When the shutter speed is set slower, only the first curtain moves when the release is depressed; the second curain follows later. The delay time is determined by the shutter speed.

On modern cameras, the shutter speed is controlled electronically. The actual movement of the curtain may be mechanical, but compared to a lens shutter, fewer mechanical components are involved, especially parts that require lubrication.

Flash Synchronization

Since a focal plane shutter scans the film area from side to side, different areas of the film are exposed to light at different times. This means that when flash is used, the flash must go off when the shutter is open over the entire film area. Otherwise only part of the film area is exposed. At high shutter speeds, the second curtain starts to move and cover up part of the film area before the first curtain has disappeared completely. Consequently flash pictures can be made only at slower shutter speeds. The flash synchronization range has been increased dramatically over the years because metal curtains can be made to move faster. Modern 35 mm focal plane shutter cameras can synchronize with flash at rather high shutter speeds. On medium format cameras, this is not the case because the curtains have to travel across an area that is about twice as wide as on 35 mm.

Some cameras allow a top speed of 1/30 sec only, a serious limitation in such applications as sports and flash fill-in. The highest flash syn-

1.   2.   3.   4.   5.

The flash must fire when the first curtain has fully exposed the film area but before the second curtain starts to move *(3)*, which occurs only up to a certain shutter speed. At higher speeds, the second curtain starts to move before the first curtain has fully exposed the film area. Part of the picture is blank, as in *(2)* and *(4)*. On some cameras, the flash fires only when the shutter is set at speeds at which it is synchronized with the flash eliminating, or at least reducing, the danger of a costly mistake.

chronization on focal plane shutter medium format cameras at present is 1/90 sec, quite an improvement over 1/30 sec.

If the shutter speed is accidently set too high on a focal plane shutter camera, the mistake is usually not discovered until the film is processed. To avoid this, some manufacturers have built a flash firing control so the flash does not fire when the shutter speed is set beyond the synchronization range, indicating to the user that something is wrong.

Distortion

Focal plane shutters, especially those moving horizontally, produce another undesirable effect when photographing moving subjects. Since the shutter scans the film, it does not expose the entire film area at the same moment. It exposes one side first, and by the time it has moved across the film area, a moving subject also has moved. As a result, a subject moving horizontally in front of the lens may be recorded physically longer than in reality if the image crosses the film in the same direction as the curtain, or physically shorter when it moves in the opposite direction. In either case, it is referred to and recognized on the film as a form of distortion. A moving round wheel is recorded as ellipses.

Focal plane shutters can distort images of moving subjects because the recording of the image is progressive rather than instantaneous. Thus an object moving in the same direction as the shutters will appear elongated; one moving in the opposite direction will appear shortened.

Shutter Speed

With the focal plane shutter being completely separated from the lens aperture, the effective shutter speed is the same whether the lens aperture is wide open or closed.

With focal plane shutters, on the other hand, exposure variations can occur across the film area. For even exposure, the curtains must travel across the entire film area at a perfectly even rate. This is difficult to accomplish since the curtains must accelerate to a very high rate within a very short time and then travel across the medium format film area at a high rate and come to an almost instant stop without tearing the curtain. Manufacturers try to keep the exposure variations within acceptable levels or have gone beyond and provided perfectly even exposure from side to side by designing the electronics so the speed of the second curtain varies from side to side to compensate for the acceleration. The width of the slit exposing the film thus changes as it travels across the film area to ensure even exposure. This important and professional feature can be found on medium format cameras using the most modern thin titanium curtains.

One other negative, though minor, point of focal plane shutters is that they tend to be noisy because the curtains moves at a rapid speed over a large area. They are also frequently associated with a metallic sound. Lens shutters are quieter and operate more smoothly.

Vibration

Focal plane curtains are often said to produce more camera vibrations than the lens type. Generally they do. Most of the motion is caused when the curtain stops, and this is not after the exposure is made, as often said. The first curtain stops while part of the film area is still being exposed, so its vibration can add image unsharpness. The starting and stopping of modern focal plane curtains, however, has been dampened to a great degree to reduce camera motion. The possibility of increased camera motion should therefore be a minor consideration when deciding between a focal plane or lens shutter.

Lens Variety and Design

There are other good reasons for building focal plane shutters into the camera body. The shutter of the camera determines shutter speed. It is therefore more likely that every lens produces the same exposure at the same aperture.

The focal plane shutter camera can be used with just about any type of lens, including special types—photomicrographic, for example—without losing the shutter control. They can also be used in applications where lenses are not needed at all—for instance, photography through a microscope or telescope. It eliminates the need for each lens having its own shutter, thus perhaps reducing the cost of the lens. More important, putting the shutter in the camera instead of the lens increases lens design possibilities. A shutter in a lens limits lens design, making it more difficult to increase the maximum aperture and the minimum focusing distance and making it almost impossible to design special lenses.

Shutter Speed Range

Fast shutter speed is another advantage of focal plane shutters. Lens shutters are efficient up to speeds of 1/500 sec, sufficiently fast for most photography. Focal plane shutters can be made to produce accurate exposure times at higher speeds. You can find speeds of up to 1/2000 sec on medium format cameras. Cameras in the future may even go higher.

Focal plane shutters in modern medium format cameras are timed electronically. On the long shutter speed end, they go at least to 1 sec but may extend up to several seconds. Exposure times longer than 1 sec can be obtained by keeping the shutter open manually for the desired number of seconds. A solution for electronically timed long exposure times is with a shutter speed multiplier accessory. Attached to the camera, it multiplies the exposure times set on the shutter by a certain factor, perhaps 60. The exposure time is then sixty times longer than set on the camera: 1 sec becomes 60 sec; 1/4 is 15 sec ($60 \times 1/4 = 60/4 = 15$).

LENS SHUTTERS

The wide choice of lens shutter models is another advantage of the medium format. Lens shutters are standard in TLR, press, and folding cameras. They operate simply: the shutter and the lens open and close when the release is depressed. Exposure times on lens shutters can be 1 sec or longer. The shortest speed is 1/500 sec, sufficient for most photography.

Shutter Design

A lens shutter adds to the cost of the lens. If there is a problem with a shutter in the lens, however, photography can continue because the user can switch to another lens.

A lens shutter complicates the design of an SLR camera. A focal plane curtain not only makes the exposure, it also keeps the film chamber completely light tight before and after the exposure. A curtain of some kind must be built in to an SLR lens shutter camera to perform the same task before and after the exposure.

The lens shutter and rear curtain operations must then be synchronized accurately so the lens shutter is fully closed before the rear curtain starts to open, and the rear curtain must be fully open before the lens shutter opens again to make the exposure. These operations are done fully automatically and within a very short time delay of perhaps 1/25 sec in a modern camera—not much longer or even shorter than the delay in a focal plane shutter SLR camera with through-the-lens light metering.

Prereleasing Cameras

Lens shutters are smooth and quiet. In an SLR camera, however, most of the sound and vibration do not come from the shutter but the mirror liftup and the protective rear curtain operation. The full benefits from the smooth and quiet lens shutter operation, especially valuable in suppressing camera noise when photographing in churches, synagogues, and museums, are obtained by prereleasing the camera. This means the mirror is lifted up and the rear curtain is opened before the exposure is made.

In a lens shutter, shutter blades open and close at the set speed, exposing the entire film area at the same time and for the same length of time. With lens shutters, distortion of moving subjects does not occur.

Flash Synchronization

Since they expose the entire film area at the same time, lens shutters can be used with flash at every shutter speed up to 1/500 sec. This must be one of the main considerations when the camera type decision is made. To overcome this limitation, some medium format camera manufacturers offer one or two special shutter lenses for focal plane shutter cameras. One medium format camera with focal plane shutter can be used with an entire line of shutter lenses, from fish-eye to long telephotos. That means

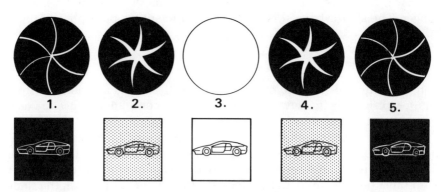

When the lens shutter is used, the entire film area is exposed immediately. During the cycle, the image becomes bright and then darkens again. There is no distortion because the entire film area is exposed simultaneously.

users have a camera with two shutters—and therefore the benefits of both. Such a camera does not exist in any other format.

Electronic and Mechanical Shutters

Lens shutters can be controlled mechanically or electronically. Electronic control is likely more accurate, especially at cold temperatures, but users have to rely on battery operation.

Mechanical lens shutters must be cleaned and lubricated more frequently to remain accurate and reliable in cold weather. This is necessary mainly because lenses cannot be sealed completely so dust will penetrate. Lubricants also work differently at different temperatures. The lens shutter operation is therefore affected by temperature, especially cold temperature. The shutter slows down when exposed to extremes, especially when lubricants are old.

Exposure Accuracy

Because the lens shutter is next to the lens diaphragm, it opens and closes in front of a large opening when the diaphragm is set to large apertures and in front of a small opening when the diaphragm is closed down. The engraved shutter speeds are calibrated as if the blades opened fully and closed again. In other words, they are calibrated for a larger aperture. When the diaphragm is closed, the small aperture is uncovered slightly sooner and covered slightly later. The effective shutter speed may be longer by the equivalent of one-half or even one f stop. On a properly lubricated lens, this happens only at 1/500 sec and only when the diaphragm is completely, or almost completely, closed.

While the variation in the effective shutter speed is correct, it is often exaggerated as far as modern lens shutters are concerned. The effect depends mainly on the relationship between the shutter and lens apertures. The closer the two are related, the more efficient is the shutter, especially at high shutter speeds.

In modern lenses, shutters are made in different diameters so they correspond as closely as possible to the maximum aperture diameter. Large diameter shutters go into the longer focal length lenses and small diameters into the wide angles. Exposure variations have been reduced to acceptable levels.

OPERATING CONSIDERATIONS

Lens shutter operation on most cameras is as automatic as the focal plane type. After the exposure, moving a lever or turning a crank recocks the shutter and advances the film. Motor operation is also possible. In some medium format cameras, however, shutter cocking and film are two separate operations—in my mind, a rather old-fashioned approach that limits the speed of shooting almost down to the view camera level.

On focal plane shutter cameras, the shutter operating knob is always on the camera body; the aperture ring, on the lens. Lens shutter types feature the same arrangement if the shutter is controlled electronically. You can also find both calibrations on the lens barrel. The latter might be an advantage; users need to look at only one place to see aperture and shutter speed setting. Both being next to each other also shows instantly the different aperture–shutter speed combinations that provide correct exposure and may make it easier to decide which combination should be used.

Self-timers do exist on focal plane and lens shutter cameras, but they are disappearing from cameras because they are used infrequently. Most photographers can live without them, and the space that was taken up by the timing clock can be used more valuably. Furthermore, self-timing accessories can be attached to the camera release.

CHAPTER 6

Films

The quality of the medium format image starts with the film loaded into the camera.

BLACK-AND-WHITE FILM

Most black-and-white films made for medium format cameras are identical to those made for 35 mm cameras. They are also processed in the same fashion. This simplifies the selection for photographers who have previously worked in the smaller format. In most cases, the film that would be used in the 35 mm camera is also the logical choice in roll film.

Photographers who frequently work in low light situations with lens apertures of $f1.4$ or $f2$ on their 35 mm cameras may be better off switching to a faster medium format film if it exists. The reason is that medium format lenses are slower. F2 lenses do exist for some cameras. For most, however, the maximum aperture of the standard lens is only $f2.8$ and even slower on the wide angles and telephotos.

There is another reason for considering a faster medium format film: depth of field. The focal length of the lens necessary for the medium format camera to cover the same area as a 35 mm lens needs to be almost twice as long. Such a lens at the same aperture produces less depth of field. To produce equal depth, it must be closed down one to two stops, depending on the medium film format.

As an example, a 90 mm lens on a medium format camera with 400 ASA at $f16$ and 1/125 sec produces an image with about equal depth of field as a 50 mm lens on a 35 mm camera at $f8$ (either with 100 ASA film at 1/125 sec or 400 ASA at 1/500 sec).

Just as in any other film format, slower medium format films tend to have a higher resolution and finer grain, thus producing a sharper image. It is obviously the choice when sharpness is the main goal or when the negative is to be enlarged tremendously or needs extensive cropping.

With the high quality of today's films, however, one should not hesitate to use the faster films, especially not in the medium format where the negative need not be enlarged as much. The fast films might allow hand-held photography where otherwise a tripod may be necessary. More important, it allows using shorter shutter speeds and thus reducing the possibility of camera shake. The sharpness of the high-speed film negative taken at a shorter shutter speed can very well be superior to that of a slower film at a slower speed. This is correct especially for the latest development, the chronogenic black-and-white films with an ISO rating of about 400. They are similar in function to color negative films but without separated tricolor response. The resulting negative is a dye image rather than a silver one. They have less apparent grain, higher resolution, and greater exposure latitude. They are developed in C-41 chemistry along with color negative films. Special developers are also available.

Since black-and-white films are of such high quality, users might be able to do all their black-and-white photography with one film.

Generally, however, for optimum sharpness, it is better to use the slowest film that can do the job and select the faster ones only when necessary. Switching from slow to fast films and vice-versa is greatly simplified in medium format cameras that offer interchangeable magazines. Two or three magazines can be loaded with different black-and-white films and switched from one to the other in the middle of the roll. Thus users are always in the position to use the film that is best for each subject by carrying one camera only.

Those interested in experimenting in the darkroom should not overlook many of the black-and-white films made for special purposes, such as high-contrast images, copying, and photomicrography.

Exposure

In addition to camera steadiness, accurate focusing, lens quality, and film flatness, the sharpness of the black-and-white negative is also affected by exposure and development. Overexposure and overdevelopment increase gain size and thus reduce apparent sharpness.

A thin negative that has just enough shadow detail makes the sharpest print. There is naturally a limit to how far you can go in changing exposure and still produce a good negative with shadow and highlight detail.

Too little exposure causes loss of shadow detail. A print from an underexposed negative has shadow areas in which even the lighter subject tones print black. In a good print, the lighter subject tones in the shadows must show detail for the picture to look natural.

In serious overexposure, some of the light and shadow effects of the subject are lost.

Subjects with high brightness ratios are contrasting subjects, while subjects with low brightness ratios—say 30:1—as in the fog or on an overcast day, are flat or low contrast. Contrasting subjects must be exposed fairly exactly, whereas flat subjects can be exposed over a fairly wide range without serious overexposure or underexposure.

Film Development

Film development provides more latitude than exposure. Developing time changes contrast. Contrast is increased by developing longer and reduced by cutting the developing time. This is a helpful control that not only produces very printable negatives but also may make it unnecessary to have a wide range of different contrast papers. Most or all negatives can have a contrast range that is printable on a standard grade paper regardless of the subject or lighting contrast. Using this contrast control requires that all negatives on a roll of film be taken of similar subjects. The shorter rolls with fewer images (usually twelve) of the medium format films have in this respect an advantage over the longer 35 mm rolls with twenty-four or thirty-six exposures. Film development time should be chosen so that normal subjects will match the contrast of medium or grade 2 papers when printed on one's own enlarger.

Proper agitation avoids mottle. Unevenly developed silver densities are caused by underagitation. Increased density along the edges of the film, or, in the case of 70 mm film, perforation streaks are caused by agitation that is too violent.

Overdevelopment at high temperatures can cause blocked highlights, particularly when the negative is overexposed. An overworked or under-replenished developer should not be used. Shadow areas in the negative may be lacking in detail as if they had been underexposed.

All film manufacturers have detailed information on their films. A film and development combination that works for you should be used; trying a different film and development each time may very well slow down your photographic progress without leading to better results.

Photographic Print

To maintain the maximum sharpness in the print, consider the quality of the enlarging lens, film flatness in the negative carrier, accurate focusing of the enlarging lens, and steadiness of the enlarger during exposure. Special attention needs to be paid to the negative carrier. The base on most medium format films is thinner than on the 35s. There is a greater tendency to buckle when exposed to the heat in the enlarger. The negative pops, no longer lies flat, or actually buckles and moves while the exposure is made. Use of a glass carrier will prevent this. All glass surfaces must be kept clean.

The tendency to buckle might also come up in film developing. The point at which the film bends can add density, creating a small crescent shape. Other points to consider for maximum print quality are correct exposure of the print; proper choice of contrast grade of paper that produces a print with deep blacks, white whites, and a full range of middle tones; and correct and full development of the print.

A glossy paper surface also produces the sharpest looking print. Papers with glossy and high-luster surfaces have longer visual scales than papers with luster and matte surfaces. Better visual tone separation is obtained when printed on glossy or high-luster papers.

Print quality is best when:

- It is exposed so that the print density is just right when it has received the full development time. Considerable print underdevelopment causes muddy and perhaps uneven image tones that may have an unpleasant brownish image color. Overdevelopment results in a lack of highlight detail, fog, or stain or all three.
- The specular highlights print as white (paper base white), with diffuse highlights printed as delicate grays.
- Dark subject tones in the shadows are reproduced as black (maximum density) in the print.
- Mid to light subject tones in the shadows are reproduced as dark but lighter than black tones in the print.
- The midtone range of the print has good tonal separation.

Enlarger Lenses

Nothing contributes toward good print quality as much as a clean enlarger lens in top condition. Sparkling highlights and rich blacks are difficult to obtain with a dirty enlarger lens or one in poor condition.

Condenser illumination yields somewhat higher contrast and slightly greater sharpness than the diffused light type. Use the one that best suits the type of work you are doing.

Condenser enlargers usually are brighter; thus exposure times can be kept reasonably short. They print with more contrast than do the diffusion type, so films for condenser enlarger printing should be developed for shorter times than those for diffusion enlarger printing. Condenser enlargers are usually preferred for enlarging medium format negatives.

Whichever type is chosen, the illumination should be reasonably even over the entire field. You can test this by making a print without a negative in the enlarger. Focus the lens on the edges of the negative carrier and stop down to your usual printing aperture. Expose the paper so that it develops out to a middle gray. If the test print varies considerably in density over the printed area, the illumination is uneven.

COLOR NEGATIVE FILM

Most that has been said about black and white applies also to color negative film. Most film manufacturers make the same films for 35 mm and medium format cameras. Slower films tend to have finer grain and better definition.

Until recently, the fastest color films were rated 400 ASA. Today's fast color negative films are 1000 ASA. These films are of high quality, far better in every respect than the 100 ASA types of some years ago.

Exposure and developing times, however, cannot be varied as in black and white. Color negatives need the correct exposures with sufficient shadow details. Some films can be exposed at a somewhat higher ASA rating and pushed in developing, although some deterioration in the image quality may occur.

Everything said about the enlarger and enlarging lens for black-and-white film also applies except the point about print sharpness between condenser and diffuser illumination. Condenser illumination does not produce sharper color prints.

Amateur and Professional Film

Color negative films made by some manufacturers come in an amateur version and a professional type with the same or a completely different name. For Kodak, Kodacolor is the amateur type and Vericolor the professional. One may be better than the other in some respects, but both produce superb color prints. Many professionals use the amateur type for some of their work, and many amateurs use the professional type. Professional films are made to a higher degree of color consistency so that each roll of film produces matched results. This is important to the professional who often exposes several rolls of film of the same subject. Professional films also are made to higher accuracy in sensitivity, so exposures are matched from roll to roll. To maintain this consistency, professional films must be stored properly as recommended by the manufacturer. This means refrigerated until they are used and refrigerated again afterward if not processed immediately. Amateur films do not need this treatment, an advantage when traveling.

The choice between amateur and professional, however, may be mainly determined by the laboratory. Many are specifically geared toward one or the other. Many professional laboratories do not process the amateur films or do not guarantee professional results from the amateur version.

Filters

Color negative films are made in the daylight version only because the majority of amateur and professional images are made in daylight or with electronic flash, both with the same color temperature. They can be used under other light sources—tungsten or fluorescent lights, for instance—and without using a filter on the lens. The necessary filtration can be

To help the laboratory produce prints with the proper color rendition, include either a gray card or a color control strip in one of the color negatives. This is advisable especially when the image does not include subjects of known color values (flesh tones, for instance).

employed when the print is made, although I recommend using the necessary filter on the camera when the picture is made. All images are then reproduced on the film as if taken under the light for which the film was made, eliminating many problems in the darkroom. The required filter is the same as required for daylight color transparency film.

The filter is especially suggested when no people are in the picture. Without flesh tones, the darkroom technician has no idea what the colors should be unless the photographer included an 18 percent gray card or a color chart in at least one of the negatives. Even with people in the picture, correct colors can only be assured because flesh tones vary from white to black. A gray card or color chart included in at least one of the negatives is highly recommended for critical work. If nothing else, it eliminates future arguments with the laboratory.

COLOR TRANSPARENCY FILM

Color slide films also come in amateur and professional versions. They may be identical films, even with the same name, and both may require the same processing. The only difference is in the aging process. The colors in an undeveloped film are not perfectly stable; they shift somewhat as the film is stored. Professional film is preaged at the factory so it produces the correct color when delivered to the store. To remain in the properly aged condition, however, the film must be refrigerated until about an hour before it is used. If it is not processed immediately afterward, it must stay refrigerated. Professional films are made so the professional has matched colors and exposure from roll to roll. The exact ASA rating of each roll of professional film is imprinted on the instruction sheet. If the color quality is beyond the manufacturer's standards, the necessary color correction filter is also indicated.

Amateur film is delivered to the store in a state where it produces the correct color after it has been stored at normal room temperature for four to six months. This is the average time manufacturers have found it takes from the moment the film is made until it is actually used.

Mounting Transparencies

Users must specify whether they want slide film returned as mounted or unmounted slides. Most professional laboratories do not mount 2 1/4 in. slides. Glass mounting 2 1/4 in. and superslides is highly recommended for projection to eliminate popping in the projector. If the slides are to be glass mounted, the film should be returned unmounted because it is a nuisance to remove slides from cardboard mounts. For presentation to a client, unmounted slides are also more effective. On the other hand, unmounted slides cannot be projected; they must be viewed on a light box.

Projection Quality

The true quality of a slide, 35 mm or medium format, often cannot be enjoyed on the screen because of the somewhat questionable quality of the projector's condenser system and projection lenses.

If you are interested in 2 1/4 in. slide projection, it is worth investigating the quality of the projector. Be prepared to spend quite a bit more than for a 35 mm machine. It is, however, a worthwhile investment because 2 1/4 in. slide projection can be very effective. Once you have seen these slides presented in a high-quality projector, it is difficult ever to be satisfied with 35 mm. Because of the thinner medium format film base and the larger surface, however, you should also be prepared to mount the slides in glass.

FILM ROLL

Medium format cameras made up to the 1950s were designed for one type of roll film exclusively. Some medium format cameras are still made that way, but the majority can take at least two types by the use of interchangeable film inserts or magazines. This is where medium format cameras differ widely from 35s. 35 mm cameras can take different lengths of film (twelve, twenty-four, or thirty-six exposures), but it is always 35 mm perforated film, loaded in the same cassette, producing the same size negatives or transparencies.

Medium format cameras with interchangeable magazines, on the other hand, may be made for unperforated roll film, 70 mm perforated film, sheetfilm, or Polaroid film packs. This not only increases versatility but gives the medium format photographer a practically unlimited selection of emulsions. If one is not available in one form, it probably comes in another.

120 Roll Film

All medium format cameras—whether they produce 2 1/4 in. square, 6 × 4.5 cm, 6 × 7 cm, or any other negative size—can accommodate 120 rollfilm. Because of its popularity, 120 film is readily available in different of types of store—something travelers may want to keep in mind.

120 roll film comes in the widest variety of emulsions. You can find just about every emulsion necessary for general black-and-white and color photography. On the other hand, many emulsions made for special purposes or applications are not made in roll film but are available in 70 mm or sheets only.

120 roll film has a paper backing from beginning to end. Its main function was for the proper film transport. That is why it has frame numbers printed on it. In the past, the user advanced the film by looking into a window while turning the film advance knob until the next number appeared in the window. In most medium format cameras today, the film transport is automatic so the numbers are no longer necessary. As a matter of fact, the paper is no longer necessary, but it is still there.

220 Roll Film

Since modern medium format cameras no longer need the paper backing for spacing, film manufacturers started some years ago to spool 120 roll film with paper only at the beginning and end of the roll just to protect the film, so loading and unloading the camera can be performed in daylight. This new film became known as 220 probably because it can record twice as many images. That is its main benefit. Leaving out the paper made it possible to put twice as much film on the same film spool. It provides twenty-four instead of twelve 2 1/4 in. square images; twenty instead of ten 2 1/4 × 2 3/4 in.; and thirty or thirty-two instead of fifteen or sixteen 6 × 4.5 cm images. 220 roll film is appreciated by photographers who want to eliminate film changing, especially in cases where film changing can mean missing the most important picture, as in wedding, sports, and stage photography.

It is used mostly by professional photographers. As a result only the most popular professional films are made in 220 and are available only in specialty camera stores that do professional business. A camera with interchangeable magazines can be preloaded with twice as many magazines with the more readily available 120 size. Most laboratories that process 120 can also process 220.

Depending on the camera, the use of 220 film instead of 120 may require an adjustment on the film insert, a different film insert, an adjustment on the camera, or a different film magazine.

Manufacturers that supply a special 220 magazine claim it provides superior image sharpness. Since the combined thickness of the film and paper on 120 is at least twice that of 220 film alone, it is not sufficient just to adjust the film transport. They feel it is much more important to adjust the springs and the pressure plate to the particular thickness of each film, and this is possible only with a different magazine design. I do not know whether tests have been made to prove this point, but it makes good sense. As various photographic editors have pointed out and have proved, film flatness is the most overlooked part in camera design.

Long Roll Film

Longer rolls of 70 mm film are also usable on some medium format cameras with interchangeable film magazines. 70 mm film is manufactured without

The 70 mm film used in most medium format cameras is the double-perforated motion picture type.

perforations and with different types of perforations known as type I and type II. Perforated 70 mm film looks like 35 mm with perforations on both sides. Both are actually motion picture films. Each camera or film magazine is made for a specific type. If 70 mm film is necessary for your photography, find out which films are manufactured in which 70 mm form. Not all come in all versions.

Most 70 mm film magazines are made for use with cassettes, which are built and look like the 35 mm cassettes, except that they are larger. A cassette holds about 15 ft of standard base film and more with films made on a thinner base. A 15 ft length of film has room for about seventy 2 1/4 in. square images.

70 mm Cassettes.   The most popular films can be purchased in cassettes, ready to be loaded into the camera. Others are available only in longer lengths on spools for home loading into the cassettes. The spooling must be done in complete darkness. It can be done by hand, but a bulk film loader is a convenience. With such loaders, complete darkness is necessary only while placing the film spool into the light-tight chamber. The cassettes can then be loaded in daylight. Those who spool their own film but have it processed on the outside can request that the cassette be returned to avoid buying a new cassette for every roll of film. 70 mm cassettes can be reused if the felt light trap is kept clean and the cassettes are not bent so they remain light tight.

The 70 mm cassettes can be loaded into the camera in daylight. Unlike 35 mm, the 70 mm film moves from the full cassette into an empty cassette on the other side, so the film does not have to be rewound at the end.

70 mm Spools.   Some cameras can also take magazines designed for 70 mm on spools. The advantage is that they can hold longer lengths of film and thus provide more exposures per roll. This advantage is not obtained without some drawbacks: the need for darkroom loading and unloading. That is the reason why 70 mm film magazines for cassettes are still the favorite.

Film Variety.   More exposures per roll is one advantage of 70 mm. Another is the access to a wider variety of films. Many special emulsions, for instrumentation, infrared, high contrast, copying, duplicating, and microscope applications that are not available in 120 or 220 can be obtained in 70 mm. Many films that are not listed in a catalog can be obtained in 70 mm but require a minimum order quantity.

Processing 70 mm.   A medium format camera designed for 70 mm can thus increase photographic possibilities, but the processing possibilities must be investigated. Only a limited number of professional laboratories are equipped to process all or at least some of the 15 ft or longer lengths of film without cutting them. Amateur labs probably will not do this work.

Equipment for home processing is available. It usually includes not only the processing tank and film spiral but also the necessary items to wind the film on the spiral. There is nothing special about the processing itself except that good agitation is important to produce even development over the entire film area and length of film.

SHEETFILM

Various medium format cameras allow you to attach a magazine for sheet-film. Its design and operation are like those made for view cameras. The film is inserted in complete darkness into the sheetfilm holder protected by the dark slide. The sheetfilm holder slides into the magazine attached to the camera, the dark slide is removed, the exposure is made, and the dark slide is inserted again.

Sheetfilm for view cameras comes precut in the proper size (4 × 5, 5 × 7, or 8 × 10 in.). Finding the correct size for the medium format camera is a problem. Either it is not made at all or not readily available. The solution is to cut your own from larger sheet sizes. Since this work must be done in the darkroom, try to simplify the process as much as possible. The following suggestions may help:

- Use a paper cutter for polyester films.
- Attach a cardboard strip or something similar to the papercutter at the proper distance (required width of film) from the cutting knife. Slide the film under the knife until it rests against this strip. The blade will now cut it to the proper width. If a rectangular sheet is necessary, you need two strips at two different distances.
- Cut a piece of thin metal, Plexiglas, or anything else that is not easily cut with scissors to the correct film size length and width. Place this target on the film and cut around with scissors.

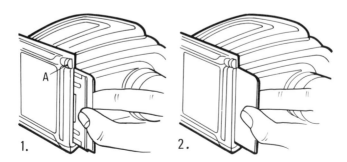

With a sheetfilm adapter attached to the camera, sheetfilm holders are inserted as on a view camera (1). Each sheetfilm holder has a dark slide that must be removed before the exposure is made (2).

Cutting your own sheets may be somewhat of a nuisance, but it should not prevent anyone from using sheetfilm if that is the only way the desired results can be obtained—usually when the particular emulsion is not made in any other form, roll film or 70 mm. There are many such films, from orthochromatic black and white to films for spectroscopy and photomicroscopy. A sheetfilm adapter thus allows using the medium format camera for special projects that would otherwise require large sheetfilm cameras.

Developing the medium format sheetfilm in tank or tray is identical to that of the larger sheetfilm.

INSTANT FILM

Instant films can be used on a number of medium format cameras. Camera manufacturers have introduced this possibility not to provide the medium format photographer with an instant snapshot camera but so that serious amateur and professional photographers can see on a print the image actually recorded through the lens. An instant print is the most reliable assurance that the camera is functioning properly, that the lens and camera settings are correct, that the flash is synchronized with the shutter, and that the correct accessories are used. It allows the photographer to experiment without guessing and to make changes before the shooting starts. It eliminates guesswork and saves on film and laboratory costs. It also serves as an excellent teaching tool since it allows the student to see instantly the results of the teacher's approach, just as videotape allows an athlete to study his motions instantly or a recording tape allows an instant test of the sound quality and effectiveness.

Professionals may want to use instant film to show an instant print to clients so they can see whether the image is as expected and give instant approval. A medium format camera equipped with a Polaroid film magazine can be used for Polaroid test shots even if the final pictures are made with another camera for which the film or the accessory to hold the film is not available (such as 4 × 5 in. or 35 mm format). It is then necessary only to transfer the lens and camera settings to the other camera and use a focal length lens that produces an identical or similar image on the other format. Depth of field will vary with the focal length.

Exposure Testing

Checking correct exposure is another, and often the most important, application. In ordinary lighting situations, you should have no problem in obtaining perfect exposures based on an exposure meter reading. Instant film is most useful under unusual lighting situations or when combining different light sources. The exposure latitude of instant films is not as wide as regular negative or slide films, and lens settings must be correct to within one-half f stop.

A *good* exposure on instant film should, therefore, be a *perfect* exposure on other film materials. Exposure tests on film can be valuable especially in extreme low-light situations, in photomicrography and photomacrography when special lenses like the Luminars are used and when photographing directly into light sources, to not only determine the most effective exposure but also check for possible flare. Exposure tests are valuable with bounced flash.

When you use Polaroid film for checking exposure, keep in mind the film in the camera. Transparency films must be exposed for the lighted areas, negative films for the shade. The lens settings are thus correct for slide film when the Polaroid test shot is properly exposed in the lighted areas. They are correct for negative film when the test has shadow detail.

Checking Light Ratios

In multiple flash setups, lighting ratios can be checked with flash exposure meters. If the modeling lights on studio units are directly related to the power of each flash unit, lighting ratios can also be checked visually. For lighting ratios, film tests are not really necessary; what they are valuable for is being able to see the effectiveness of the lighting, how and where shadows fall on the subject and the background, and detect possible disturbing highlights on eyeglasses or other shiny surfaces. When the light from different light sources is combined—flash fill-in, for instance—Polaroid material becomes still more valuable.

An instant picture is a must for determining exposure as well as the effectiveness and evenness of the lighting when painting with light.

Producing Special Effects

An electronic flash unit fired several times while the camera shutter is open produces multiple images. For example, dancers can appear several times in different positions, in different areas of the film in the same size or smaller or larger each time, perhaps even in different colors. The effectiveness of such pictures depends mainly on the positioning of the various images within the frame. They can be completely separated or overlap partially or completely. An image on film is the best or only way to check this. When double or multiple exposures are made in the camera, the final result can also only be seen on film, not in the viewfinder of the camera.

Effects of Shutter Speeds

There is no way that you can see with your eyes or in the viewfinder how the shutter speed affects or changes the image of a moving subject. If you want to stop action, you can follow written guidelines, which indicate how short the shutter speed must be to record some of the common moving subjects completely or reasonably sharply. Such guidelines are difficult to give when it is desired to record the moving subject with a blur to enhance the feeling of motion.

There are two solutions: either photograph the moving subject at different shutter speeds and pick the best shots when the film comes back from processing, or make a test on instant picture film at one shutter speed; if the results are not satisfactory, shorten or lengthen the shutter speed to get more or less blur, and repeat the process until the instant picture shows exactly the desired results.

It is also a good idea to use instant film when the camera is moved to produce the blur; when the focal length of a zoom lens is changed while the shutter is open to produce a zoom effect; when the focusing ring on the lens, vignettes, or other accessories in front of the lens are moved; or when electronic flash is combined with slow shutter speeds.

As a Teaching Tool

Instant film material helps you to create the desired image on the film. A special advantage in using this photographic material is for teaching and training. The value here is not in the photographer's being able to see the results but in giving others visual proof of the happening immediately. This can be for the purpose of showing photography students immediately the result of a photographic approach under discussion, for showing a model's performance in front of the camera, or for showing a scientific or other happening that cannot be repeated over and over or may be too fast, too slow, too dangerous, or too far away to be studied by the naked eye.

Instant film material allows you to show to an entire group things that normally can be seen by one person only, such as a view through a microscope. Other valuable applications are for showing a client or an art director a layout with actual images instead of sketches. The film can be used to make photographic instead of pencil notes in the classroom, especially valuable when time-consuming sketches would be involved.

Adjusting for Film Sensitivities

In the majority of cases, the negative or transparency film used for the final image will have a different exposure index than the instant film material used for the test. For correct exposure, therefore, something must be adjusted. The following possibilities exist:

1. *Change shutter speed*, to be done only when the shutter speed is not a deciding factor in creating the image. For blurred motion effects, the same shutter speed that produced the proper results on the test shot must be used.

2. *Change aperture.* Recommended when the shutter speed cannot be changed and/or when depth of field is not the deciding factor.
3. *Use neutral density filters* either when making the test shots or when making the final shots, depending on which film has the higher sensitivity. The use of such filters allows identical lens settings with any combination of films.

The amount of correction necessary is shown on the chart below, which is based on an instant film sensitivity of 70–80 ASA, 19 DIN, the most common film used for test shots.

EXPOSURE CORRECTIONS OF 70–75 ASA POLAROID FILM FOR FINAL FILM

Final Film		Change in Aperture	Multiply Shutter Speed	Use Neutral Density Filters
ASA	DIN			
25	15	Open 1½ stops	3 ×	0.50 with instant film
40	17	Open 1 stop	2 ×	0.30 with instant film
50	18	Open ½ stop	1.5 ×	0.10 with instant film
64	19	None	1 ×	None
100	21	Close ½ stop	⅔ ×	0.10 with final film
125	22	Close 1 stop	½ ×	0.30 with final film
160	23	Close 1 stop	½ ×	0.30 with final film
200	24	Close 2 stops	⅓ ×	0.60 with final film
400	27	Close 2½ stops	⅕ ×	0.60 with final film
800	30	Close 3½ stops	⅒ ×	0.90 with final film

Shutter speeds are multiplied as follows:
Original shutter speed 1/125 sec.
2 × : 1/125 × 2 = 2/125 = 1/60 sec.
½ × : 1/125 × ½ = 1/250 sec.

Polaroid Film Magazine

The instant film image is obtained by attaching a special magazine to the camera. It should be possible to switch magazines at any time, even in the middle of a roll of film. Instant film is of limited value when the Polaroid magazine can be attached only at the end of a roll of film. Regular Polaroid film packs are used. The sheet of film is larger than the image produced by the medium format camera so you waste some film, but the image and image size are the same as recorded on the roll film, and that is more important.

Care of Film and Magazine

Once a film pack is unwrapped, protect it from bright light; if possible, keep it in a closed box to guard against light leakage. When handling film packs during loading, be careful not to press against the center of the pack at any time as this may damage the film. Hold the film pack only by its edges at all times.

The Polaroid Land film process uses a caustic jelly, which is safely packed inside sealed containers within the film packet. If you should accidentally get some of this jelly on your skin, wipe it off immediately, and, to avoid an alkali burn, wash the area with plenty of water as soon as possible. It is particularly important to keep the jelly away from eyes and mouth. Keep the discarded materials, which still contain some jelly, out of the reach of children and animals and out of contact with clothing and furniture. There is usually some leakage of jelly inside the film packs, which can cause problems. It is therefore important to keep the rollers of the developer spreader clean. They should be checked and cleaned frequently, preferably after every film pack.

Developing Temperature

Polaroid films may be exposed successfully at any temperature, but the temperature of the film and film holder at the time of processing has an effect on the picture. The ideal processing temperature is 24°C (75°F) for all Polaroid materials, but satisfactory results can be obtained when it is warmer or cooler. For critical results on Polacolor Professional film, the 24°C (75°F) temperature should be maintained whenever possible.

Acceptable results with this film may be obtained at 16–38°C (60–100°F), but the processing temperature affects both the effective film speed and the color balance, so that some correction may be necessary. When film is to be processed at 16°C (60°F), increase exposure by about one-half an f stop. If prints have weak tones and a reddish tint, extend the processing time by 10–20 sec for better results. When film is to be processed at 38°C (100° F), decrease exposure by about one-half an f stop; in addition, magenta filtration may be required.

Overextended processing will yield richer, more saturated colors and deeper blacks. Also, the print may adopt a slight blue-green color bias, requiring warming filtration. Use of a CR decamired or 81 Wratten filter is suggested.

Reciprocity Law Failure

When light reaching the film is of low intensity or of very short duration, reciprocity law failure will occur. To correct for it, the normal indicated exposure should be increased. The color balance generally also needs correction. The following table shows the approximate correction needed over a range of indicated exposure times, in daylight or with electronic flash.

APPROXIMATE CORRECTIONS FOR RECIPROCITY LAW FAILURE

Indicated exposure (sec)	1/1000	1/100	1/10	1	10	100
CC filter	None or 05C	None	05R + 05Y	10R + 20Y	30R + 20Y	30R + 20Y
Exposure increase	None	None	⅓ f stop	1½ f stops	2½ f stops	3 f stops

Flash of very short duration (less than 1/1000 sec), as is given by some automatic electronic flash units at normal portraiture range, will cause a further shift in color balance. You can generally avoid this by setting the flash unit for manual operation.

Polaroid Black-and-White Film in Bright Light

The 3000 ASA or 36 DIN exposure index of the Polaroid black-and-white films is of great advantage when used in available light situations. It is generally too fast for use in daylight or with studio lights or electronic flash. Neutral density filters, however, can be used to reduce the sensitivity as follows:

Filter Type	Density	Film Sensitivity	
		ASA	DIN
Gr 2	0.6	800	30
Gr 3	0.8	400	27
Gr 6	1.8	50	18

Care of Prints

Some Polaroid films need coating; others do not. In either case, do not touch the face of the print after separation from the negative until it dries to a hard gloss. Polaroid color prints have good colors stability but as with all colors and any type of color film, prints should not be subjected to prolonged exposure to strong light, which can produce premature fading.

Polaroid Instant Films

Some film magazines use what is known as the amateur film types 87 and 88. They are less expensive than the Polaroid Professional films and mainly meant for snapshots:

Polacolor Type 88. Equivalent to 75 ASA, 20 DIN. Color film balanced for 5500 K–DM 18 and therefore made for color pictures in daylight or with electronic flash. Developing time: 60 sec.
Type 87, black and white. Equivalent to 3000 ASA, 36 DIN. Developing time: 30 sec. Black-and-white film for instant images in existing light.

For serious testing, use a magazine that takes the other films, known as the professional types, which are also readily available:

Professional Color Land film 669. Equivalent to 75 ASA, 20 DIN. Balanced for 5500 K or DM 18 (daylight and electronic flash). Developing time: 60

sec. Most light sources other than average daylight or electronic flash will require special filtration. In general, the basic rules for filtration are the same as those for wet-process color films that are balanced for daylight.

High-Speed black and white. Land film 667. Equivalent to 3000 ASA or 36 DIN. Developing time: 30 sec. Pictures are completely finished as soon as they are away from the negative. Prints do not require coating.

Positive-negative Professional black and white. Land film 665. Equivalent to 75 ASA or 20 DIN. A professional film that produces a print and a fixable negative simultaneously in about 30 sec. Both develop on the spot, and no darkroom is needed. It allows instant viewing of the results on a print, and at the same time gives a fine-grain negative with a very high resolution, which can be used to make high-quality enlargements the standard way on regular enlarging papers.

LOADING FILM

120 and 220 roll film is sold on spools. On the majority of medium format cameras, the film goes on a separate insert, which after loading is inserted into the camera or a film magazine. The spool with the film goes on the feed reel, and the beginning of the film is attached to an empty take-up spool. On some cameras, the film moves from reel to reel in its natural curl, as rolled on the spool; on others, it moves in the opposite way. It has been mentioned occasionally that this inverse film movement reduces film flatness, but I have never seen proof that the natural curl results in better film flatness and thus better sharpness and must assume that it is nothing more than an advertising statement.

Film flatness is a matter of designing the pressure plate and the rest of the magazine accordingly. Films have been running through motion picture cameras in the inverse curl since motion picture cameras were invented.

On many cameras, the film is loaded on an insert, which is then put

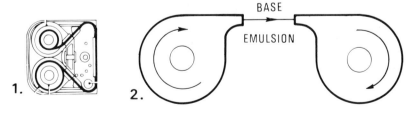

70 mm film is usually used in daylight loading cassettes of the same design as those used in 35 mm cameras. Unlike 35 mm film, 70 mm film runs from one cassette to another so it need not be rewound. (1) If the film loading path is opposite the wind in the cassette, the film must come out of the cassette with the emulsion side shown in (2).

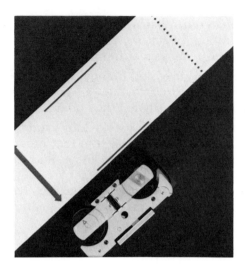

On modern film magazines and cameras, the arrow on the roll film must be set opposite an index.

into the camera or film magazine. Roll film must be advanced to a certain point to ensure proper spacing. On 120 and 220 films, the thick arrow on the paper is set opposite an index engraved on the film insert before the insert goes into the camera or magazine. Some 220 films have a dotted line on the paper backing before the black arrow. Do not put the dotted line opposite the index. You will lose the first two frames.

Medium format images should be spaced more or less evenly, with sufficient space between for cutting. The first image should be about 1 in. from the paper leader. 70 mm film comes perforated and unperforated. The perforated type is used in most medium format cameras.

Before a picture can be made, the paper leader must be moved through the camera. This is usually done by turning a crank until it stops. On some cameras it is done by a built-in motor. The beginning of the actual film is now behind the aperture, and spacing between the images should be fairly even from here on. *Spacing* refers to the blank space between the frames. On some cameras designed for the 6 × 4.5 cm format, however, the space between frames changes, which is the reason you can obtain only fifteen images instead of sixteen on a roll of 120 film. On a well-designed camera or magazine, the space may vary somewhat, but it should never be so wide that the last image falls into the paper trailer, and there should always be sufficient space between to cut the film.

On older cameras and magazines, there was no automatic stop at frame 1. The film had to be wound to 1 by watching the paper through a window and turning the crank until 1 appeared in the window.

While loading is simple, a few suggestions need to be made. Always remove the paper that holds the film tight on the spool completely. Otherwise it may become loose and wedged in the film aperture, acting like a mask in front of the film. Although roll film is designed to be loaded in daylight, do not do so in bright sunlight. Keep the film in the shade and the film tight on the spool during the entire process; otherwise light can fog the edges. Practice so you can load quickly without exposing the film to daylight longer than necessary. After the last picture on a roll is taken, the paper trailer must be wound up before the film can be removed. The now-empty feed spool becomes the take-up spool for the next roll of film.

Film Magazines

On some cameras, the film is loaded directly into the camera body. That means the roll of film must be finished or at least run through the camera before the film can be changed. Roll film cannot be rewound in the camera.

With an insert that goes into the camera body, you can preload inserts before going on a job. Reloading the camera can be quicker because it involves only running the paper leader to frame 1. It offers no other benefits. The roll of film still must be finished or at least run through the camera before the film can be changed.

If the insert, on the other hand, is part of a film magazine or, said in a different way, if the camera offers interchangeable film magazines, you have many other, and in many cases very valuable, benefits, including changing from one type of film to another in mid-roll or changing a loaded magazine from one camera to another without wasting a frame.

Cameras with interchangeable magazines are likely more expensive because they require a greater precision so every magazine fits on every camera and couples to the camera mechanism as if it were part of the camera itself. But the versatility—allowing you to do things with one

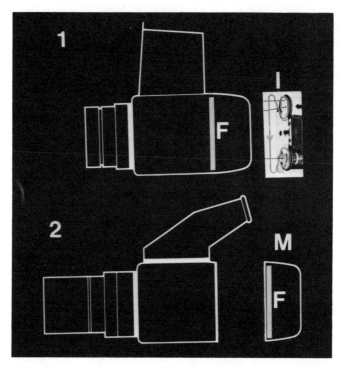

In some medium format cameras, the entire film magazine is removable *(1)*; in others, the film insert only is removable. The latter *(2)* is less expensive, but the advantages are limited. (*F* = film plane; *M* = magazine; *I* = insert.)

camera that otherwise require two or three cameras—may well be worth the additional cost.

Before a loaded film magazine is removed from the camera, a dark slide must be inserted so the film is not exposed to light. The purpose of a dark slide is the same as the dark slide in a sheetfilm holder of a view camera: to protect the film when the magazine is off the camera. It serves no purpose as long as the magazine is attached to the camera. Well, not quite. Some cameras cannot be released until the dark slide is removed, at least partially. It thus can be used to prevent accidental releasing. There are differences in this respect. On some cameras, the release works when the slide is only 1/16 or 1/8 in. pulled out—not enough to be clearly visible. The photographer could very well take pictures without being aware that the slide is still in the camera. The result: no pictures. A camera that requires the slide to be pulled out at least halfway is a safer choice.

Rotatable Film Magazines

Most medium format cameras made for rectangular pictures must be turned for verticals just like 35s. Another solution in the medium format is a rotatable film magazine. Only the film magazine is rotated for verticals. It is a convenience, especially when working on a tripod, but the camera body needs to be considerably larger—at least as wide as the long side of the negative in either direction. What is gained in versatility may be lost in convenience.

OPERATING SIGNALS

Medium format cameras, especially those offering interchangeable film magazines, should have operating signals and controls to prevent mistakes and to make it unnecessary for the photographer to do a lot of worrying while shooting. A frame counter that shows the number of exposed pictures is taken for granted. Most frame counters are coupled to the gears and work whether there is film in a camera or not. The camera or the film magazine should have a signal that shows whether there is film in the camera or magazine. The signal must work whether the magazine is on or off the camera, and to be reliable it must be controlled by the film itself, not the gear.

The camera or magazine should have a place where you can mark the type of film and its ASA rating. Mark every magazine, and mark it all the time. Mixing up magazines is too easy. There should furthermore be a signal that indicates whether the film is advanced, and this signal must work with the magazine on or off the camera. It is also helpful if you can tell whether the shutter is cocked without having to try to turn the crank or knob.

Photographers should not have to check the frame counter continuously just to ascertain that they did not run out of film. The camera should have some arrangement whereby the release cannot be depressed after the last frame has been exposed. This warning should preferably come right after the last frame is shot. On some cameras, you will not find out you are out of film until you try to depress the release again, which

Unless you use the same film all the time, always indicate what film is in the camera or magazine.

can be annoying. My own camera has this arrangement. I have never missed a picture, however, because I have found that winding the film from the second to last to the last frame feels different because the paper trailer runs over the roller. The sound and feel is sufficient for me to know when I advance the film to the last frame. This is even the case on my motor-driven model where the film is advanced automatically.

CHAPTER 7

Lenses

The medium format camera best suited for your photography may be, and often is, determined by the lens or lenses. If you are in the market for a camera, consider:

Type and make of lenses.

Range of lenses available.

Simplicity of changing lenses.

Possibility of using the same lenses on other camera models.

Convenience of reading the scales and operating the lens controls.

Extent and desirability of automation.

Lens quality.

LENS COST

Lenses are an expensive part of a good camera system, with a single lens possibly costing more than the camera body. Medium format lenses may cost more than equivalent 35 mm lenses because everything—the lens elements, lens mount, and diaphragm—is larger, and increasing the size of a lens element increases the cost drastically. The lens requires a larger piece of glass, and more time is needed to grind and polish the larger surfaces to perfection.

Selecting a high-quality lens is a wise decision, especially in the medium format. Most people probably select the larger format to get better image quality, so it makes no sense to sacrifice some of the benefits of the larger negative with an inferior lens. The larger medium format negative or transparency will also show up lens deficiencies more than the 35 mm frame. The films available today are capable of resolving more detail than most of the lenses, so lenses, not the film, are the limiting factor in sharpness. This is again more prominent in the medium format. Films will likely be improved further, so be prepared for the future by investing in the best-quality optics.

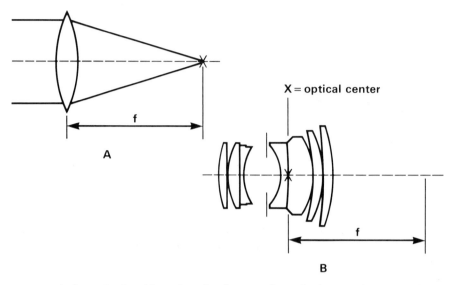

On a single lens, the focal length is the distance from the lens to the point where the lens forms an image of a subject at infinity (A). On a compound lens, the focal length is measured from the rear nodal point, which is known to the lens designer only (B).

FOCAL LENGTH

Lenses are distinguished and separated mainly by their *focal length*: the distance at which a lens forms an image of a distant subject. For a single lens element, it is the distance from the element to the image point. On a compound lens (a lens consisting of several elements), the focal length is measured from the rear nodal point (or principal plane H), which can be anywhere inside the lens or even outside its physical size. Since the focal length is engraved on every lens, there is no need to know the position of the principal plane.

Focal length is an optical characteristic built into the lens. It is the same regardless of whether the lens is used on camera, enlarger, or projector. Focal length is also unchanged by adding extension tubes or bellows (they simply move the lens physically farther away from the film plane) or by switching a lens from one camera to another or using a lens for different film formats. For example, a 150 mm lens remains a 150 mm lens whether used on a 4 × 5 in., 6 × 6 cm, or 35 mm camera.

Focal lengths can be changed only by adding or removing optical components, such as a teleconverter. A Proxar or close-up lens is also an optical component. It changes the focal length, but the change with the normally used Proxars is so small as to be negligible. The purpose of adding close-up lenses is not to change the focal length but to allow photography at closer distances.

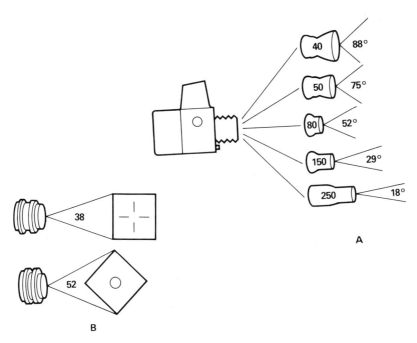

The focal length of a lens in relation to the picture format determines its angle of view. The longer the lens is, the narrower is the angle of view for the same format (A). The angle of view can be expressed in relation to the picture diagonal or to the horizontal or vertical. The two are different (B).

On zoom lenses, focal length can be changed within a certain range by moving some of the components inside the lens.

To classify lenses into standard, wide angle, and telephoto, consider the focal length in relation to the format. A lens is considered standard when the focal length is about equal to the diagonal of the picture format for which it is used; for example, 80 mm is normal on a 2 1/4 in. square camera because the diagonal of the 2 1/4 in. square is 78 mm. Lenses with shorter focal lengths are classified as wide angles and those of longer focal lengths as telephotos.

When the 80 mm lens is used for superslides, it can no longer be considered standard because the diagonal of the 40 × 40 mm superslide is only 58 mm, so the 60 mm lens, which is a wide angle for the 2 1/4 in. square, becomes the standard for the superslide.

ANGLE OF VIEW

The *angle of view*, as the name indicates, is the angle the lens "sees" when used on a specific camera. The angle of view can be related to the

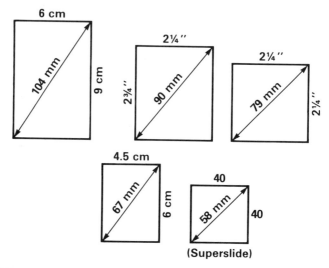

A standard lens has a focal length approximately equal to the length of the format diagonal. This is about 79 mm for a 2¼ in. square. The length of the diagonal, and thus the standard lens for the various medium formats, is shown here.

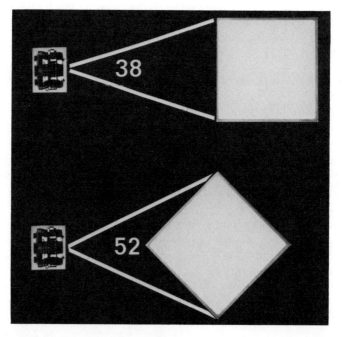

On an 80 mm lens, the diagonal angle of view is 52° but only 38° in relation to the vertical or horizontal of the 2¼ in. square.

picture format in three ways: in relation to the diagonal, the vertical, or the horizontal side. On the 2 1/4 in. square format, the vertical and horizontal lengths are equal. For example, the 80 mm lens used with the 2 1/4 in. square has a horizontal angle of 38° and 52° diagonally. Used on 4 1/2 × 6 cm, the view is still 38° horizontally but only 46° diagonally and 28° vertically. For any specific format, the angle of view is inversely proportional to the focal length. Any lens that has a diagonal angle of approximately 50° is considered standard; when the diagonal angle is larger, the lens is considered wide angle, and when it is smaller, telephoto.

Lens makers commonly give diagonal angles of view. This makes sense for the lens designer because the lens produces a circular image that must cover the square or rectangular format. For practical picture taking, however, it is useless. As a photographer, you must think of horizontal or vertical coverage. What you normally need to know is what focal length is necessarry to cover the same width on a smaller or larger negative.

The chart here shows equivalent focal lengths for 35 mm; 6 × 6 and 6 × 4.5 cm; the superslide; 6 × 7 cm; and 4 × 5 in. The figures are based on the horizontal coverage (that is, the long negative side). As an example, to cover the same width of an area as an 80 mm on 2 1/4 in. or 6 × 4.5 cm (angle of view 38°), you need a 58 mm lens for a superslide, 52 mm on 35 mm, 100 mm on 6 × 7 cm, and 175 mm on 4 × 5 in.

EQUIVALENT FOCAL LENGTHS FOR DIFFERENT FILM FORMATS

	Focal Length of Lenses (mm)				
Horizontal Angle of View (degrees)	4.5 × 6 cm and 2¼ × 2¼ in. (54 × 54 mm)	Super-slide (40 × 40 mm)	35 mm (24 × 36 mm)	6 × 7 cm (54 × 68 mm)	4 × 5 in. (98 × 120 mm)
84	31	23	20	38	67
72	38	27	25	48	83
69	40	29	26	50	87
65	43	31	28	54	93
62	46	33	30	58	101
58	50	36	33	63	109
54	54	39	35	68	117
49	60	43	39	75	130
40	76	55	50	96	167
38	80	58	52	100	175
36	84	61	55	105	183
32	100	73	65	125	218
30	105	76	69	131	229

Horizontal Angle of View (degrees)	*Focal Length of Lenses (mm)*				
	4.5 × 6 cm and 2¼ × 2¼ in. (54 × 54 mm)	Super-slide (40 × 40 mm)	35 mm (24 × 36 mm)	6 × 7 cm (54 × 68 mm)	4 × 5 in. (98 × 120 mm)
26	120	86	78	150	261
24	130	95	85	163	283
23	135	97	88	169	295
21	150	108	100	190	330
15	206	150	135	259	450
13	250	180	163	314	545
10	306	220	200	383	667
9	350	255	229	439	763
7	458	330	300	575	1000
6½	500	365	327	627	1090

AREA COVERAGE

The angle of view determines (1) area coverage and (2) magnification. The area coverage for any lens is directly proportional to the subject distance. At twice the distance, a lens covers an area twice as wide; at half the

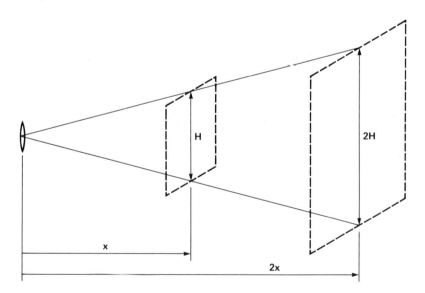

Area coverage at different distances can easily be calculated when it is known for one distance. At twice the distance, the lens covers an area twice as wide and four times as large in area.

distance, half as wide. The larger area coverage means that the subjects are recorded smaller; the magnification is lower.

An aerial photographer may need to determine the necessary flying altitude for covering a certain area. This can be done easily with the following formula:

$$\text{altitude} = \frac{\text{focal length} \times \text{subject width}}{\text{image width}}$$

(image width = length of negative side).

For example, to cover an area 2500 m (8200 ft) wide with a 50 mm lens,

$$\frac{50 \times 2500}{55} = 2272 \text{ m (7455 ft)}.$$

The same formula can be used to determine the necessary focal length of a lens or the area that will be covered from a certain altitude with a specific lens:

$$f = \frac{\text{altitude} \times \text{image width}}{\text{subject width}}$$

$$\text{subject width} = \frac{\text{altitude} \times \text{image width}}{\text{focal length}}$$

Covering power of a lens is the diameter of the circle within which satisfactory image quality and illumination are obtained.

The same formula can be used to determine distance or width of area coverage when photographing anything else.

COVERING POWER

Covering power is not the same as area coverage. Lenses are designed in the factory to cover a certain negative size. Lenses for 2 1/4 in. (55 × 55 mm) square cameras are designed to produce the promised image quality and corner illumination on the 2 1/4 in. (55 × 55 mm) square and not beyond. They are not likely to perform properly for the larger 2 1/4 × 2 3/4 in. format. This is called *covering power*. The covering power depends on the design of the lens, not the focal length; for instance, 50 mm lenses are made for 35 mm, 2 1/4 in. square (55 × 55 mm), 4 × 5 in. (98 × 120 mm), and perhaps even larger format cameras. Since all lenses produce a circular image, the covering power of a lens can be indicated by the diameter of the circle in which definition and illumination are satisfactory. If lenses designed for a small format camera are used on a large format camera, the corners are beyond the covering power of the lens. They may be completely cut off, or the illumination and image quality in the corners may be unsatisfactory. Lenses designed for a large format camera, however, can be used for a small format; for example, 4 × 5 in. (98 × 120 mm) lenses could be used on a 2 1/4 in. (55 × 55 mm) square camera, and medium format lenses can and are being used on 35 mm cameras with adapters.

LONG TELEPHOTOS AT CLOSE RANGE

As the focal length increases, so usually does the minimum distance at which the lens can be focused. The relatively long focusing distances of telephoto lenses give some photographers the impression that these long lenses are meant for long distance photography only. This is not so. The focusing distances are limited for mechanical design reasons. Telephoto lenses can be used at all distances and at closer range in combination with close-up accessories, Proxars, or extension tubes.

MAXIMUM APERTURE

The *lens aperture* determines how much light reaches the film at a given moment. The *f* number is the focal length of the lens divided by the working diameter of the lens. It used to be said that the working diameter was the diameter of the front element. This can be the case on some lenses but does not apply to other lens designs. The working diameter is the diameter of the entrance pupil, known only to the lens designer.

TRUE TELEPHOTO

It is common in photography to classify all lenses with a focal length longer than normal as tele or telephoto lenses. This is not so in the optical field, where such lenses are separated into long focal length types and optically true telephotos.

An optically true telephoto is a specific design of a lens with a positive front and a negative rear section. The principal plane, from which the focal length is measured, is not within the physical dimension of the lens as on an ordinary design but somewhere in front of the lens. The advantage is that the physical length of the lens can be much shorter than its focal length, so these lenses are shorter, lighter, and easier to carry and use. Because of these advantages, practically all long focal length lenses used in photography are optically true telephotos.

RETROFOCUS LENSES

From an optical design point of view, there are also two types of wide angle lenses. In an optically true wide angle lens, the rear nodal point from which the focal length is measured is within the physical dimension of the lens. The shorter is the focal length, the closer the lens must be to the film plane.

On SLR cameras, lenses cannot be placed close to the film because the mirror needs space to swing up and down between the lens and film, making the use of lenses below a certain focal length impossible. Lens designers have found a solution by designing lenses where the rear nodal point is behind the lens.

For the very best in corner-to-corner sharpness, for architectural, product, or scientific photography with a super wide angle, or for photogrammetric purposes that require view camera quality without distortion, true wide angles should be considered. Their superb image quality is maintained at close distances. They are therefore also good lenses for photographing large documents. Such wide angle lenses are, however, found only on special wide angle cameras; they are not interchangeable types for SLR cameras. If you want this quality, you must select a special wide angle medium format camera. Practically all wide angles, and definitely those of shorter focal length, on all 35 mm and medium format SLR cameras are retrofocus types.

Retrofocus lenses are sometimes also called *inverted telephotos* because the front section is negative and the rear is positive—the opposite from a true telephoto. The front element of retrofocus lenses is larger than one would expect of a short lens and larger than on an optically true wide angle of the same focal length and speed.

Because wide angles are mostly used for long shots, retrofocus lenses

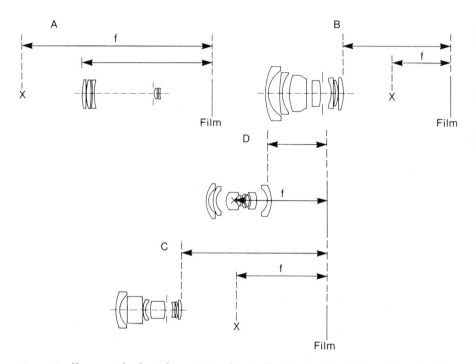

An optically true telephoto lens (A) is physically shorter than its focal length. The point from which the focal length is measured is in front of the lens. Practically all long focal length lenses used on cameras are of the optically true design. In a retrofocus design (B), the rear nodal point from which the focal length is measured is not inside the physical dimension of the lens but behind it. The retrofocus wide angle design (C) is necessary on an SLR camera. The rear element of the lens is far enough from the film plane to clear the mirror. An optically true wide angle (D) does not provide this space.

are designed to produce the best image quality at long distances. There is a visible loss of sharpness, especially at the edges when used at close distances, and they are therefore not recommended for that purpose, at least not at large apertures. Closing down the diaphragm will restore some of the quality loss. Unfortunately, this shortcoming is not always pointed out by the lens or camera manufacturer.

FLOATING LENS ELEMENT

In recent years lens manufacturers have been trying to improve the close-up quality of retrofocus-type wide angle lenses and have succeeded by incorporating what has become known as a *floating lens element*. When an ordinary lens is focused, all elements move together at the same rate. In the floating element design, one or several elements are moved separately, so there is a somewhat different lens construction at the close focusing distance than at infinity. It is somewhat like a zoom lens where some elements are moved when changing the focal length.

On some retrofocus wide angles, the floating elements are moved automatically when the focusing ring is turned, but this can be a rather complicated lens mount design. Others have a second focusing ring that operates the floating part. This is a less costly design and has no disadvantages except that both focusing rings must be adjusted. The floating element ring is adjusted first either for long distances or close-ups; the fine focusing is then made with the regular focusing ring. Although the floating element design improves close-up sharpness, it is not likely to affect other qualities, such as sharpness at long distances, distortion, and illumination.

LENS NAMES

The names of most lenses today simply refer to the manufacturer rather than the lens design, as it used to be. Years ago when most lenses were designed and made in Germany, the lens design determined the name, which often was the name of the designer (Gauss). When the designer came up with a new development, he also gave the lens a new name. As a result, lenses made by the same manufacturer for the same camera may have different names, such as Planer, Sonnar, and Tele-Tessar. Also, different makes of cameras might have been supplied with the same lens. European lens manufacturers still use this system today. It has no specific advantage to the photographer except perhaps to specify the design. For example, if the lens has a Distagon name, it is a retrofocus type, if it is engraved Biogon, it is an optically true wide angle.

TELECONVERTERS (EXTENDERS)

Teleconverters are negative optical components consisting of at least four lens elements. They are mounted between the lens and camera like an extension tube and thus move the camera lens farther from the film plane.

1

2

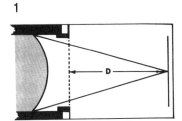 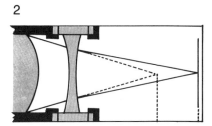

The lens without teleextender forms an image on the film plane, distance D from the lens mount (1). A tele-extender moves the lens forward by the distance L, the length of the extender. The image formed by the lens also moves forward for the equivalent distance. The negative lens components in the tele-extender diverge the light rays so the image again falls on the film plane (2).

The negative lens component in the teleextender moves the image back to the film plane. They can be combined with various focal length lenses. They increase (usually double) the focal length of the lens used in front of it so that, for example, a 150 mm lens becomes a 300 mm. Instead of purchasing a longer focal length lens, you can purchase at less cost a teleextender, which you can then use to increase the focal length of all lenses. Such an addition cannot be made without losing something, and the main sacrifice is loss of two f stops for a $2 \times$ converter. For example the $f4$ 150 mm lens becomes a 300 mm $f8$.

When lens components are added to a lens, the quality changes. In what way and by how much it changes depends on the quality of the teleconverter and the quality of the lens with which it is combined.

Prerequisite for good image quality with any teleconverter is a high quality of the camera lens used in front of the converter. A lens of questionable quality is likely to be unsatisfactory when used with any converter.

A teleconverter's performance is also determined greatly by the design of the lens. It varies from one lens to another so it is impossible to make a general comment. It can be said, however, that a converter made by the same company as the lenses, if available, is likely to perform better since it is designed with these lenses in mind. Such a converter can produce an image quality that is equal, or almost equal, to that of a prime lens, especially the longer focal length lenses with which it is usually combined. Such a teleextender may have as many as, or more lens elements than, a prime lens.

If there is a quality falloff, it is mainly at the edges and may not be

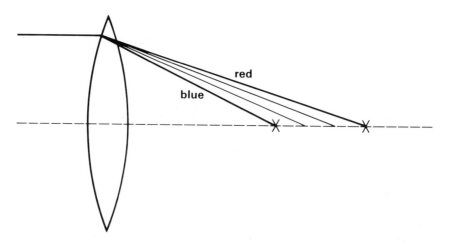

When white light goes through a single lens element, it is dispersed into its different colors. Blue is reflected more than red and thus forms an image closer to the lens. This so-called chromatic aberration is reduced by adding lens elements.

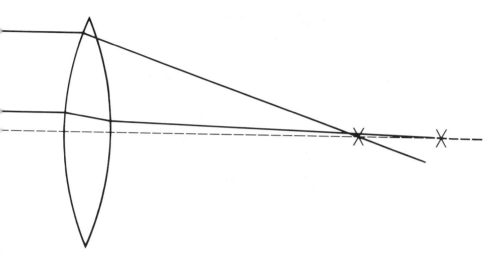

Spherical aberration is another lens fault the lens designer has to contend with. Light rays entering a single lens on the outside form an image closer to the lens than the light rays that go through the center of the lens.

objectionable (in portrait photography, for instance). The quality can also be improved by stopping down the lens.

LENS ABERRATIONS

A single lens element produces an image affected by all kinds of faults called *aberrations*: spherical and chromatic aberration, coma, astigmatism, field curvature, and distortion. A faulty image is hardly acceptable to serious photographers. The aberrations can be reduced by combining various lens elements with different curvatures and thicknesses made from different glass and arranged in different ways within the lens mount. The lens designer's job is to find a combination that reduces all aberrations to a point where they are not visible or objectionable in the applications for which the lens is made.

Perhaps one might conclude that a greater number of elements automatically means better quality. Although large aperture lenses and extreme wide angles do require more elements, the quality of the complete lens is not determined by the number of elements but by the skill of the designer in combining the minimum number of elements to produce the maximum in quality, using the latest types of glass and design techniques. The quality of the final lens is determined even more by the accuracy with which each lens element and each mechanical component of the lens mount is made and assembled and how carefully and thoroughly the finished lens is tested.

The overall sharpness or quality of a lens used to be, and still is in many cases, expressed by *resolution*: the number of lines per millimeter a lens is capable of reproducing as separate lines. Lens and photo tech-

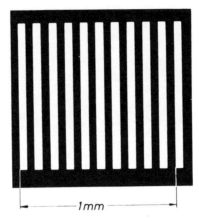

The quality of a photographic image is not so much determined by the number of lines that are resolved but by the edge sharpness, which is called *acutance*. High acutance means a sharp line between white and black or two different colors *(A)*. With a low acutance lens, there is a gradual transition between the two *(B)*.

nicians have found, however, that image quality in a photograph is not so much determined by the resolution of fine detail as by the manner in which the more easily perceptible, larger structural elements in the picture are reproduced. This is more a question of contrast rendition. Edge sharp-

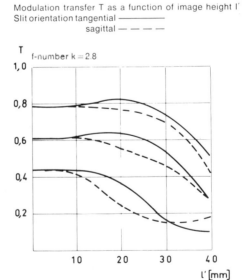

An MTF diagram shows contrast transfer curves for three spatial frequencies: 10 *(top)*, 20 *(middle)*, and 40 line pairs per mm *(bottom)*. The solid line shows the contrast transfer of sagittal surface, the dotted line for the tangential image surface.

ness (called *acutance*), not resolution detail, is what gives a photograph the appearance of sharpness. Frequently high acutance goes together with high resolution—but not always. A poor photograph can result even with a high resolution, and a good picture can result with a lens with moderate resolution. Resolution frequently fails to conform to the subjective judg-

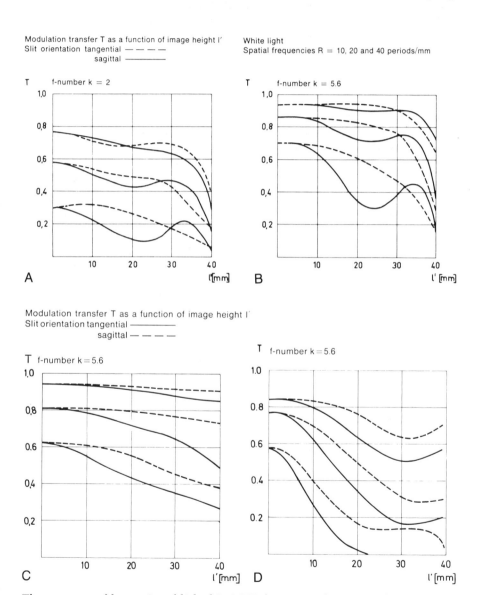

The acutance of lenses is published in MTF diagrams. The center of the image is at the left and the corner at the right. These diagrams allow a quality comparison among different lenses (bottom) or at different apertures (top).

ment of overall sharpness, while values of acutance correlate very well with the observer's feeling for sharpness.

The image-forming qualities are expressed through the rendition of contrast with MTF (modulation transfer function) diagrams. Unfortunately, MFT diagrams are not readily available from most lens manufacturers. Zeiss is one of the few companies that publish them. If they were published by all lens manufacturers, you would know what you were getting for your money and see why one lens may cost more than another.

IMAGE QUALITY

Image sharpness improves as the lens is stopped down; however, beyond certain limits, the nature of light affects the sharpness. Light pouring through any opening spreads slightly at the edges, an effect known as *diffraction*. This becomes a problem in photography only when the aperture is very small. The minimum aperture of high-quality lenses is usually limited to a point where the degradation of the image is not noticeable. For all practical purposes, on a high-quality lens, you need not be concerned about closing the aperture too far and losing quality, so do not hesitate to stop the lens down completely if the depth of field requires it. The lack of sharpness caused by limited depth of field would be more noticeable than the loss of overall definition caused by diffraction.

As a general rule, the best image quality appears not at the smallest aperture but two to three f stops below the maximum ($f5.6$–$f8$ for an $f2.8$ lens). Because MTF diagrams are not readily available for many lenses and are of little practical value to anyone except optical experts, you must determine the quality with your own film test.

Making your own test is not a drawback or nuisance; it is the most reliable quality measurement. It is made with your lens, on your camera, and takes into account not only the performance of the lens itself but other sharpness-determining elements as well, especially the film flatness in the camera.

Load the camera with the highest resolution film that you can find. This is probably a low-speed, or special type, black-and-white film. I have found that sharpness differences can be seen easier on black and white than on color. Photograph a subject with fine detail. Brick walls always come to mind first, but they actually are poor subjects. The brick itself has little fine detail, and the contrast range is very narrow. You need high contrasts for easy evaluation, such as white window frames against darker walls, a black railing in front of a light building in the distance, newspaper pages, or good lens test charts at close distances.

While you make the test, test the lens at different apertures and in the center and the edges.

For a reliable test, you must keep a few other points in mind:

1. When comparing different focal length lenses, move the camera to different distances so each lens covers the same area.
2. Make certain that each negative or transparency has exactly the same exposure and development.
3. Make certain that the test target is lighted evenly and identically for each lens.
4. The test target must be flat or the subject far enough away so you need not worry about depth of field. The film plane must be parallel to the test target.
5. Eliminate any possibility of camera motion.

Always evaluate the actual negative or transparency with an 8× or 10× magnifying glass. Never evaluate prints made from a negative or slides projected on a screen because too many other factors can enter and distort the results. Evaluate the center and corners.

COLOR CORRECTION

Simple lenses bring lights of different colors to different points of sharp focus, unsatisfactory for most photography. One of the main reasons for using a complex lens is to reduce this problem. Most photographic lenses are *achromatic*, which means that they are corrected for two colors. This is good enough for most photography.

Apochromatic Lenses

Apochromatic lenses are corrected for three colors and show an improvement in reproduction of fine detail. For this reason, they are necessary for high-quality copy reproduction and for color separation work. In most other work, you would have to be extremely critical to appreciate the quality improvement. Apochromatic lenses may also be corrected for infrared radiation (from 700–1000 mμ). They do not require the focusing adjustment necessary with ordinary lenses and thus simplify infrared black-and-white photography. The necessary black-and-white film for this work is, however, difficult to obtain in the medium format. In most areas, it is available only in sheetfilm.

Fluoride Elements

Apochromatic lenses often have one or more lens elements made from fluoride to simplify the apochromatic design or to make the improved color correction possible. Fluoride is affected by temperatures and actually changes with temperature more than regular glass does. The change affects the distance setting, which is why on such lenses, the focusing does not

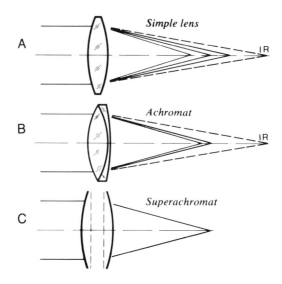

With a single lens element each color forms its image at a different distance, the infrared wavelength farthest from the lens (A). Most photographic lenses are achromatic, which means they are corrected for two colors, sufficient for most photography (B). An apochromatic lens is corrected for three colors, which reduces the secondary spectrum. An apochromatic lens may also be corrected for infrared, so even the infrared radiation forms the image at the same plane (C).

stop at infinity. It goes beyond. Always focus the image visually on the ground glass, even if the subject is at infinity.

MULTICOATING

For over thirty years, good photographic lenses have been coated, meaning that glass-air surfaces are covered with a thin layer of a fluoride, which reduces the amount of reflected light. When light hits an uncoated glass surface, about 5 percent is reflected, and the transmitted light is therefore reduced to 95 percent. A 5 percent loss of light is not serious. In a good photographic lens, however, there may be eight, ten, or even more surfaces where glass meets air, or vice-versa, and if each surface reflects 5 percent, the total light loss may amount to 40 to 50 percent.

Of even more concern than the loss of light is what happens to the reflected light. It probably reaches another lens surface and is reflected back to another lens or part of the lens mount. The reflected light causes *flare*, a haze over the image that reduces contrast. A single coating over the lens surface reduces light reflection to about 1 percent. Applying several layers to each surface further reduces reflections to about 0.3 percent. In a multicoated lens, each element has several coatings, each of a different thickness, so that each eliminates the reflection caused by a different wave-length of light. Light transmission is increased, and the

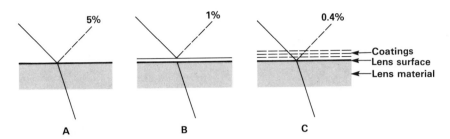

An uncoated glass surface reflects about 5 percent of the light *(A)*. Coating *(B)* and multicoating *(C)* reduce the amount of reflected light, resulting in a reduction of flare. Actual benefits depend on lens design.

reduction in flare can be significant. Reduction of flare, however, depends greatly on the design and focal length of the lens. The improvement is more noticeable on wide angle lenses and least noticeable on those of longer focal lengths. With some multicoated lenses, you can photograph directly into the sun or other light source without picking up objectionable flare. Multicoating is most helpful when photographing against white backgrounds or directly into a light source when a lens shade cannot protect the lens. In all other cases, a lens shade can do more to prevent flare.

LENS SHADES

Multicoating has not reduced or eliminated the need for lens shades. They are still important for maximum contrast, especially when photographing

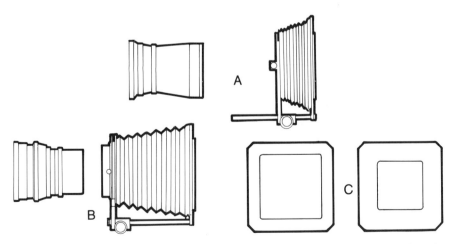

A bellows shade can be extended more or less to provide maximum shading for different focal length lenses, from wide angle *(A)* to telephoto *(B)*. Masks *(C)* can be inserted in the front of the bellows shade for even better shading when using long lenses. The rear of the bellows shade may have a slot for gelatin filters *(B)*.

A

A bellows shade over the 150 mm lens *(A)* eliminates the flare caused by the sun shining directly on the multicoated lens *(B)*.

toward light sources or against white backgrounds or bright areas in general (including overcast white skies, water, sand, and snow). Regardless of what camera, type, and focal length lens you are working with, equip it with the best possible shade, even purchasing a separate shade for each lens, though the front lens diameter may be the same. The reason is that the longer is the focal length of the lens, the longer is the required shade to provide maximum protection.

The shape of the shade should also be considered. Square or rectangular shades are more effective because they correspond to the image format. Round shades are least effective. They provide maximum shading only in the corners, not at the top, bottom, and sides. If the round type is the only shade available for your lens, you can improve its efficiency by placing black tape across the four sides. Check carefully that it does not vignette.

Regular metal or plastic shades are the most compact types. For most medium format cameras, you can also buy the type with a flexible bellows, usually referred to as a professional lens shade. They provide better shad-

B

ing of the front element. The bellows can be extended to suit the focal length of the lens. Therefore one shade can be used for a wide range of different focal length lenses. The permissible maximum extension may be engraved on the rail. The front may be designed to take masks to give even better shading for longer focal length lenses—the lenses where a shade is most important.

Although you should use the longest possible shade for each lens, also make certain that it does not vignette the corners. Usually a check on the ground glass is sufficient; a film test, photographing evenly lit surfaces, is better. In either case, make the test with the lens completely closed down because vignetting in the corners becomes more visible at small apertures.

A bellows shade also makes a good holder for masks, vignettes, and other special effect devices that must be placed a few inches in front of the lens. A bellows shade, furthermore, may have a slot at the rear for gelatin or other square filters. The higher cost of the bellows shade is therefore justified. In my mind, if there is one accessory that should be on every medium format camera, it is the professional shade. Sunshades can also protect a lens from possible physical damage and protect it from rain or snow.

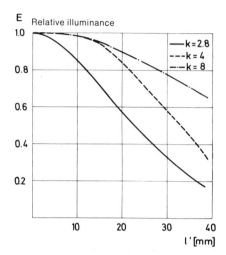

The relative illuminance of lenses can be illustrated. The center of the image is shown on this graph as having a greater relative illumination *(left)* than the corners of the image *(right)*. The three lines represent different apertures.

RELATIVE ILLUMINANCE

Every lens has a lower illuminance at the edges. Wide angles have a higher falloff than normal lenses and telephotos. The difference between center and corner can easily amount to one or two *f* stops, perhaps even more. This is unacceptable in serious photography because the difference is visible and objectionable. A difference up to one-half *f* stop is not objectionable. Unfortunately, illumination curves, like MTF diagrams, are published by few lens manufacturers. The falloff is something you must find out by a film test. Contrary to sharpness, light falloff is more easily recognized on color films. Illumination changes with the aperture and must therefore be evaluated with the lens wide open and closed down.

COLOR RENDITION

Many types of glass used in modern lenses are not absolutely clear but have a color tint and therefore act as a color filter. Although the eye adjusts easily to different colors when viewing individual images, accurately matched color rendition in all lenses is important when you photograph the same subject with different lenses. With unmatched lenses, the images cannot be combined or projected after each other because the slight color variations become objectionable. If you use lenses of the same make, color matching is more likely to be the same. If you do not, try to match colors with color balance filters.

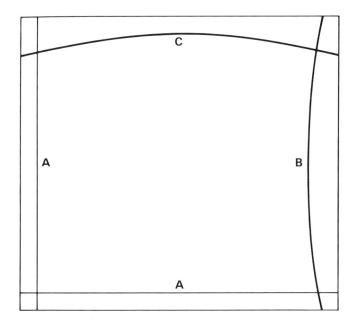

A lens corrected for distortion records straight lines straight over the entire image area. Insufficient distortion correction shows up as curved lines near the edges *(A)*. An inward curvature is referred to as *pincushion distortion (B)* and an outward curvature as *barrel distortion (C)*.

DISTORTION

Distortion is the lens's inability to record straight lines as straight lines over the entire film area. Straight lines near the edges appear curved either inward *(pincushion distortion)* or outward *(barrel distortion)*. In some photographic fields, such as portraiture, the degree of correction is less critical than in architectural, product, and scientific photography. Even slightly curved lines on a skyscraper are noticeable and distracting and certainly unacceptable in professional architectural work. In this type of photography, distortion should be determined in a film test because distortion curves are difficult to obtain from lens manufacturers. For the test, photograph a subject with straight lines so the straight line is very close to the vertical or horizontal edges of the frame. This test can be made at any aperture because distortion does not change by closing or opening the diaphragm.

Retrofocus-type wide angle lenses have more distortion than the optically true wide angles, which architectural photographers use on view cameras. If you want to do architectural work or any other photography where distortion is unacceptable with a medium format camera, you may

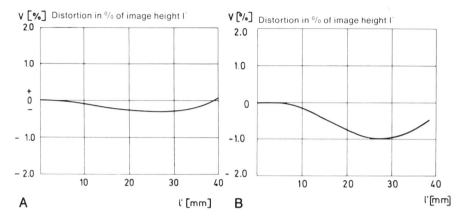

In a lens designer's diagram, distortion is shown as a percentage of image height. The two diagrams show the difference in distortion between an optically true wide angle type (A) and a retrofocus type (B).

have to refrain from using an SLR type and use one of the special cameras equipped with an optically true wide angle.

Photographers call various other effects in a photographic image distortion and usually blame the lens. When subjects that were closer to the camera, like the nose in a portrait, appear too large in proportion to the rest of the image (the eyes or ears, in this case), the short focal length of the lens is usually blamed—and incorrectly. This so-called foreshortening is caused by shooting from too close. It is caused by the distance, not the lens.

Slanting Lines

Slanting vertical lines—on a building, for instance—are caused by tilting the camera. This is not a fault in the lens or camera, it is a normal way of seeing. When you look up at a skyscraper, you will see that the lines converge as they recede into the distance. A wide angle lens can enhance the slanting.

Perspective Control Lenses

Recording straight and parallel verticals is simplified or made possible with the use of perspective control (PC) lenses, which are available for a few medium format camera models. PC lenses have a larger covering power than the negative format of the camera, which allows the lens to be moved up or down (or sideways) without cutting off part of the image.

The film plane is made parallel to the subject being photographed, which may cut off the top or bottom of the subject (the top of a tall building, for instance). If that is the case, the lens is shifted up or down until the entire subject is recorded on the film (until the top of the building is in the film area). The same control is possible sideways if the PC lens has both controls or by turning the camera sideways.

The range of the shift movement is limited by the covering power of the lens and also mechanical reasons, so it will probably not cure all situations, especially in architectural applications. A PC lens, however, can solve many problems that otherwise would require a view camera.

Shifting the lens or part of the lens components requires a complex and delicate lens mount, which must be made with great precision. This is the main reason for the cost.

Some PC lenses offer only shift control, which means simply moving the lens parallel to the film plane. Some PC lenses are more complex, offering a certain amount of lens swing in addition to shift. *Swing* means tilting the lens in relation to the film plane. Although swing control could also be used to straighten lines, it is not the suggested method because it likely creates sharpness problems from top to bottom. The main application and use of this swing is for increased depth of field along one plane.

The same swing motion can also exist in a camera where a regular (non-PC) lens is mounted in front of a bellows rather than in the camera body. The swing motion is now accomplished with the bellows.

Wide Angle Distortion

Another type of distortion occurs when three-dimensional subjects are photographed with wide angle lenses. The objects near the edge of the picture appear wider than those in the center. This is objectionable when photographing groups of people, interiors, and many other subjects. The distortion is created mainly because the lens views the people in the center of the group from the front, and those at the outside from the side. A second reason is that the film plane is flat rather than curved. A perfectly round bowl thus appears stretched out when geometrically projected on a flat plane. This so-called perspective distortion happens with all lenses but becomes obvious only with wide angles; the distortion with a 50° angle of view lens is only 10 percent but increases to about 40 percent with an 85°–90° wide angle.

Even a 10 percent distortion can be objectionable in some types of photography—for example, in commercial photography when known symmetrical objects are shown at the edges or in photographs of an architectural interior. The solution is to frame the area so that such objects are away from the edges of the photograph or to use a longer focal lens to decrease the angle of view. In group pictures, the people at the edge should be turned toward the center or they should be arranged in a curve so all are photographed from the front.

ZOOM LENSES

In a zoom lens the focal length can be changed by moving some of the lens elements in relation to others. This is done by turning or moving a zoom control. The image that is produced at each focal length can be checked on the ground glass or, in the case of a projector, by the size of the projected image. The ratio between the shortest and the longest focal length is known as the *zoom range*.

If the lens goes from 140 to 280 mm, for example, it has a 2:1 range, which is the minimum range to make a zoom lens a worthwhile investment. Zoom lenses on 35 mm cameras come with considerably higher ranges. Medium format zooms are (at least at the present) more limited, and they also tend to be large and heavy. Zoom lenses must be larger and heavier because they require more elements; fourteen to seventeen is not uncommon. Weight and size are the main disadvantages to zooms. This is not so much a consideration for carrying because one zoom lens replaces at least two fixed focal length lenses. The two together may weigh as much and take up as much space in the case. Mounted on the camera, it is a different story. The larger zoom limits portability and hand-held shooting capability somewhat. Likely to be of a larger diameter, they also require larger filters, shades, and other accessories.

Aperture must also be considered. The maximum aperture of the zoom may very well equal that of an equivalent fixed focal length lens at the long end but be slower at the shorter focal length. *f* 5.6 on a 140–280 mm zoom is good at the 250 mm focal length but probably one *f* stop slower than a 150 mm fixed focal length lens. On a modern zoom lens, the aperture remains the same over the entire zoom range.

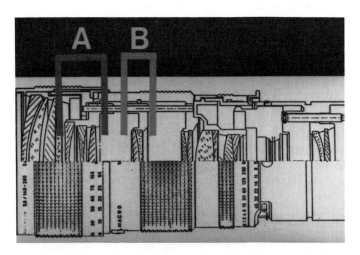

The focal length of a zoom lens is changed by moving some of the lens components while turning the zoom ring. Effective aperture does not change, and in the case of an optically true zoom, the image remains in focus.

Optically True Zooms

Better zoom lenses are of the optically *true zoom* type. That means they remain in focus while zooming. On less expensive zooms, especially those used on projectors, the image moves out of focus when the focal length is changed. Each time you change image size, refocusing is necessary, which I consider unacceptable. These lenses should really be called variable focal length lenses, not zooms. Although an optically true zoom stays in focus and thus could be focused at any focal length, this is not the recommended focusing procedure.

The image stays in focus only if the focusing is accurate. To be assured of this, always focus on the ground glass with the lens at the longest focal length, regardless of the focal length actually used. At the longest focal length, the image is at its greatest magnification, the depth of field is at the minimum, and focusing is therefore most accurate.

Zoom Image Quality

In the early developmental stages in the 1960s and 1970s, zoom lenses were generally of somewhat questionable quality, certainly inferior to fixed focal length types. The introduction of new types of glass, in some cases combined with aspherical optics, and the use of the computer, which decreased the developing time of a new lens drastically, has changed this picture. Certainly poor-quality zooms are still on the market, but you can find zoom lenses today that closely match the sharpness of a high-quality fixed focal length lens. High-quality zooms are costly. They require not only many lens elements but also an elaborate mechanical and optical construction. The quality, sharpness, distortion, and illumination naturally vary from one focal length to another. If you want to evaluate a zoom lens, you must test it at different focal lengths. The color rendition, however, is the same, which is another advantage of a zoom: long shots and close-ups are always color matched.

Close-ups

Some zoom lenses have macrofocusing, but at macro, zooming is no longer possible. The lens is locked at one focal length, usually the wide angle. As a matter of fact, the zoom ring frequently becomes the focusing ring in the macrosetting. The built-in macrocapability nevertheless can eliminate the need for close-up accessories in many cases.

If you want to zoom in the close-up range, however, you must still invest in close-up accessories. A Proxar or close-up lens is the only close-up accessory usable with most zooms. The power of the close-up lens and the shooting distances are described in chapter 16. Extension tubes do not work with most zoom lenses. Because these tubes are mounted between camera and lens, they change the back focus (the lens seat to film plane distance). When this happens, the subject does not stay in focus when the focal length is changed.

FISH-EYE LENSES

Fish-eye lenses are constructed to produce curved images of all straight lines that do not pass through the center of the image. The effect is exaggerated barrel distortion, resulting in curved images that can be strangely beautiful. To most photographers the typical fish-eye image is a round circle covering only the central area of the frame. That is one type of fish-eye image produced by one type of fish-eye lens. The effect can be striking, but it is largely the circular image that attracts attention. The subject, usually reproduced on a tiny scale, is often secondary. The effect wears off quickly, and the pictures start to look alike. The possibilities for cropping are slight, and therefore, such lenses have very limited applications.

Other fish-eye lenses cover the entire format with no visible light falloff in the corners. The focal length is still long enough to produce a relatively large image in the center, yet it also embraces surrounding subjects from corner to corner, usually within a 180° field. Since the entire image format is used, part of the image can be used and enlarged. The distortion of the fish-eye lens is completely unrelated to sharpness. Good sharpness is obtained from corner to corner even with the lens wide open.

FILTERS AND SUNSHADES

The 180° diagonal angle of view of most fish-eyes does not allow the placing of any accessories, filters, or shades in front of the lens because they would cut into the field of view. Multicoating and the optical design of some fish-eyes might allow you to photograph directly into light sources without picking up objectionable flare. Nevertheless, be careful when photographing into the light, toward bright backgrounds. Watch the image closely on the ground glass. If you require the use of filters, you need a fish-eye lens that allows attaching filters inside the lens. The front section on such a lens is completely removable, and small filters can then be attached to the front or rear section. In such a design, the filter is actually part of the lens. This means that the lens must always be used with a filter or a clear glass of the same thickness; otherwise image sharpness suffers. All filters must also have the same thickness.

CHAPTER 8

Lenses and the image

The focal length determines area coverage. The shorter is the focal length, the wider is the coverage. Wide angle lenses thus can be used to cover a large area without having to move the camera; telephotos allow one to photograph and thus enlarge a distant detail.

Changing lenses is frequently more convenient than moving the cam-

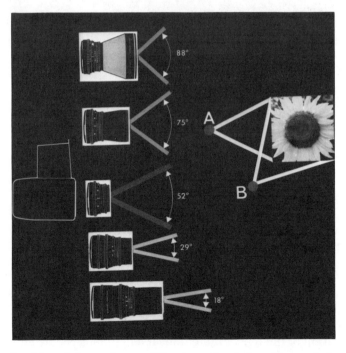

Different focal length lenses have a different angle of view. The angle is sometimes indicated in relation to the diagonal of the negative format *(B)* and sometimes to the horizontal or vertical *(A)*. The two are different.

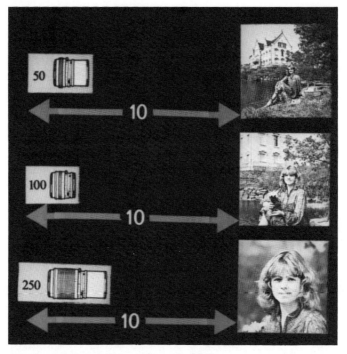

Because different focal length lenses cover different sized areas, you can take a long shot, a medium shot, and a close-up without moving the camera by changing from wide angle to standard to telephoto.

era, especially on a tripod. Often it is the only possibility; the size of a room may prevent you from moving farther away. Lenses can do much more than just covering larger or smaller areas. They are major tools for creating effective, beautiful, unusual, and interesting images.

PERSPECTIVE

Perspective refers to the size relationship between subjects close and far away. With our eyes, area coverage and perspective do not change. We see everything in one way. This usual perspective allows us to judge distances. In photography, we can change the size relationship between foreground and background by changing camera distance and lens. Perspective is determined by the viewpoint, which is the position of our eyes (or the position of the camera lens). Although perspective is determined by the position of the lens, different focal length lenses play an important part because they now determine how much of the area is included on the frame from that particular point of view. To cover a large area from a close distance, you need the wide angle or extreme wide angle; to cover a small distant area, you need a long telephoto. The normal focal length

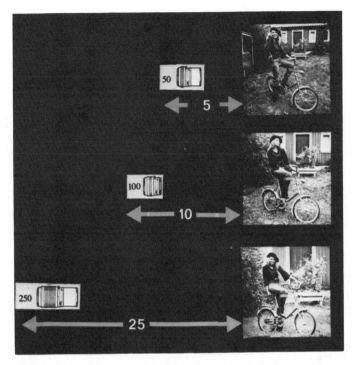

Different focal length lenses can be used from different distances so the foreground subject is recorded in the same size. The wide angle picture *(top)* includes a much larger background area than the one with the standard lens *(center)* and even greater than the telephoto shot.

lens records images in a perspective quite close to our eyes. That is the main reason for calling it *normal*. If we want to create images as everyone else sees the world, photograph the scene with the standard lens. For many images, this is the most effective or only way. In legal photography, it is important that the scene be presented in court in the normal perspective. If it cannot be recorded in that way, the judge must be aware and must have the facts. A distorted perspective might present the facts to the court in a completely different light.

On the other hand, wide angle lenses used from a close distance and long telephotos used from a long distance allow you to record images that are completely different from the way we see, providing an opportunity to record scenes in an unusual way.

VIEWING DISTANCE

Perspective is not only the viewpoint when the picture is taken but the viewpoint selected when viewing the print or slide. The perspective in the final image—the photographic print or the transparency—is deter-

A

Distance determines the size relationship between foreground and background (perspective). When a wide angle lens is used from a close distance, the foreground subject appears much larger in relation to the background (A), and the background subject appears to be farther away than it does when photographed with a telephoto (B). A standard lens records the scene as we see it with our eyes.

mined by the viewing distance. Every image, regardless of focal length lens used, appears in the normal perspective if the viewing angle equals the taking angle. The size of the recorded subject, then, has the same ratio to the viewing distance as the actual subject had to the camera distance. The correct viewing distance for true perspective can be determined from the following formula:

$$\text{distance} = F \times M,$$

where F is focal length of the lens and M is degree of enlargement of the print or slide. According to this formula, the correct viewing distances for some common print sizes made from 2 1/4 in. square negatives are as follows:

B

CORRECT VIEWING DISTANCES

	5 × 5 in. Print		8 × 8 in. Print		16 × 16 in. Print		Slide on 5 × 5 ft. Screen	
Lens	*in.*	*mm*	*in.*	*mm*	*in.*	*mm*	*feet*	*Meters*
40 mm	3½	90	6	150	12	300	3½	1.1
50 mm	5	120	7¼	180	15	370	4½	1.3
80 mm	7	180	12	300	24	600	7	2.2
120 mm	11	280	17	440	35	890	11	3.3
150 mm	14	350	22	550	43	1100	13	4.0
250 mm	23	580	37	920	73	1850	22	6.8
500 mm	46	1160	74	1840	146	3700	44	13.6

The figures in the table apply when the full negative is enlarged. If only a portion from the negative is used, the magnification is higher, and the viewing distance must be correspondingly longer. If you come right down

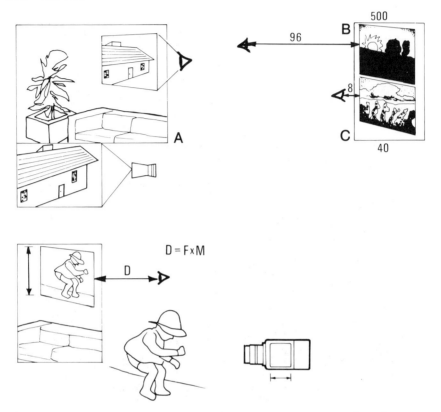

Every photographic image is seen in the correct perspective when the viewing angle corresponds to the angle under which the image was photographed. This would mean that an 8 × 10 in. print taken with a 500 mm lens would have to be viewed from 96 in. (8 ft., 2.5 m) (B). To see correctly the same sized print but made with a 40 mm wide angle lens, the eye must be down to 8 in. (20 cm) (C). The proper viewing distance, D, can be determined by multiplying the focal length of the lens, F, by the number of times the negative or transparency was enlarged, M: $D = F \times M$. The formula can be used to determine the focal length of the lens necessary to record a subject so that it appears in proper perspective when enlarged to a certain size. By juggling the equation, we get $F = D \div M$. For example, for a 16 × 16 in. image made from 2¼ and viewed from 36 in. $M = 16 \div 2\frac{1}{4} = 7.1$ and $F = 36 \div 7.1 = 5$ in. a 120 mm lens should be used.

to it, perspective in photographs looks different because we view all prints of a certain size from the same distance. An 8 × 10 in. print is viewed from about 2 ft regardless of what lens was used. If we viewed such a print made with a 500 mm telephoto from 6 ft, it would appear in normal perspective. If we could view the same sized print made with a 40 mm lens from only 6 in., it would also appear normal. This, however, is more theory. More important is how we use the different lenses to create good images.

With telelenses, background subjects are recorded larger; they appear closer, and perspective is compressed. A car photographed in this way, for instance, appears shorter than we see it with our eyes. Long telephotos are perhaps the greatest tool to give outdoor scenics a special look.

With wide angles used from a close distance, the subjects in the foreground are oversized in relation to the rest of the image. For example, flowers and leaves can be just a few inches in front of the extreme wide angle. With wide angles, distant subjects appear much farther away because they appear smaller than we see them with our eyes. Rooms photographed with wide angles appear longer because the furnishings in the back are smaller.

FORESHORTENING

The exaggerated size of foreground subjects, also referred to as *foreshortening*, is frequently referred to as distortion, but the wide angle should not be blamed for the distortion. It is created by photographing from too close a distance, not by using a wide angle. Although this type of perspective can be very striking, it can also be distracting or even unacceptable, especially with portraits. Photographing people from less than 3 ft makes the nose, the feature of the face closest to the camera, appear too large in relation to the eyes and ears. A short telephoto, about 150 mm on a 2 1/4 in. square camera, is usually selected for portraits to cover only head and shoulders from 3 ft or a longer distance.

SELECTIVE BACKGROUNDS

Different focal length lenses can also be used to change the background area without changing the size of the foreground subject, unfortunately a technique often neglected by photographers. Yet it should be one of the major reasons for selecting a specific lens. Backgrounds are a very important part of most images, and the effectiveness of many photographs and slides is determined mainly or completely by the background. Turning the statement around, too many photographic images are ruined by the type, size, and sharpness of the background area. This applies in black and white and color.

Instead of photographing a subject with a standard lens from, say, 10 ft, you can photograph it with a 150 mm telephoto from about 18 ft. The size of the subject is the same, but the background area is smaller.

Long lenses permit us to cut down background areas and eliminate

A

By using different lenses, you can cover smaller or larger background areas without changing the size of the main subject. A short lens from a short distance covers a large background area; a longer lens from the necessarily longer distance covers a smaller background area. The size of the main subject is the same with both lenses. The 150 mm telephoto includes only a small part of the church in the background (A). With the 50 mm wide angle, you can see almost the entire church while the model in the foreground is the same size and standing in the same place (B).

distracting background elements, such as billboards, cars, people, or direct light sources. These lenses are valuable in the studio because they allow smaller paper backdrops to be used. In a formal outdoor wedding picture, the longer lenses may be preferable because they produce a small, blurred, undisturbing background. In a candid shot, however, a large background may be desirable to identify location. By photographing the wedding couple with a wide angle, you might be able to have the entire church in the background, not only the entrance steps. Do not hesitate to use a wide angle in such an application if it gives the desired background coverage. Just stay at least 3 ft away from the people, as you do in portraits.

B

VERTICALS

Vertical lines—of a building, for instance—appear in the finished picture vertical and parallel to each other only if the camera was level. As soon as cameras are tilted up or down, the verticals slant toward each other.

Such an effect can be disturbing, or interesting visually, depending on how much the camera is filtered. Tilting the camera slightly up for no other reason than getting the whole building in the picture is a poor use of the camera. The result looks like a mistake. Either have the camera level or tilt it excessively so the audience gets the feeling it was done purposely. Such images can be beautiful and different especially because few people ever tilt their heads to get this view. Such images can be exciting because slanted, diagonal lines can produce moving images.

Slanted verticals happen with all lenses. The shorter focal length lenses simply add to the effect. This means that leveling is more critical and must be done more accurately with short focal length lenses. The slightest tilt that may not be noticeable with a normal lens becomes objectionable with an extreme wide angle. Vertical and horizontal guidelines

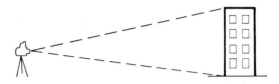

A longer focal length lens used from a longer distance requires less tilting of the camera to cover the same area as a shorter focal length lens does from a shorter distance. Slanted verticals can be corrected in the darkroom by tilting the easel or, better, tilting the easel and negative carrier so that their planes meet in the plane of the enlarging lens.

on the ground-glass screen can help. But because the image on the screen is enlarged only about three times, even this help may not be sufficient for critical work. A spirit level is most accurate; that is why they are built into view cameras. If one is available as an accessory for your medium format camera or even built into the camera, use it.

There are other ways straight verticals can be obtained without the use of swings and tilts. With negative material, the verticals can be straightened when the prints are made. One other method is to use a shorter focal length lens or to shoot from farther away to enable you to cover a larger area and thus get the entire subject into the frame without tilting the camera. As long as the film plane is parallel to the subject being photographed, lines are straight and parallel. The wider angle of the lens, however, also covers more on the bottom—perhaps too much to make a pleasing picture. The bottom can be cropped out later, perhaps making a horizontal out of the square. If possible, try to have an interesting foreground—a flower bed perhaps—at the bottom of the picture, so cropping is not needed.

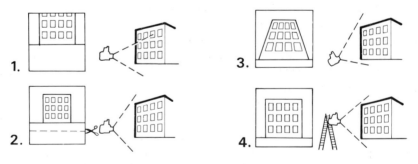

When the camera is too close to include the top of a building (1), a shorter focal length lens may solve the problem, but a large, undesirable area may then be included at the bottom (2). A solution is to tilt the camera (3), although this results in slanted lines. Raising the camera slightly (for example, with the use of a step ladder) frequently removes the necessity to tilt the camera (4). With extreme wide angle lenses, the camera need not be raised very much.

Including an effective foreground can make the wide angle shot more attractive and eliminate the need for cropping the bottom. One way to fill the foreground is to have a major subject, such as the lamppost, extending from the bottom of the picture to give the feeling that the image "had" to be composed in this fashion.

A more effective solution, when it is possible, is to use a longer lens from a longer distance. This allows covering the same area as a shorter lens from a shorter distance but without the need of tilting the camera as much or tilting it at all. If you cannot move farther away, try to raise the camera. Carry a small stepladder so you can shoot from higher than eye level. Raising the camera just 2 or 3 ft can make a great difference with extreme wide angle lenses. Professional architectural photographers use this technique to do architectural photography, especially interiors, with a medium format camera where normally larger view types would have to be used. Another possibility is to attach the medium format camera body and magazine to a view camera body. Such special adapters exist for some view cameras. This technique allows the use of swings and tilts yet records the image on roll film, and you still have the SLR's benefit of ground-glass viewing and focusing. To get the full benefits from medium format view camera photography, study a good book on large format photography so you understand the view camera movements—what they are for and how they are used to obtain the desired results.

LENS CONTROL

Another method for straightening verticals is with PC lenses available for some medium format cameras. The PC lens is shifted up, down, or sideways, parallel to the film plane so it covers more of the subject on top, bottom, or side without the need for tilting the camera. Since the film plane remains parallel to the subject, the lines are straight and parallel.

A more elaborate PC lens may also provide a certain amount of tilt where the lens moves but not parallel to the film plane. It also changes the angle in relation to the optical axis.

The same swing motion can also exist in a camera where a regular (non-PC) lens is mounted in front of a bellows, rather than in the camera body. The main application of this lens is for producing more depth of field along one plane. It is explained in detail in the chapter on depth of field.

CREATING IMAGES WITH ZOOM LENSES

A zoom lens can replace at least two fixed focal length lenses, and it gives an unlimited range of focal lengths between the minimum and maximum. This gives a practically unlimited control of composition and is easier and faster to operate. It gives the fastest, easiest method to see what the composition looks like at a wide range of focal lengths.

In sports, action, and news photography, a zoom lens has a more important advantage: it reduces or eliminates the need to change lenses. Lens changes are time-consuming because each change also needs resetting to the correct aperture and distance and perhaps even shutter speed. There is also the problem of what to do with the lens that is removed and where to put it. While a lens is being changed, the camera is unusable, and this may be when the most startling action takes place. On a zoom lens, the focal length can be changed without disturbing the lens setting. You are always ready to shoot and can take a long shot followed almost instantly by a closer view.

Zoom lenses not only duplicate the uses of fixed focal length lenses, they also have the unique capability of creating images that are completely different from the way we see the world. These images are created by zooming while the shutter is open. The change of image size is recorded on the film in the form of streaks, which can go from the center to the outside, or vice-versa. They go to the outside when zooming from the short to the long focal length because image size increases. Going the other way, the image becomes smaller, so the streaks radiate toward the center. The image recorded on the film depends on other factors. If you alter the focal length for the entire exposure time, the image consists of streaks only; the subject itself is hardly visible. Most zoom shots are more effective when the subject can be recognized and is simply surrounded by streaks. To produce this effect, keep the focal length at a fixed setting (usually at either the shortest or longest) for about half of the exposure time, and change it during the second half only. If the total exposure time is 1 sec, wait about 1/2 sec before moving the zoom control.

Effective zoom shots require subjects with bright areas because these are the areas that produce the streaks. The streaks produced by the highlights are most visible if they cross darker image areas. You can vary the length of the streaks by zooming over the entire focal length range (for long streaks) or over a part only (for short streaks). Fast zooming produces faint streaks and slow zooming more pronounced ones. Because exposure times must be long enough to be able to rotate or move the zoom ring during the time the shutter is open, a camera mounted on a sturdy tripod makes zoom shots easy. It is possible that 1/8 sec may be sufficient, but the results may be questionable; 1 sec gives greater control.

In low light levels, these long shutter speeds can be obtained without a problem, but what about outdoors in bright sunlight? With 64 ASA film the diaphragm cannot be closed down enough to obtain a 1 sec or even 1/2 sec exposure; so the amount of light reaching the film must be cut down in another fashion. Neutral density filters are excellent for this purpose in color and black-and-white photography. With a 0.9 density filter (three f stops), you can shoot in bright sunlight with 64 ASA film at $f22$ and 1/4 sec with a 1.8 density filter, six f stops at $f16$ and 1 sec.

Other zoom effects are possible. Instead of a continuous zoom, you can superimpose two or more images of the same subject but at different focal lengths of the zoom. Photograph the subject with the zoom lens at one focal length; then change the focal length without moving the camera and superimpose a second image, larger or smaller, of the same subject. Double exposures are mostly or only successful when photographing a light subject against a dark background because of the need for contrast. These exposures work well indoors with electronic flash and a light subject against a black background. A dancer dressed in white is a good example. Photogaph the dancer at one focal length, change the focal length and perhaps also the pose and position of the dancer for the second exposure, and repeat the process a third or fourth time. You can add more variety by taking each image through a different color filter. Rather than making multiple exposures with flash, you can make just one exposure but multiple flash. Open the shutter and keep it open while firing the flash two or more times, changing the focal length and model in between. There can be no other light in the room with this process.

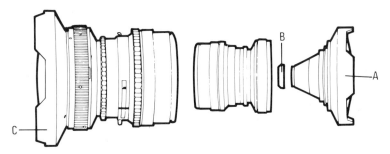

Fish-eye lenses with a 180° diagonal angle of view do not allow the use of a shade. A shade (C) may be part of the lens. The lenses also do not allow attaching filters to the front. The lens may be designed to take filters (B) inside the lens after detaching the front section (A).

Fish-eye images are characterized by curved lines, which give them an attention-getting quality.

FISH-EYE LENS PHOTOGRAPHY

While circular fish-eyes have limited use as a creative tool, the full-frame fish-eye lenses do. The beautiful curved lines are an attention-getting device, making every fish-eye image different from the way we see the world. The curved lines also make a more moving and dynamic image than straight horizontals or verticals. Try to compose the curved lines to enhance the visual effect and excitement of such images.

With a full-frame fish-eye design, lines need not necessarily be curved; images need not have the distorted fish-eye look. All straight lines that intersect the center of the field are recorded as straight lines.

The fish-eye look in scenic pictures is avoided, or at least reduced, by aiming the camera so that the horizon crosses the center of the field. You can avoid obvious curves by careful placing of other subjects. For example, an image of trees in a forest can look like a wide angle shot if the fish-eye lens is pointed up to the sky and the tree trunks are composed to go from the corners toward the center. Circular subjects centered on

In a full frame fish-eye lens, lines that intersect at the exact center of the frame are straight. The tree extending diagonally from the bottom was framed to intersect the center and thus avoid curvature.

the focusing screen remain as perfect circles. A doughnut, a balloon, the face of a clock, or a round plate are recorded as they appear to the eye. Why, then, use a fish-eye? Because the fish-eye covers a 180° angle diagonally and therefore includes a much larger background area than any other lens.

The most interesting fish-eye images are often those where the viewer is not aware that they were made with a fish-eye lens. Its use is practically unlimited for images with or without the fish-eye look.

There are three main reasons for using a full-frame fish-eye:

1. To cover large areas. The large horizontal or vertical angle covers an area larger than the shortest wide angle lens. The 180° diagonal coverage, usual on most fish-eyes, covers an area twice as large as the widest wide angle lens.
2. To create an eye-catching image that presents an unusual view of a subject.
3. To produce images that are unusual because of the large diagonal angle, not because of distortion.

DEPTH OF FIELD

Turning the aperture ring on a lens controls not only exposure but also depth of field, which is equally important.

Depth of field is a calculated figure not based on the design or workmanship of a lens. It is simply based on an assumption that an object

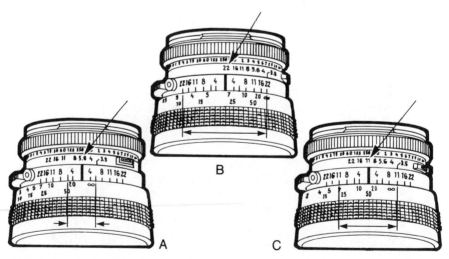

At f5.6, depth of field is from 50 ft to infinity (A). Depth of field increases as the lens aperture is closed down. At f11, it goes from about 20 ft to infinity (B) and at f22 from about 11 ft to infinity (C). Depth of field should always be determined from the depth of field scales on the lens, not the ground-glass image.

point still appears sharp even if it is imaged as a blur below a certain size on the negative. The acceptable blur is around 1/50 mm for critical consideration. A less critical manufacturer may base the depth of field tables on a larger 1/40 mm. That is why depth of field scales may vary from one manufacturer to another. It does not mean one makes better lenses than the other but just that the one that shows more depth of field at the same focal length and apertures uses lower standards.

How critical you should be about depth of field depends on your own standards and how much you plan to enlarge the negative or transparency. For very critical work or when negatives are enlarged beyond normal sizes, you may want to consider a somewhat smaller depth of field range; for less critical work, when enlargements do not go beyond 8 × 10 in. (20.3 × 25.3 cm), a somewhat larger range can be considered acceptable.

At normal distances, the lack of sharpness increases more rapidly in front of the subject and more gradually behind it. As a result, about one-third of the total depth of field is in front and two-thirds behind. This can be seen clearly on the engraved depth of field scales.

Focal Length and Depth of Field

It is generally accepted that wide angle lenses have more depth of field and telephotos less, but this statement needs some investigation.

When you photograph a subject with different lenses from the same camera position, the short focal length lenses give more depth of field than the longer telephotos. The statement is therefore correct. Although the depth of field is the same, what is recorded on the film is not. Used from the same distance, each lens covers a different area. If the standard lens covers a country cottage from the foundation to the top of the chimney, the telephoto shot includes just the entrance, and the wide angle shows the cottage surrounded by blue sky and gardens with trees and flowers. Thus there are three completely different images.

In some cases, this approach to obtaining more or less depth of field works; in most cases, it does not. Usually you work the other way around: you know the size of the subject you want to photograph, so the area coverage is predetermined. Then you can decide whether to cover that area with a standard lens, or to go closer and use a wide angle, or to go farther away and switch to a telelens. If you work this way, different focal length lenses no longer provide different depth of field ranges. When you are covering the same sized area, every focal length lens gives the same depth of field.

The focal length of the lens, then, really does not affect depth of field. Depth of field is determined by two factors only: the lens aperture and the area coverage, which we call *magnification* in close-up photography. Depth of field thus can be changed only by opening or closing the lens aperture or by changing the area coverage. Open the aperture for less depth; close it to obtain more depth. If you run into a situation where even the smallest aperture does not provide enough depth of field, which often happens in close-up photography, the only solution is to photograph a larger area than necessary and crop later. This works only with negatives; you probably do not want to crop slides. Knowledge of depth of field is most helpful in close-up photography. In close-ups, the area coverage is almost always predetermined because you want to fill the frame with a subject of a specific size—a piece of glassware, a tool, a flower. Regardless of what lens is used, the depth of field is the same; and regardless of what close-up accessory is used to cover that area, depth of field remains the same. Close-up accessories do not determine the range of sharpness, as is often thought.

Medium Format Depth of Field

Those switching from 35 mm to medium format must be prepared for one fact: the medium format provides less depth of field. Focusing must be more accurate; thus checking depth of field scales is more important. The smaller depth of field can best be explained by the difference in magnification.

At life-sized magnification with any camera or focal length lens, for instance, the depth of field is about 2 mm at $f11$. Life-sized magnification with a 35 mm camera means covering an area 24 × 36 mm—the size of the 35 mm frame. To fill the larger medium format frame with the same area—24 × 36 mm—means a magnification of more than life size—to be exact, about one and a half times, which reduces the depth of field down to half, or 1 mm at $f11$.

There are two ways to increase the depth of field: (1) close the aperture or (2) do not fill the negative, in which case you lose the benefits of the larger medium format.

Setting Depth of Field

When depth of field is unimportant, simply focus on the main subject— the eyes in a portrait, for example. But when you need a particular range of sharpness, you have to manipulate the focus and aperture settings. Alter these settings until the range of distances you need falls within the engraved aperture marks on a lens. Focus the closest subject and the farthest subject that need to be sharp, read the two distances on the focusing scale, and then set aperture and focusing ring so the two fall within the depth of field scale.

If the range of distances is beyond the depth of field range even at the smallest aperture or at a usable aperture-shutter speed combination (for instance, at a shutter speed short enough for hand-held work), you have to compromise. Decide whether it is more important to have the background or the foreground sharp or whether it is better to have both beyond the depth of field range.

Camera Controls for Increased Depth of Field

Depth of field can be increased in some instances by using the swing and tilt controls built into view cameras and a few medium format models. The camera must have a lens or a film plane that actually tilts in relation to the optical axis and can now produce more depth of field along one plane. This is based on the Scheimpflug theory and can be applied whenever a subject is photographed from an oblique angle. To swing the lens to this point on a view camera or a bellows medium format camera with this capability, try to visualize the two lines extending from the film plane and the subject, and try to determine where they would meet. Since the film plane is tilted in relation to the subject plane, they meet somewhere. If you adjust the lens so that its extended line meets in the same point, you are set for maximum depth of field. This procedure is not as complicated as it sounds, and you can always check on the results on the ground-glass screen. The Scheimpflug setting not only provides more depth of field than any other setup but can give it at relatively large apertures so shutter speeds are shorter. It produces increased depth of field only when the subjects are more or less along one plane.

Another method of increasing depth of field along one plane is with a PC lens, which has built-in shift control and also a certain amount of lens swing. These lenses are available for medium format cameras, but they are costly. Tilting a lens or part of a lens requires a complex lens barrel that must be machined to precision.

HYPERFOCAL DISTANCE

If you want distant hills or mountains in sharp focus and, at the same time, have the maximum depth of field, set the distance ring so that the infinity mark is opposite the depth of field indicator on the right. The lens is then set for what is know as the *hyperfocal distance*. It is, in fact, also the near limit of depth of field when the lens is set at infinity. With the focusing ring set at the hyperfocal distance, the depth of field is at its maximum. It extends from the far distance to half the hyperfocal distance. For example, the 80 mm lens at $f22$ has a hyperfocal distance of 16 ft, and the nearest point of sharp focus is then 8 ft.

CREATIVE USE OF LENS APERTURE

Now comes your most important decision: how much depth do you want or need in a picture? That is where technical thinking must end and creative ideas must enter the photographic approach. Before you snap the shutter, you must decide whether everything from foreground to background should be sharp or whether one or both should be blurred.

With our eyes, everything usually appears sharp. They focus practically instantly when looking from one subject to another. There are good reasons why images should be sharp from foreground to background. Many subjects look best or most satisfactory only when sharp from front to back. Keep in mind, however, that such images are the most ordinary ones because they represent the world as we see it. The lens aperture provides one of the most powerful means to make images different by concentrating sharpness on one narrow plane with the rest of the image blurred. That is often the main attraction of the image on the camera's screen. So think before you lose the effect by stopping the lens down to make everything sharp.

Background Sharpness

The lens aperture also determines the degree of unsharpness of subjects in front and beyond the depth of field. It dictates how sharp or how blurred the background appears in the photograph. Since backgrounds form a large portion of many images, this is an important consideration. Therefore do not set apertures just for depth of field. Evaluate the image on the ground glass at different apertures, and check the degree of sharpness in the background.

If the backgrounds are beyond the depth of field and therefore unsharp, the focal length of the lens determines the degree of unsharpness. As longer lenses magnify backgrounds, they also magnify the blur. Such backgrounds therefore are less sharp. If you use a short focal length lens, your backgrounds may be just slightly out of focus. At the same diaphragm opening but with a longer focal length lens, you can have backgrounds completely blurred, forming a subdued, undisturbing backdrop behind the main subject.

Foreground Sharpness

What has been said about background sharpness applies to subjects closer to the camera. The focal length of the lens determines whether foregrounds are sharp or become a patch of diffused colors. The blurred foreground approach usually works on color film but not in black and white. The blurred patches can add a touch of color or can be used to frame the main subject. Suitable objects for blurred foregrounds can be found almost everywhere outdoors, but they can also be placed artificially; a tree branch or flowers can be held in front of the lens, for example.

Out-of-focus foregrounds are generally best when blurred completely so that they are not even recognizable rather than blurred just a little when it might almost look like a mistake. If the standard lens does not provide enough blur, go to a longer lens.

MANUAL DIAPHRAGM STOP-DOWN

On SLR cameras, the diaphragm is normally wide open to provide the brightest viewing image. The image on the ground glass is therefore the image as it appears on film if taken with the lens at the maximum aperture. The manual diaphragm stop-down allows you to see the effect of closing down the aperture.

The stop-down lever is one control most photographers should use more often. Too often the image is focused and viewed with the lens wide open, allowing the camera to close the aperture down and snap the picture while the photographer has no idea what the image will look like on the film. When you operate the stop-down mechanism, the lens closes down to the aperture preset on the ring. The ground-glass image becomes darker and the grain on the glass somewhat more pronounced, but you can see the image as it will be recorded on the film. Once the stop-down lever has been depressed, the diaphragm usually moves as the aperture ring is turned, so you can see how the image changes as the diaphragm opens and closes.

ACTION AND SHUTTER SPEED

The shutter speed may be predetermined from the point of view of exposure or to allow hand-held camera operation. The speeds that can be chosen with reasonable assurance of sharpness in hand-held photography depend on the focal length of the lens and one's ability to hold the camera steady. A fairly safe rule is to use a shutter speed fraction not longer than the focal length of the lens. A 60 mm lens is satisfactory at 1/60 sec or shorter; a 250 mm lens is preferably used only at speeds of 1/250 sec or shorter. You may be able to go to speeds twice as long.

When you are photographing stationary subjects, you can decide on shutter speed on these considerations alone. But when you are photographing moving subjects, the shutter speed should be chosen from the image-creating point of view to determine how the subject is recorded on the film. You must decide whether the motion is to be frozen, recorded with a little blur, or completely blurred.

Freezing Action

A moving subject recorded with a high shutter speed appears to be standing still. This produces interesting and sometimes curious pictures. The

A

High shutter speeds record moving subjects in the ordinary way (A). Slow shutter speeds—1 sec in this case (B)—produce an image different from the way we see moving subjects.

shutter speed necessary to stop action depends on the speed of the moving subject but also on the magnification of the subject as recorded on the film. If a particular subject fills the entire frame, its image moves farther across the film in a given time than it does when it fills only half the frame.

The movement also depends on the angle at which the object is photographed. The image moves the greatest distance when the subject is recorded from the side moving across the picture. It moves relatively little when recorded from the front and moving towards or away from the camera. Between these limits, the movement varies. A change in camera angle to 45° or to straight on can therefore stop action in a way that would not be possible from the side.

Another way to stop motion is to photograph at the peak of the action. This works well with all sports or actions that are not continuous but have a beginning and end or are repeated. In golf or tennis, shoot at the end of the stroke; with people on a swing, shoot at the maximum height

B

as they change direction. There is a peak of action on many rides in amusement parks, in jumping on a trampoline, in ballet dancing, and other stage and circus performances. If such actions are caught at the peak, a shutter speed of 1/500 sec is more than good enough with most lenses. To stop continuous motions, such as skiers, motorcycles, cars, horse races, divers, and rollercoasters, 1/2000 sec is frequently necessary, especially with long focal length lenses.

Following Moving Subjects

You can use another approach to stop moving subjects by following the subject with the camera and trip the shutter while the camera moves. This approach is good not only for stopping motion but also for the purpose of being different. If you move the camera at the same speed as the subject, only the background is blurred.

The amount of blur depends on the shutter speed and focal length of the lens. You can also move the camera slower or faster than the subject, creating a blur in the background and in the subject. With many subjects,

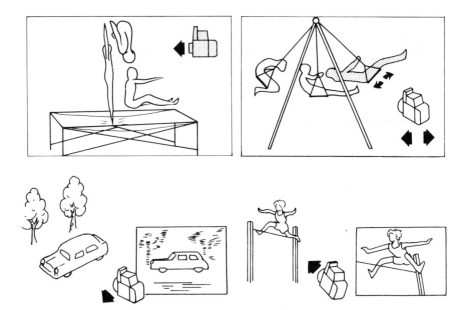

One method to reduce blur when photographing moving subjects is to release the shutter when the subject is momentarily still—for example, at the end of a swing or at the top of the bounce from a trampoline. Another method is to follow the movement of the subject in the viewfinder. When the exposure is made, the subject appears sharp against a blurred background.

some elements are moving in all different directions and at different speeds for instance, the spokes of a wheel, the legs of a bicycle rider or horse, the wings of a bird, the arms of a ballet dancer or ice skater. So even if the camera is moved at the same speed as the subject, these elements may then also be blurred in addition to the background, which adds to the impression of motion. If several subjects move at different speeds, there is still more choice of creativity. For example, with two or three runners or bicycle riders, each could travel at a different rate, and the camera speed can be adjusted so that one is recorded sharp and the others blurred.

Because the desired effect on film is frequently a personal choice, it is difficult to give recommended shutter speeds. For a bicycle rider or runner, start around 1/8 sec. Polaroid film can be used to make a test shot.

Choice of background is important. With a completely plain background, such as a blue sky, an empty wall, or a dark theater set, camera movement is not noticeable. To bring out the feeling of motion, the streaking effect must be obvious. Highlights and bright areas create the most noticeable streaks, so select a contrasting background, such as trees against the sky, sunlight on water, or crowds of spectators.

Cameras can be moved hand held or on a tripod. Many photographers

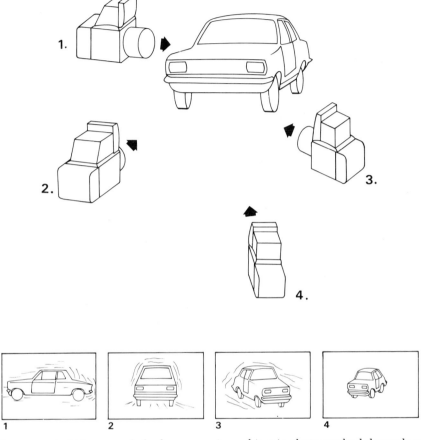

The amount of blur recorded when a moving subject is photographed depends on the position from which the photograph is taken and the size and distance of the subject. Using the same shutter speed, blur is greatest when the subject is moving at right angles to the camera view (1). A subject moving at the same speed straight toward (2) or at an angle (3) to the camera view is less blurred. Viewed from a greater distance (that is, when the image area of the subject on the film is smaller), there will be less blur, even at the same shutter speed.

find it easier to follow with a hand-held camera, especially when the subject changes speed or direction, as birds or ice hockey players do. If the subject, on the other hand, moves along a straight line—for example, a racing car, an athlete in a 100 m sprint, a bicycle rider on a straight road, or an object falling to the ground—a tripod-mounted camera is more likely to produce a successful result. The gunstock is an excellent accessory for a moving camera equipped with long telephoto.

Looking straight down on the ground glass with the regular finder or magnifying hood cannot be recommended, mainly because left and right are reversed. All prism viewfinders reverse the image. Many photographers find sports and frame viewfinders the best choice. The simple mechanical frame or mask makes it easy to follow the subject, not an image, and therefore you see everything as bright as it actually is. An even more valuable feature of frame and sports finders is that they show the surrounding area, and you can see where the subject might be going and where the camera is moving.

Blurred Motion Effects

The feeling of motion can be visually conveyed in a still photograph by recording any moving subject partially or completely blurred. These subjects can include reflections, clouds, smoke, wind-blown trees, flowers, grass, and rain, as well as more common subjects, such as rides in amusement parks, racing cars, and football games.

Shutter speed is one of the greatest creative tools available in photography. It is a tool that allows you to record on film any moving element in an unusual way. The eye cannot stop fast-moving action nor can it blur movement, which is why blurred-motion effects are fascinating and attract attention. They have impact. Instead of always trying to capture everything sharply, why not make a second exposure at a shutter speed slow enough to blur the motion?

It is not easy to be certain how blurred the image will be; it cannot be seen directly through the camera's finder. Evaluating the image on the ground glass can help, or you can watch how far the subject moves within a certain length of time. Even these aids, however, cannot indicate the effectiveness of the image. Try to photograph the subject not only at the speed you calculate but at two slower and two faster shutter speeds. Keep a record of the shutter speeds for future reference. Even better, make a test on instant film material. Slow shutter speeds are one of the most valuable applications of instant film. Within a minute you can see what the image looks like and make the necessary adjustments in shutter speed while the camera is still set up.

CHAPTER 9

Seeing the image

The medium format image is only as good as the view through the finder. The type of finder and the method of viewing, framing, and focusing are important elements for creating the image.

On nonreflex cameras—the rangefinder, press, folding, and special wide angle types—the finder is a permanent part of the camera body and there is no choice of finder, not necessarily a disadvantage. These finders are usually well designed and serve their purpose of framing the view. If the finder is designed for focusing as well, a split image rangefinder is used.

These separate optical finders have their own advantage. The image is very bright, as bright as seen with the eyes, because there is no lens, mirror, and ground glass to cut down the light. On the other hand, they show only the area coverage and provide no idea how the image will be recorded on the film.

For satisfactory viewing, two things are important: that you can place your eye close enough to see the full frame and that the view through the finder is sharp. The viewing window of such cameras is usually above the lens or to one side, so you must worry about parallax.

PARALLAX

The finder is adjusted to show the same area as covered on the film. However, because the finder is located above the camera lens, it sees the subject from a slightly different point of view than the lens, so parallax needs to be considered. It concerns one only when photographing at closer distances. The finder is adjusted in the factory, so its field of view is that covered by the lens at long distances, where these cameras are used mostly. Parallax thus is seldom a problem. Parallax must also be considered in TLR cameras.

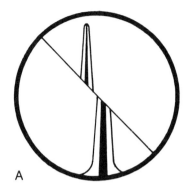 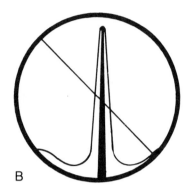

Accurate focusing with a split image rangefinder is obtained when a straight line in the subject crossing the split is not broken (A) but is continuous (B). The split line can be horizontal, vertical, or diagonal. The rangefinder area can cover the entire viewing area or only a portion of it.

RANGEFINDER FOCUSING

Rangefinder focusing is part of a few medium format cameras. The subject is viewed through two windows, on the left and right of the camera body. Each window views a somewhat different area, so you can see a double image over the entire field, or, in the case of a split image rangefinder, the two images are separated along the split. A horizontal or vertical line appears split. It is brought together by turning the focusing ring. When the line appears unsplit, the lens is focused on that subject.

Split image rangefinder focusing is extremely accurate as one can easily see whether a line is split or continuous. It is also rather reliable because even a user with impaired eyesight can usually see the line with sufficient sharpness. This is one of the reasons why many SLR users like screens with split image focusing.

TWIN LENS VERSUS SINGLE REFLEX

Practically all medium format photography today is done with TLR or SLR cameras. On both, the image is viewed and focused on a ground-glass screen that equals the negative size. It is viewed from the top through a folding-type finder with magnifier, which in most cases is interchangeable with prism finders. Ground-glass screens may be interchangeable on both. But here the common points end. On SLR types, the same lens forms the image on the ground glass and film; therefore what you see is what you get, assuming the mirror is properly aligned. This applies regardless of what lens is on the camera or what accessory might be placed in front of the lens or between the lens and camera. The image also can be viewed at any aperture. All it needs is closing down the diaphragm manually.

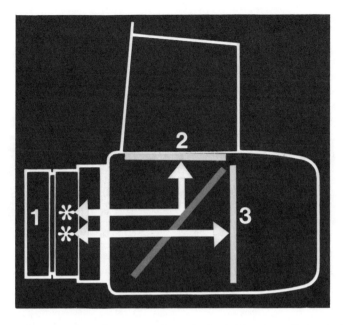

SLR cameras let you view the scene through the taking lens. It is vital for the mirror and ground-glass screen to be accurately aligned so the distance from the lens *(1)* to the screen *(2)* is identical to the lens-to-film distance *(3)*.

The TLR camera uses different lenses for viewing and photographing. The lenses move together when the focusing knob is turned, so accurate focusing is no problem. The two lenses, however, see different images, so parallax must be considered at close distances. The ground-glass image is always and only viewed with the aperture wide open, so image evaluation is somewhat limited.

You may have to be satisfied with one lens because lens interchangeability does not exist or is limited to one or two additional lenses. Close-up photography is limited to the use of Proxar lenses. On the other hand, the TLR type has advantages. The brightness of the ground-glass image is often increased by making the viewing lens with a larger aperture than the taking lens, an advantage in low light photography.

The ground-glass image never disappears because the viewing mirror does not move. It is the only camera besides the rangefinder and optical finder types that allows you to see the subject in the finder the moment the exposure is made. There is no delay; the image is recorded on the film the moment the shutter is depressed. When you depress the release on the TLR type, only the lens shutter opens and closes, thus providing quiet operation. And since only the lens shutter is involved in creating the image, the TLR camera mechanism is very simple. The simplicity, how-

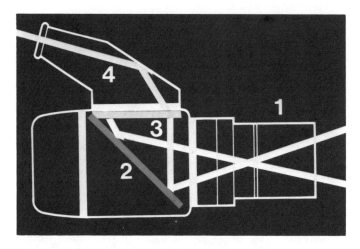

On an SLR camera the image recorded by the lens (1) is reflected by the mirror (2) to the viewing screen (3). The purpose of the viewfinder (4) is to magnify the ground-glass image for accurate focusing.

ever, also limits not only the use of different lenses but other accessories, such as film magazines.

SCREENS

Ground-Glass Screens

Most modern medium format SLR and TLR cameras allow you to select the type of ground-glass screen and change from one screen to another at any time. On cameras that offer this interchangability, each screen must rest in the same position so the lens-to-screen distance remains exactly the same.

The choice of screen must be a personal one. Do not purchase one specific screen simply because someone else uses or recommends it. If at all possible, check the different screens to determine which is best for your eyesight and for the lighting conditions, the lenses, and the accessories you use most.

You may very well end up acquiring two or three different screens and change them depending on the subject, the lens, and other considerations. The purpose of interchangeable focusing screens is to match the focusing and composing qualities of a screen with specific subjects and lenses. The right screen can assist critical focusing. Focusing screens in a modern camera are easy to change, but be careful not to touch or scratch the surface. Also make certain the new screen is inserted properly.

All focusing screens used alone provide an image that is brighter in the center than the corners. This deficiency was resolved by adding a Fresnel brightener to the ground-glass screen. It consists of closely spaced, very finely beveled concentric circles. The rings bend the light, striking the corners back toward the center so they can be seen through the eyepiece. The Fresnel lens thus brightens the corners of the viewing area.

Plain Ground-Glass Screen

The standard plain ground-glass screen is considered the most satisfactory by many photographers. It provides an image that, with the exception of perhaps some fine black marks for centering, is uninterrupted by circles and clear areas, making it the best choice for evaluating image effectiveness. This is especially true when photographing faces. The presence of a focusing aid in the center of the screen, as found in microprism and split image screens, obscures facial features. Faces also do not provide the image characteristics that favor split image or microprism focusing.

You can preview the image over the entire screen or any part of it. On the other hand, seeing whether the image formed by the lens falls accurately in the plane of the screen is not as easy with a plain screen as it is with other types. For this reason, screens with microprisms and split image rangefinders have become very popular.

Fine Line Focusing Screen

For some cameras, a so-called fine line focusing screen is available. The ground-glass itself is the same as the standard screen, but the circles on the Fresnel lens are more closely spaced, so they are less obvious. The closer spacing of the lines does not make it brighter, but finely detailed subjects are easier to focus, particularly in macro and micro work.

Fine Matte Screen

The overall matte surface of a standard screen dims image brightness. New technology using lasers and fiber optics has resulted in focusing screens that are noticeably brighter than their predecessors. This great improvement in brighteners justifies the higher cost, especially for those who work extensively in low light levels or wedding photography or for those who work with slow lenses. When investigating those new screens, however, compare not only the brightness but the focusing accuracy as well. Some photographers have found that they do not focus as accurately on some of these bright screens because the etching on the screen is very fine. Accurate focusing, not viewing, is still the main reason for using the ground-glass screen.

Focusing Screen with Split Image

You might also have a choice of a ground-glass screen with a central split image, which can be horizontal, vertical, or diagonal. The image can then be focused either in the clear split image center circle or on the surrounding ground-glass area. For split image focusing, the camera must be aimed at the main subject, perhaps an inconvenience in action photography or when photographing moving subjects in general. Focusing with the split image also needs a straight line crossing the split area because focusing relies on the eye's ability to detect breaks in otherwise continuous lines. When the points come together and the lines are continuous, the focus is correct. With a diagonal split, you can focus vertical or horizontal lines.

A screen with a split image is not a good choice when photographing subjects with a lot of texture and detail—flowers, for instance—and an equally bad choice for photographing people, especially their faces. The split image screen should be investigated especially by photographers who are having problems of focusing on a plain ground glass or are unable to see the screen sharply.

The main limitation of the split image screen involves lenses. When the aperture of the lens is smaller than about f4, one of the two halves of the split image field blacks out. Thus focusing is impossible except on the ground-glass area. The split image screen should therefore not be considered when you use f5.6 or f8 lenses extensively. It also means that focusing is not possible with a lens manually stopped down, although this is not recommended. Focusing is always most accurate with the lens

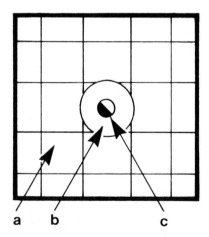

A popular screen combines a split screen center (C) with a surrounding microprism (B) and groundglass (A). Screens with grid lines help in aligning vertical and horizontal lines but are not as accurate for leveling a camera as a spirit level, especially when wide angle lenses are used.

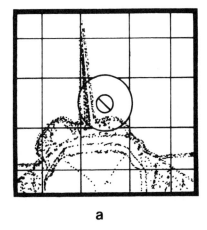

a   **b**

The focusing ring on the lens is turned back and forth until the unsharp image
(A) appears sharp on the ground-glass and microprism area (B) or with an unbroken
line across the split in the rangefinder.

aperture wide open, providing the brightest image with the minimum
depth of field.

With f4 or faster lenses, both fields of the split image field are clear
only when your eye is in the optical axis. If one of the fields is blacked
out, move your eye slightly up, down, or sideways.

Ground-Glass Screens with Microprism

This popular screen has a large microprism focusing area in the center of
the screen. It is usually brighter than the ground-glass area, an advantage
when working in low light levels.

The microprism area must be aimed at the subject for focusing, but
because its diameter is usually larger than a rangefinder area, it presents
no special problems. As the name indicates, the center area consists of
many tiny prisms that shatter the image when it is out of focus, making
it appear blurred. It blurs much more quickly than the image on the overall
matte field. Microprisms thus appear easier for focusing because the image
seems to jump more readily and rapidly into place than it does on the
standard screen.

Screens with microprism centers can be used with lenses of all focal
lengths and apertures, and consequently focusing can also be done with
the lens stopped down.

Combination Focusing Screen

Because each of the screens discussed has its own advantages and disadvantages, it makes sense to combine all three. Such screens are almost

standard in 35 mm SLR cameras and are also available for most medium format cameras.

A split image in the center of the ground-glass screen is surrounded by a microprism, permitting focusing with the rangefinder, the microprism, or the surrounding ground-glass area. The split image in most of those screens is split diagonally, which makes for faster focusing. By having these different types of focusing aids, one of them has to be right for every purpose.

Clear Glass Screens

Some camera manufacturers offer a screen of clear glass, not ground-glass, with some etched reference marks, lines, points, and circles, usually in black. It is by far the brightest screen because the image is not dimmed by the ground glass, but it is the most difficult to focus. For focusing, the eye must remain focused on the reference mark, which is difficult unless you are used to focusing through optical instruments. The image appears sharp whether the lens is in focus or not, so focusing is accomplished by parallax sighting using the cross-hairs etched into the glass. You move your eye back and forth sideways. When the lens is not focused, the aerial image moves against the cross-hairs. Turn the focusing ring until the image remains stationary. This is obviously difficult and time-consuming. This screen can be recommended only for special applications—when photographing through a telescope, for instance, but especially for photomicrography where accurate focusing of fine detail in a specimen is almost or completely impossible with a ground glass.

Screen with Grid Patterns

These screens, also called *checked screens*, have lines engraved. They are usually vertical and horizontal guiding lines, helpful when the subject lines have to be parallel to the edges of the image, as in architectural photography. These screens are sometimes offered as a specialized screen for architectural use with perspective control lenses. The grid screen, however, can also be an excellent aid to improving composition in general photography. It helps to keep horizons straight and buildings vertical. It is useful for still lifes with rectangular shapes that must be reproduced without distortion and also in aligning flat art for copying.

Other screens or screen masks for square format cameras may have guiding lines to show the vertical and horizontal 8 × 10 in. paper proportions. Such a screen should be used by every photographer who plans to crop square negatives into vertical or horizontal prints. It simplifies the work in the laboratory and eliminates the need for special cropping instructions. Simply tell the lab to use the center area of the negative.

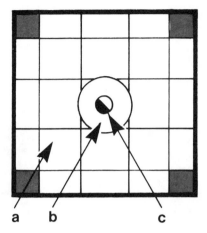

The 8 × 10 in. proportions are best marked off on a square screen by darkening the four corners with translucent tape or colored foil so you can still see out into the corners for square framing. The image is focused as usual, either on the ground glass *(A)*, the microprism *(B)*, or with the rangefinder *(C)*.

To make the 8 × 10 proportions more pronounced while viewing, you can darken the four corners with black lacquer or cement a gray filter foil over it. A screen mask of this type shows both the vertical and horizontal 8 × 10, as well as the superslide area.

Cleaning Focusing Screens

Ground-glass screens can be made from glass or plastic. Plastic does not necessarily indicate a cheaper quality and has the advantage of being unbreakable. Lens cleaning fluids must never be used on plastic screens. Glass screens can be cleaned like lenses, with lens cleaning fluid if necessary. If the screen is combined with a Fresnel lens, however, probably the Fresnel is plastic, and lens cleaning fluid or any other chemical should not be used.

Since screens rarely get finger or grease marks, they usually need nothing more than brushing or blowing the dust away. Wipe them only if absolutely necessary and if so, very gently with a soft cloth, perhaps slightly moistened with water or a mild soap and water.

VIEWFINDERS

The viewfinder serves two purposes: to magnify the image on the screen for accurate focusing and to shield the screen from extraneous light and thereby make it easier to see the image from corner to corner, even in bright sunlight.

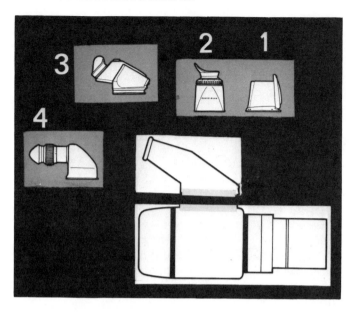

The choice of finder for most SLR cameras includes the standard foldable waist-level type *(1)*; a magnifying finder, which may include a metering system *(2)*; a 45° prism finder *(3)*; and a 90° prism finder *(4)*. The last two may also include a metering system.

The method of viewing also must be considered. Some viewfinder types allow you to view the screen while holding the camera in many different ways; with others, viewing and focusing are possible only while holding the camera one specific way. In hand-held photography, the proper viewfinder can be a great help for camera steadiness.

Viewfinders to Improve Camera Steadiness

Movement is eliminated or reduced when two forces work against each other. With a hand-held camera, the two forces are the hands pressing the camera in one direction and the photographer's head, with the eye pressed against the viewfinder, pushing the opposite way. The viewfinder and its eyepiece are therefore used not only for viewing; they are used for holding and steadying the camera. A firm contact between eye and viewfinder is necessary. For hand-held photography, select a finder that allows steady and convenient holding of the camera. A finder equipped with large, comfortable rubber eyepieces is recommended.

This firm contact is lost when eyeglasses are worn because they prevent pressing the camera against the eye. They also prevent placing the eye right behind the eyepiece. Thus, the user may not see the entire ground-glass screen area. Light may also enter between eyepiece and eyeglasses, flaring the screen and reducing the apparent brightness of the screen. Try to find a way that allows you to view and focus without eyeglasses. Perhaps you may have to take off and put on glasses constantly, but I still feel it is the most satisfactory solution, at least in hand-held photography.

Film Format and Viewfinder

A medium format camera designed for the square format offers a wide choice of finders. Since the camera never needs to be turned, the ground-glass image can be viewed straight down with a waist-level finder, a sportsfinder or from 45° or a 90° with prism finder. This is obviously a great advantage for anyone interested in photographing from different camera angles.

A camera made for the rectangular 6 × 4.5 cm or 6 × 7 cm format without a rotating film back needs to be turned for shooting verticals. Once turned, only one viewfinder, the 90° prism finder, is practical. The choice of finder is thus practically eliminated. That is also the reason all these cameras, as well as all 35s, come equipped with prism finders and consequently are designed for eye-level photography. Square format cameras, on the other hand, usually come with a foldable waist-level finder.

Prism versus Waist-Level Finders

If you move from 35 to the medium format, your first choice of finder may very well be the 90° prism type because it is the type used in the small format. There is nothing wrong with this type as long as viewing and focusing by placing the camera in front of your eye is satisfactory. For tripod work, a prism finder is a definite advantage because it allows putting the tripod on a higher level. Some photographers feel that this is the logical or only approach for fast shooting. This opinion is undoubtedly based on the fact that it is the normal 35 mm approach. But I see no reason why you cannot shoot as fast with a so-called waist-level finder if the finder is pressed against the eye, as it should be. Prism finders are often considered necessary for eye-level viewing. This again is not necessarily so. A folding-type finder, unfortunately called waist level, need not and should not be used from waist level. Pressed against the eye for hand-held shooting, the lens is only about 2 inches lower than it would be with a prism finder.

With this folding-type finder, right is left, left is right. This consideration is unimportant in most photography. You get used to it quickly and are hardly aware of the reversed image. But it becomes objectionable when photographing moving subjects. If the subject moves to the left, the viewfinder image moves to the right. You turn the camera the wrong way and probably miss the shot. Following action through the waist-level

Prism finders are advantageous when following a moving subject. They reverse the ground-glass image so the camera is moved in the same direction as the subject.

finder is impractical. But with a prism finder, the image is not only right side up but also laterally correct, so what is left is left and what is right is right.

The folding-hood viewfinder is the simplest, lightest, and least expensive interchangeable viewfinder. When folded down, it adds very little to the size of the camera, and it protects the focusing screen from dirt and scratches. When you unfold it, folding sides snap into place around the screen to exclude stray light from the focusing screen.

A prism viewfinder on a medium format camera can add quite a bit of bulk and weight to the camera and costs more than the folding type, especially if it is made of prisms, not mirrors. A true prism finder, however, is rugged and likely to have good image quality. Prism viewfinders are also made with built-in light meters, which by itself can be a good reason for selecting this finder.

Somewhat of a compromise between prism and folding-type finders is a magnifying hood. The image is viewed from the top through a built-in magnifying lens, which may have a diopter correction built in so it is adjustable for individual eyesight. It does not fold, so the camera is bulkier, but not having a prism, it is lighter and much less costly.

With a prism finder, the screen image must be viewed with one eye, undoubtedly considered by many the standard and ideal way to view an SLR image. It is an excellent approach for framing and focusing but I feel not the best way to evaluate the effectiveness of the image. Viewing the screen with both eyes open, as you view the ground glass of a view camera, is far better; probably because we then view the image on the ground glass as we view the finished print or projected slide.

This is another great benefit of the medium format: the ground-glass screen is large enough for this two-eye viewing process without the need for magnifying it.

Viewing with both eyes is possible with the waist-level finder, a great benefit. For focusing, the magnifier that is part of most waist-level finders should be flipped over the top and the eye placed right on top of it so you see the entire screen and eliminate stray light. Once focused, you can leave it in place for shooting, or you can flip the magnifier out of the way for viewing with both eyes.

45° Finders

Prism viewfinders with 45° viewing are a good compromise between the standard and the 90° finders. You can hold the camera extremely steady because your hands normally press the camera diagonally upward toward

Viewing from the top has great advantages when photographing—for example, from low angles (1), from the knee (2), straight down (3), from over the head (4), sideways (5), or from a vertically mounted camera (6).

When the camera is too high to view from above and it is inconvenient to view from below, use either an eye-level finder or turn the camera sideways and view from the side (1). For the 4½ × 6 cm format, a 90° finder and bracket allow steady and convenient holding and viewing for vertical and horizontal arrangements (2).

your slightly tilted head. Viewing is very comfortable from eye level and also from fairly low and high angles. It is excellent for tripod photography. Like the waist-level types, they are practical only on cameras that need not be turned.

Advantages of Viewing from the Top

While eye-level viewing with prism viewfinders has become almost the accepted standard for hand-held cameras, especially in 35 mm, important advantages can be pointed out in favor of viewing from the top. One is the possibility of viewing with both eyes open. The other has to do with photography from different angles. Viewing from the top offers the most convenient viewing at low camera angles. Focusing and framing is done easily, even if the camera is on the floor or ground and without the photographer having to lie on the floor, especially appreciated in snow or slush. In a nightclub or restaurant, for instance, you can place the camera on the table and view the image on the ground glass without anyone else being aware of your actions. When kneeling down, you can photograph with the camera on your knee for steadiness. You look right at the ground glass from the normal working position when the camera is mounted on a copy stand or microscope.

If the tripod-mounted square camera is too high for viewing from the top and an eye-level finder is not available, tilt the tripod head 90° to the side so that the ground glass can be seen from the side, no problem with the square format camera. This camera position also allows you to see the lens controls.

Candid photography of people—without their being aware of the photographer—is frequently more successful with the camera turned to the left or right instead of straight ahead. Just turn the camera sideways at waist level and view through the standard finder.

Viewfinders for Accurate Focusing

Besides convenient corner-to-corner evaluation of the image, viewfinders must show exactly and quickly when the lens is set at the correct distance. For that, you must be able to see the screen sharply. If the subject focused on is not critically sharp when viewing the negative or transparency through an 8 × magnifying glass, probably the lens was not focused accurately. The fault is not in the camera but your eyes. As we get older, our eyes do not adjust at all distances. There are other indications of seeing problems: if you are never certain whether the image is in sharp focus, if it takes a long time focusing a lens, if you do not see the image jumping in and out of focus when turning the focusing ring, or when the focused distance is different every time you focus on the same subject. If you have any of these problems, see how you can match your eye to your finder.

Built-in Diopter Correction Eyepieces

Viewfinders may be equipped with an adjustable eyepiece like a pair of binoculars. This feature could be a good reason for selecting a particular finder.

Turning the correcting eyepiece of a prism viewfinder is like putting different eyeglass lenses in front of the eyes. Turning the ring to + 1, for instance, is like viewing through a + 1 diopter eyeglass lens. Adjusting

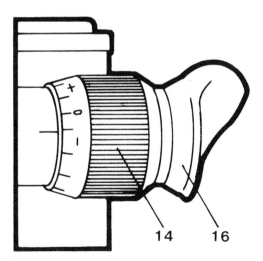

A built-in diopter correction eyepiece is adjusted to the photographer's eyesight by turning the eyepiece (14) until the groundglass looks sharp. The diopter correction can be read on the scale opposite the index. A rubber eyecut (16) shields extraneous light.

the eyepiece has nothing to do with focusing the lens or with photographing at different distances. It is simply an adjustment to provide a sharp view of the ground-glass screen. The adjustment is therefore best made without a lens on the camera. Point the camera without the lens at a bright area and turn the diopter ring until the grain on the ground glass or the engraved lines appear absolutely sharp. After adjusting, take the eye away from the finder, view a subject at infinity, and recheck the adjustment once more to see if it is still sharp. This ensures that the eyepiece is adjusted for a relaxed eye (viewing at infinity). This adjustment is made once only, and if possible the ring is then locked. It is not changed when switching lenses or taking pictures at different distances. The correction eyepiece needs changing when someone with different eyesight uses the same finder or perhaps after a few years when the eyesight has changed enough.

Diopter Correction Lenses

Other viewfinders solve viewing problems either with interchangeable eyepiece lenses or by adding diopter correction lenses to the existing eyepiece lens. Most manufacturers supply the necessary lenses, in different diopter powers, so it is not necessary to have them specially made. The installation usually consists of nothing more than dropping the lens in place as described in the instruction sheet. Adding this correction lens should allow one to focus accurately without eyeglasses. The correction lens selected must have the proper diopter power. This may have nothing to do with the diopter power of one's eyeglasses or bifocals.

With a prism viewfinder you no longer look at the ground glass but at an image of the ground glass which usually appears to be several feet away. This apparent distance is known only to the camera designer; if you need it and it is not mentioned in the instruction book, call the camera manufacturer.

The correction lens you need is one that allows you to see well at the distance at which the apparent image of the ground glass is located. If the image is 5 ft away, you need a lens through which you can see clearly at 5 ft.

Here are the suggested ways of selecting the correct diopter correction lens. If the manufacturer has different diopter lenses available, go to the camera dealer with your camera and finder.

1. Place different diopter lenses into the viewfinder eyepiece and determine by looking through the finder which lens provides the sharpest image and most accurate focusing. Make this test again without a lens on the camera.
2. If the apparent distance of the ground-glass image is known, ask an optometrist what correction you need to see sharp at that distance.

3. Assuming the distance is known, stand at a distance equal to the distance of the ground-glass image (at 5 ft if is 5 ft away) from a subject with fine detail like a newspaper page. Hold different diopter correction lenses in front of your viewing eye and determine which lens provides the sharpest image.

Diopter correction lenses are simple lenses and are not corrected for astigmatism. In most cases, this is not necessary. Only in severe cases may it be necessary, and if so you need a special lens ground to the proper diameter by an optician. As eyes change, correction lenses may also need to be changed after a few years.

Cleaning Viewfinders

The magnifying lenses are in an exposed position, and grains of sand and dust can accumulate in the hood crevices. Blow and brush away all dust particles before wiping with lens tissue and, if necessary, lens cleaner.

The same approach can be used on the exposed bottom prism surface unless the manufacturer advises against it. Clean, and especially wipe, lens or prism surfaces only when absolutely necessary. Off the camera, the prism viewfinders should always be protected with the cover that slides over the bottom plate and usually comes with the prism finder.

THE IMAGE

Seeing the Image as It Appears on the Film

SLR cameras offer the great advantage of being able to see the image as recorded on the film. This is correct if you do not forget one of the important controls on the camera: the manual stop-down or preview button or lever.

On SLR cameras, the lens aperture is always wide open to provide the brightest ground-glass image for framing and focusing. The image you normally see is thus the image as it will be recorded on the film if you take the picture with the lens wide open. If you take the picture at any smaller aperture, things change completely. It seems to me that many photographers have forgotten this or have never been told. They view and focus with the lens wide open and press the release without checking what the image might look like at the preset smaller aperture or they do not check what aperture is set on an automatic lens.

Depth of field and foreground and background sharpness depend completely on the aperture, which means the aperture, more than any other control on the camera, determines what the image on the film looks like. The aperture is the greatest and most important control factor in creating images and making them different. To use it in a creative fashion, you must not only know but also see what you are doing. You must use the manual stop-down control found on most medium format SLR cameras (unfortunately omitted on some). This control stops the normally wide-open diaphragm down. The image on the ground glass becomes darker, but that is a small price to pay for being able to evaluate the image at smaller apertures, to get a good general idea of how the image and the foreground and background sharpness change by closing and opening the aperture, and to be able to determine visually which aperture creates the most effective image.

Evaluating the image with the lens closed down is necessary with many special effect devices that can be placed in front of the lens. With vignettes, the sharpness of the outline and the size of the cutout in the vignette change with the aperture. With partial filters, the dividing line between the filtered and nonfiltered areas shifts. You must use the manual stop-down control. With multiprisms, the images overlap more at large apertures and become more separated at smaller ones. On some diffusion devices, the aperture has no effect, and on others, different degrees of softness are produced at different apertures. Because the viewing lens on a TLR camera has no aperture, this image evaluation at the shooting aperture is impossible—in my mind, the greatest disadvantage of the TLR type.

What You Cannot See

There are some things you can never see in the SLR finder. You cannot see how much blur a slow shutter speed created or what image is produced when you move the camera while the shutter is open—for the purpose of following a moving subject, for example. The finder cannot show what a zoom effect or a double exposure will look like. These effects can be seen only after being recorded on the film, so you have to experiment with different lenses and camera settings or make a test on Polaroid film.

Depth of Field

The ground-glass viewing screen of any SLR camera gives some indication of depth of field but, contrary to general belief, cannot show depth of field accurately and should never be used for that purpose. To explain this we must know what depth of field is and how it is determined.

When you focus the lens at a certain distance, say 10 ft, the only subjects that are as sharp as the lens is capable of reproducing them are subjects exactly 10 ft from the film plane. Anything closer and everything farther away is not as sharp. The falloff in sharpness is gradual. The closer or farther away the subjects are from the set distance, the less sharp they will be recorded.

Because the falloff in sharpness is very gradual, there is a certain range in front of and beyond the set distance where the degree of unsharpness is not noticeable, or at least not objectionable to our eyes when the final print or projected slide is viewed. This range is known as *depth of field*.

Depth of field is not based on the design of a lens but is a figure calculated from a formula. The formula is based on the so-called *circle of confusion*, basically the diameter of the circle of unsharpness that can still be considered sharp when the negative or transparency is enlarged to a certain size. Acceptable sharpness or depth of field is thus not based on the size of the negative or slide that comes out of the camera but on an enlargement made from the negative or slide. Considering this, how can you possibly see on a 2 in. camera screen whether the sharpness will be acceptable on a 16 × 20 in. or 30 × 40 in. print? Your impression of sharpness in the finder is based on a 1 or 2 in. contact print, not the enlargement made from it. What criteria could you use to determine what will have satisfactory sharpness and what will not? The finder eyepiece enlarges the ground glass perhaps three times, but what may appear sharp on the screen may be badly blurred when the negative is enlarged ten or twenty times.

The ground-glass screen itself makes the situation even worse. The ground-glass perhaps combined with microprism and/or rangefinder is necessary for focusing and is excellent for this purpose. The grain of the ground glass, however, makes it difficult, if not impossible, to see fine details. That is why ground-glass screens are practically never used in photomicrography; you cannot focus on the fine details of a microscopic specimen. Clear glass screens are used for this purpose.

Seeing depth of field on the ground glass is made still more difficult because the ground glass darkens as you close the aperture to a point where even focusing becomes practically impossible. If you want to see the image as it will appear on the print, you must close the diaphragm to the shooting aperture.

In summary, SLR viewfinders are great for accurate framing and focusing. They are also excellent for evaluating the effectiveness of an image, to see how much blur is in the foreground and background, to see what special effect devices do to the image, and to see what lens aperture produces the desired results; but do not waste your time trying to determine depth of field through the SLR finder. Consult the depth of field scales for this purpose. That is why they are still there on practically every SLR camera.

Frame and Sports Viewfinders

Many medium format cameras also provide the possibility of viewing through sports or frame viewfinders. They may be separate accessories,

A frame viewfinder with diagonals crossing the center is excellent for following moving subjects.

which are attached to the camera body, the lens, or the lens shade, or they may be built into the folding hood viewfinder.

With such a finder, the camera becomes a point-and-shoot camera. You view the subject through a mask in the finder that indicates the approximate field of view for that lens. The masks may be changeable or engraved for different lenses or film formats. The finder is sufficiently accurate for most applications, provided your eye is in the optical axis as described in the instruction sheet. Some sports finders have an adjustment for parallax. The lens is either prefocused on the ground glass, or distances are estimated using small apertures.

Frame and sports finders have advantages. The type with cross-hairs makes it easy to follow a moving subject. Sports and frame finders also make viewing with both eyes open easy. More valuable, you see the area in the finder and also the area around it. You can see more than what is included on the film. You can see what exists and what is happening outside the area and whether a subject is about to move into the picture. When panning with the camera, you can see where the camera is moving to, how far to move it, and when to press the release. In low light levels, a sports or frame finder shows the view as brightly as it is seen with the naked eye, without the grain of the ground glass between the viewer and the subject.

When the prerelease is depressed and the mirror locked up, sports and frame finders provide the only possibility for viewing and framing.

LEVELING THE CAMERA
While the guidelines on a checked screen can help in leveling the camera, they do not provide a guaranteed solution. The ground-glass image is not

sufficiently large to see whether verticals or horizontals are perfectly aligned. A spirit level is a better solution. If the camera does not have it built in, one might be available as an accessory.

COMPOSING THE IMAGE

Medium Format Image

The effectiveness of an image is greatly determined by *composition*: the arrangement of lines, shapes, and colors within the image area. Regardless of what camera and viewing system or viewfinder is used on the medium format camera, you must try to arrange the subject elements within the outlines of the finder so it forms a well-composed image.

Complete books have been written on this subject, and whatever information is provided is undoubtedly helpful to all photographers. Occasionally, however, the principles of composition are described as rules that must be followed, and photographic images are eliminated in competition simply because they do not follow those rules. That, to me, is going too far in the wrong direction. I consider the principles of composition as guidelines that usually make a well-balanced image. They should be considered. Photography, however, is not a science but a form of art and, even more, a form of personal expression. So rules of composition are to be broken if your intent is to do something different or do something that is more likely to attract attention. A foremost point to keep in mind is that attention is attracted by anything that is different from the ordinary, different from the way we usually see things, and that applies to composition as well.

Composition in Different Film Formats

Depending on the medium format camera or film magazine, the scene may have to be composed in a square (2 1/4 × 2 1/4 in. and superslides) or in rectangles with different aspect ratios between width and length (about 1:1.4 for 4.5 × 6 cm; 1:1.25 × for 6 × 7 cm; and 1:1.5 for 6 × 9 cm and 35 mm). The aspect ratio is even greater for panoramic formats.

The principles of composition are usually explained in relation to the rectangular image format, which many consider the normal or standard for photographic purposes. All of these principles, however, apply as well to the square format. One-third from the left side, for instance, is the same in the square as it is in a vertical or horizontal.

Photographers who are used to the square will probably even go a step further and say that the square offers the greatest freedom of composition, the greatest cropping possibilities (leaving the final image as a square or changing it into a vertical or horizontal). That is why many art directors prefer square images. If you plan to crop square negatives into rectangular prints, I recommend masking the screen with the proper cropping guidelines.

Square negatives sent to a laboratory for producing rectangular prints should be accompanied by the proper cropping instructions. Many laboratories supply masks for that purpose. However, if you compose the subject to fit into the proper guidelines on the ground-glass screen, the laboratory can simply print the center area. No special cropping instructions, except to specify a vertical or horizontal, are needed.

Composing in the Square

I hear of photographers having problems composing in the square. If so, it can only be because they have become accustomed to looking at a rectangular ground-glass screen. Whatever the shape or format, you must try to fill the entire frame area effectively, so the composition cannot be improved by cropping the image. If that is the case, you always have a well-composed and well-balanced image. This requires photographing a subject differently in the square than you would in a rectangle, just as you would photograph it from a different angle and/or distance in a vertical than a horizontal.

Any subject can be composed in the square at least as effectively as in a vertical or horizontal, especially because it is a good compromise between the two. The statement I hear occasionally—that a full-length bride and groom photograph has to be vertical and a group photograph of the bridal party has to be horizontal—has no place. They can be vertical and horizontal, but they could also be square or even reversed (the bride and groom as a horizontal, the bridal party as a vertical) by changing the camera position and making foreground and background elements part of the composition.

Attention-Creating Elements

Good composition means not only a well-balanced image but also an image where the eye is attracted to the important element, the main subject, and stays within the picture without being distracted by unimportant elements. When you evaluate the image in the finder, watch for those elements that attract the eye, and either use them to emphasize the subjects that are important or avoid them in areas that are unimportant. Always view the finder image from side to side, top to bottom, and look all the way to the corners. Distracting elements are especially objectionable near or at the edges.

Evaluating Composition

Composition can be studied in any type of viewfinder, even a simple frame finder, but the ground glass of SLR or TLR cameras must be con-

Indoor portraits require careful lighting not only to maintain the color balance but also to create the proper mood. Note the excellent composition with the strong diagonal created by the bow. Diffusion is created with a diffusion device over the lens. *Vericolor* negative film in 2¼ × 2¼ in. (6 × 6 cm) format. Photograph by Richard C. Cann (2×).

Photographs need not necessarily be exact reproductions of reality. Photographic images are often more interesting if the subject is reproduced differently from the way we see it with our eyes. Limiting depth of field is one of the simplest, yet most effective, means of creating such images. Standard lens with extension tubes. Framed in 6 × 9 cm format. Photograph by Ernst Wildi (2×).

A shaded area produces a soft, even light for portraits. Sunlight, as a backlight, not only adds life and color to the background, but can also be used as a hairlight. A small amount of fill/flash can be helpful just to bring some light to the eyes. *Ektachrome Professional ASA 64* in the 2¼ × 2¾ in. (6 × 7 cm) format. Photograph by Ernst Wildi (2×).

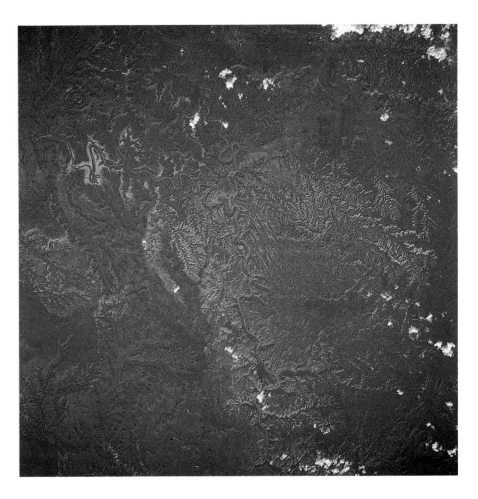

The medium format has been used since 1962 in the American space program mainly because the format provides a superb image quality as is proven by this image of the Colorado and Green River junction in Utah taken with a handheld camera on *Ektachrome 64* film from the space shuttle, flying about 160 miles above the earth, in the 2¼ × 2¼ in. (6 × 6 cm) format. Photograph courtesy NASA (2×).

Successful fashion photography means creating an attention-getting image while showing the garment to its best advantage. This image is basic flat studio lighting enhanced with carefully placed key and accent lights that create the necessary shadows and highlights on the outfit. Since many such illustrations are used full page, the subject must be composed to fit into the vertical rectangular page format. Photographed on *Ektachrome Professional*. Framed in the 6 × 4.5 cm format. Photograph by Marco Glaviano (2×).

Infrared color film provides a multitude of color effects simply by changing the color filter on the lens. Orange, yellow, red, and green filters normally used in black-and-white work are fine for this purpose, as can be seen in these two 2¼ × 2¼ in. format photographs reproduced at exact image size. Photographs by Ernst Wildi (1×).

Commercial illustrations not only require top professional models but also a *professional looking* setting with every object carefully placed and arranged. Note the eye-catching red color used in the center and the repetition of red throughout the image in this square (2¼ × 2¼ in.) format. Reproduced by special permission of PLAYBOY Magazine: copyright © 1981 by PLAYBOY (2×).

A panoramic, or wide-field, camera, 6 × 17 cm in this case, can produce exciting images even if not every part of the film area is filled with *image detail*. It gives you, in a way, a sense of presence, especially in horizontal views. Photograph by Lief Ericksenn on *Ektachrome 64* (1.5 ×).

1000 ASA film is not essential for well-lit buildings, fountains, or neon signs, but it allows short shutter speeds and handheld photography. Taken on *Agfachrome 1000* at ƒ4, 1/60 sec., in the 2¼ × 2¼ in. (6 × 6 cm) format. Photograph by Ernst Wildi (2×).

The lighting in a commercial illustration must show the product to best advantage and in an attention-creating fashion. The red color is, furthermore, used to attract the eye and to add a touch of reflective color on the polished bits. *Professional Agfachrome ASA 100* in the 2¼ × 2¼ in. (6 × 6 cm) format. Photograph by Agfa (2×).

A good full-frame fisheye lens covers the entire medium format negative or transparency without a noticeable light fall off in the corners. The curved lines with the diagonal 180° angle of view creates attention. *Kodak Ektachrome Professional 64 ASA* in the 2¼ × 2¼ in. (6 × 6 cm) format. Photograph by Ernst Wildi (2×).

Polarizing filters should be used in outdoor photography not only to darken blue skies but also to eliminate reflections, increasing contrast and color saturation. The polarizing filter can improve especially distant views, as in this case on the West coast of New Zealand, with 250 mm lens in the 2¼ × 2¾ in. (6 × 7 cm) format. Photograph by Ernst Wildi (2 ×).

Window light as a sidelight—or even as a backlight—can be very beautiful and is ideal for creating a solemn mood for a wedding day. If the window itself is in the picture, make certain it does not overpower the scene through overexposure. You must see details in the window or in the outdoor background outside the window. Either change the angle or control the lighting with fill-in flash, as in the 6 × 9 cm format image. Photograph by David Smith (2×).

This subject required careful attention to lighting. A very large source of light (a 6½ in. box) was used to create form with the spectacular highlights on the hands. Shadows were used to create form on the pearls. The background was created with a second exposure in this 2¼ × 2¼ in. (6 × 6 cm) format on *Fujichrome Professional ASA 50*. Photograph by Dean Collins (2×).

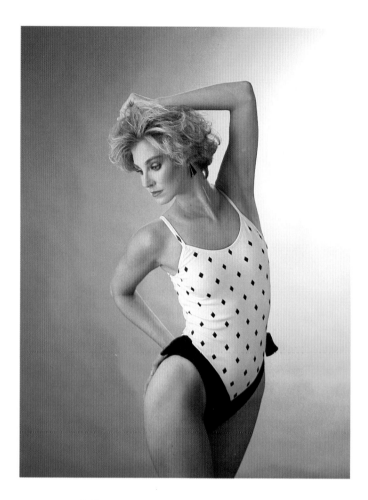

Carefully controlled lighting highlights the model's facial features with a colored backlight separating the body's outline and the hair from the background. Framed in the 6 × 4.5 cm format on *Professional Fujichrome ASA 50*. Photograph by Dean Collins (2×).

sidered best. Through an optical finder, everything is sharp. On the ground glass, what is sharp and what is not depends on the lens and lens setting. This is especially important regarding distracting elements. A highlight may be hardly noticed as a sharp point but becomes distracting as a large, blurred circle. On a ground glass, the positioning of the elements in re- lation to the frame becomes clearer, and engraved lines on the screen can help in placing lines and subjects at specific points. This is true especially for the large medium format screen. Although composition on the ground glass can be evaluated with one eye through a prism viewfinder, I still feel that the two-eyed evaluation through the standard, open waist-level finder is more effective and definite. There is a difference in seeing the ground-glass image with one or two eyes.

CHAPTER 10

Exposure

The technical quality of photographic images is determined mainly by sharpness and exposure. Exposure is determined by the amount of light, sensitivity of the film, lens aperture, and shutter speed. The amount of light is usually predetermined. The sensitivity of the film is decided by choice of film, which leaves two major controls for exposure: the aperture and the shutter speed. The two must be set so that the proper amount of light reaches the film in the camera.

APERTURE

The aperture ring opens and closes the diaphragm built into each lens. The size of the diaphragm opening is engraved on the lens in *f* stops or numbers. A large opening, letting more light onto the film, is indicated by a small number, such as *f*2.8; a small opening letting less light onto the film is a high number, such as *f*16. The *f* number is the ratio between the diameter of the entrance pupil and the focal length of the lens.

A 150 mm lens is *f*4 because the entrance pupil is 37.5 mm in diameter (150 ÷ 37.5 = 4). On some lenses, especially those made in Europe, the aperture is engraved as a ratio; 1:4 means *f*4. A smaller entrance pupil results in a higher fraction (a higher number) when related to the same focal length. In order to let more light onto the film, therefore, set the aperture to a smaller number; to cut down the light, use a higher number.

Aperture numbers are multiples of 1.41 (for example, *f*4 = *f*2.8 × 1.41, *f*22 = *f*11 × 1.41) because 1.41 is the square root of 2, and light intensity increases or decreases in the proportion of the square root of 2. If you want twice as much light from a light source, move the light 1.41 times (not two times) closer to the subject. If you want half the amount of light on the film, decrease the distance 1.41 times. The *f* numbers work in the same way.

A change in aperture from one figure to the next doubles or halves the amount of light reaching the film. It doubles when moving to the next lower number (from f5.6 to f4). It is reduced to half when going to the next higher number (to f16 from f11).

The maximum aperture of a lens is frequently referred to as the *speed of the lens*, and large aperture lenses are known as *fast lenses*.

SHUTTER SPEED

Shutters can be part of the camera body (focal plane type) or built into the lens (leaf shutter). In either case, the shutter controls the length of time the light coming through the lens shines on the film. Aperture and shutter speed together therefore determine the total amount of light that goes onto the film. The same amount of light can reach the film with many different combinations of aperture and shutter speed. As aperture numbers double or halve the amount of light, it is very easy to compensate for these changes by adjusting shutter speed.

If the aperture is closed one number (from f4 to f5.6 for example), only half the amount of light goes through the opening. If this amount of light goes through the opening for twice as long—the shutter speed is doubled from 1/250 sec to 1/125 sec—the exposure is the same. If the aperture is opened one number (from f16 to f11) the shutter speed must be halved (to 1/30 sec from 1/15 sec).

EXPOSURE VALUES

Some camera lenses and most exposure meters also have an exposure value scale (EVS) in addition to aperture and shutter speed. Exposure value (EV) is a single figure that indicates how much light exists for the film in the camera. It is somewhat like the guide number in flash, also a single number indicating how much light the flash produces again based on the film in the camera. In a way, we can say that the exposure value is a single figure that represents all the combinations of lens aperture and shutter speed that give correct exposure on a film of a particular sensitivity in lighting of a particular intensity. The various aperture–shutter speed combinations for EV values, 2 to 18, are found in the chart. The EV reading at a given light level depends on the sensitivity of the film in the camera because the meter has been set for the film speed prior to taking the meter reading. If the EV is 12 for 100 ASA film, it will be 14 for 400 ASA.

The exposure value system in some way offers simplicity; it is easy to remember a single number and to transfer that from one lens to another. It is also a simple way to remember the exposure values for a particular film when used in standard lighting conditions.

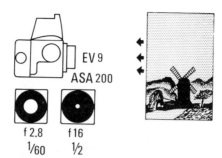

Exposure values (EV) are an indication of the amount of available light. A low EV number indicates a small amount of light; a high number indicates a greater amount. EVs are also related to the speed of the film in the camera. For example, for 400 ASA film, the EV may be 10, while under the same lighting conditions using 200 ASA film, the value would be 9. Once the exposure value has been determined, several aperture and shutter speed combinations will give the correct exposure—for example, $f2.8$ and ¹⁄₆₀ sec or $f16$ and ½ sec.

CONVERSION FROM EV TO SHUTTER SPEED–DIAPHRAGM COMBINATIONS

EV Setting				Equivalent Diaphragm and Shutter Speed Combinations (sec)					
	$f2$	$f2.8$	$f3.5$ $\&f4$	$f5.6$	$f8$	$f11$	$f16$	$f22$	$f32$
2	1	2	4	8	15	30	60	125	250
3	1/2	1	2	4	8	15	30	60	125
4	1/4	1/2	1	2	4	8	15	30	60
5	1/8	1/4	1/2	1	2	4	8	15	30
6	1/15	1/8	1/4	1/2	1	2	4	8	15
7	1/30	1/15	1/8	1/4	1/2	1	2	4	8
8	1/60	1/30	1/15	1/8	1/4	1/2	1	2	4
9	1/125	1/60	1/30	1/15	1/8	1/4	1/2	1	2
10	1/250	1/125	1/60	1/30	1/15	1/8	1/4	1/2	1
11	1/500	1/250	1/125	1/60	1/30	1/15	1/8	1/4	1/2
12	1/1000	1/500	1/250	1/125	1/60	1/30	1/15	1/8	1/4
13	1/2000	1/1000	1/500	1/250	1/125	1/60	1/30	1/15	1/8
14		1/2000	1/1000	1/500	1/250	1/125	1/60	1/30	1/15
15			1/2000	1/1000	1/500	1/250	1/125	1/60	1/30
16				1/2000	1/1000	1/500	1/250	1/125	1/60
17					1/2000	1/1000	1/500	1/250	1/125
18						1/2000	1/1000	1/500	1/250

The greatest benefits of EV, however, are derived when aperture and shutter speed rings on the lens are coupled. Once such a lens is set to the EV, any of the aperture and shutter speed combinations of the coupled rings will give correct exposure.

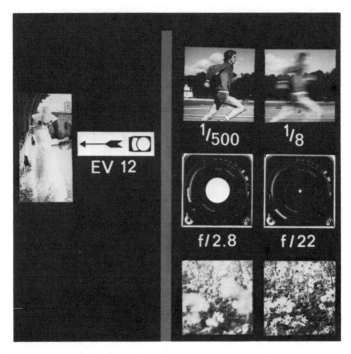

Using EV, you are more likely inclined to set aperture and shutter speed to create pictures rather than just for exposure. At the same EV value, you can photograph at a large aperture (little depth of field) and high shutter speed to freeze the action *(left)* or blur the action at a slow speed but use a small aperture for increased depth of field *(right)*.

Once the lens is set for EV, you can see all the possible aperture and shutter speed combinations. Since the depth of field scale is most likely next to the aperture, you can also see the depth of field range that every aperture produces. As long as aperture and shutter speed rings are left coupled, they can be moved in any way and always produce the same exposure. You can take two or more images with different depth of field or with different shutter speeds almost instantly and be assured that they will all be equally exposed.

In a way, coupled aperture and shutter speed rings offer the same automation found on built-in meters. If you change shutter speed from 1/30 to 1/125, the aperture changes automatically, say from f8 to f4. If the lens is set to 1/500 at f2.8 and you want f8, turn the aperture ring four notches, and the speed is automatically set to 1/60 sec.

FILM SENSITIVITY

The lens settings depend also on the sensitivity of the film. If you use a meter, separate or built into the camera, the film sensitivity must be set on the meter before the reading is made. The sensitivity, also called *speed of film*, is usually indicated in two ways: DIN (the German standard) and ASA, or now ISO, the international standard. ASA and ISO numbers are identical. 40 ASA = 40 ISO.

A film that has double the ISO or ASA is twice as fast. The aperture is closed one *f* stop to compensate for the difference. If 100 ISO or ASA requires *f*5.6, *f*8 will give the same exposure on 200 ISO or ASA. In the DIN system, a film twice as sensitive is three numbers higher. DIN 24 requires *f*8 if *f*5.6 is correct for DIN 21.

ESTIMATING LENS SETTINGS

Many seasoned photographers, especially those working frequently under similar light conditions, decide on the lens settings based on experience or the instruction sheet supplied with the film and end up with accurate results. In many situations, the light is extremely constant, so it makes no sense to meter every time. Such situations exist inside where there are no windows. Most living and working areas are lit to a fairly even level. A constant light situation can also exist outdoors on clear, sunny days. The amount of sunlight that falls on the subject is the same everywhere and most of the day except early morning or late afternoon. The so-called sunny 16 rule works well, at least for slide film for front- or side-lit scenes; in sunlight, set the aperture at *f*16 and the shutter speed at the inverse value of the ASA film speed. For 100 ASA it is *f*16 at 1/100; for 400 ASA, *f*16 at 1/400 sec or the closest to it. If you work with exposure values, EV 14 is correct for 64 ASA and EV 16 for 200 ASA. This setting not only works but frequently is more accurate than a meter reading. It eliminates some of the mistakes made with the meter, especially the reflected type— on the seashore or in snow, for instance.

Exposure charts work well, especially with many dim lit or special subjects, as shown here (for 200 ASA negative film or 400 ASA slide film):

Living room at night: 1/30 at *f*2 to *f*2.8

Interiors with fluorescent light: 1/60 at *f*4.

Close-up in candlelight: 1/15 at *f*2.

Stage-lit shows, circuses spot lit: 1/250 at *f*2.8 to *f*4.

Indoor sports: 1/125 at *f*2.

Outdoor sports at night: 1/125 at *f*2.8.

Fires: 1/60 at *f*4.

Neon signs: 1/60 to 1/125 at *f*4.

Lighted buildings, monuments: 1/15 at *f*2.

Amusement park rides: 1/30 at *f*2.8.

EXPOSURE METERS

Most photographers base lens settings on the reading from an exposure meter—a meter built into the camera or a separate accessory. Both types and all light meters made by all companies produce good results if used properly. More important than the make is the metering method. You must learn in detail how the meter measures the light and how it must be used to provide the best results in all situations.

Metering Cells

Cadmium sulfide (Cds) cells were most common in all types of meters until a few years ago. They are still around. They are accurate but react slowly to different light levels—in low light levels often frustratingly slowly.

Before Cds selenium cells were used. They are not as sensitive and thus not recommended or usable in low light levels. They have, however, an advantage: they do not need a battery. It is the light itself that produces the current to move the needle.

Modern exposure meters use silicon cells. They are extremely sensitive and adjust instantly to different light levels. They also react more or less equally to different colors, valuable when the light is measured through color filters. The battery must be checked occasionally, and carrying a spare battery is recommended. One point worth checking is that the meter shuts off automatically after a few seconds to eliminate wasting battery power. It is easy to forget to turn it off after each reading. Next time you take the camera out, the battery may be drained completely.

Meters as Part of the Camera System

Most modern medium format cameras also offer some way of measuring the light in the camera. The metering system may be in the camera body or in an accessory viewfinder. Both types measure the light reflected off the subject, but they measure it through the camera lens, which has a few advantages. The viewfinder shows what area is measured, and when the lens is changed, the measuring angle of the meter also changes. This is especially valuable when working at long focal lengths and photographing distant subjects that may not permit a close-up reading with a separate meter. Because the meter reading is seen in the viewfinder, changes in brightness can be seen while viewing the subject. The light is also measured through any accessories placed in front of the lens (such as filters) or any accessories placed between lens and film (such as extention tubes and bellows). Built-in meters therefore provide exposure readings that do not require consideration of filter or exposure factors.

Built-in meters also eliminate the need to carry a separate meter. But

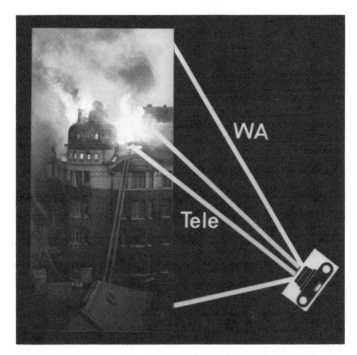

With a built-in meter, the reading is made through the lens that actually takes the picture. The reading is thus based on the reflectance of the area covered by that particular lens.

on the other hand, a repair of the meter also requires giving up the camera or that particular finder.

Built-in Measuring Method

Although all built-in meters measure the light through the lens, they can measure it in different ways. The meter may measure the entire area seen in the finder equally from center to corner—the averaging method. It is the same as measuring with a separate meter. There are built-in meters that work more like a spot meter, measuring only a certain area of the viewfinder image. The area may or may not be in the center. There can be a combination of the two—a method known as the center-weighted. The meter measures the entire ground-glass area, but it favors the center (or quite often the lower center). This last has become almost the standard on 35 mm and medium format cameras.

If your camera measures the light off the ground-glass screen and the camera offers interchangeable screens, ascertain from the manufacturer or through your own tests whether all screens provide the same reading—

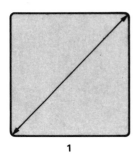 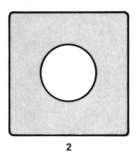 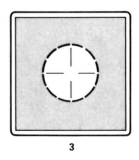

An averaging built-in meter measures the image evenly from center to corner *(1)*. A spot meter measures only a specific area indicated on the ground-glass screen *(2)*. The popular center-weighted system measures the entire area but not evenly. The major reading is made in the central area *(3)*.

or at least that the screen you are using does not require an adjustment. This is most likely so but should not be taken for granted.

Transferring the Built-in Reading

Meters in the camera system vary in the way the meter reading is transferred to the lens aperture and shutter. Major changes have taken place in the last few years. Medium format cameras have followed the path of 35s with more and more automation. Until recently the metering system in most medium format cameras was part of the finder rather than the camera body. Now they are more often part of the camera. In most up-to-date systems, the metering system is coupled to aperture and shutter speed ring. You can preset one or the other and then adjust the other until the indication in the finder shows correct exposure. With even more advanced automation, often aperture or shutter speed is preset; the other sets itself automatically.

Lens settings, which used to be indicated with moving needles, are indicated today with electronic displays or light-emitting devices (LEDs). Because there are no moving parts, they are more rugged and can take shocks and some abuse. The moving needle type, common until a few years ago, can be as accurate, but the delicate moving parts need more care. In this field of exposure automation, new developments are made constantly.

Although medium format cameras more and more are going the automatic route of 35s, they have not gone (and are not likely to) to fully programmed mode—that is, full automation where the camera, not the photographer, decides all the settings. They still let the photographer decide whether to choose automation and provide the settings. That is the way it should be on medium format cameras, which are used for more serious photography.

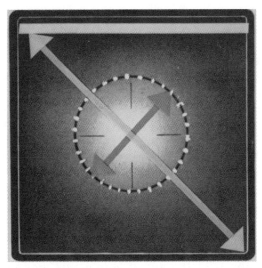

Most built-in meters are center weighted, measuring the full viewing area but favoring the center.

viewfinder indications

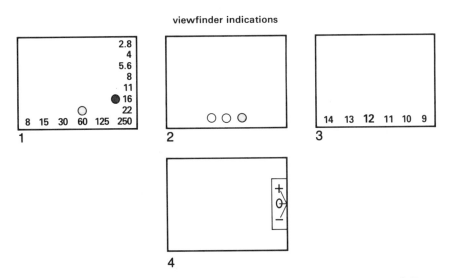

Lens settings in a built-in meter are indicated in the viewfinder in many different ways: actual stops and shutter speeds (1); with diodes next to lens setting (2); with exposure values lighting up (3); and with diodes simply lighting up or lighting up in a different color when the setting is correct or incorrect (4).

The medium format camera should allow the photographer to preset both aperture and shutter speed. In other words, it must offer aperture and shutter speed priority. Whether the other sets itself automatically or must be changed manually is unimportant. The system must, however, allow the user to override either. The latter may simply be in the form of full manual setting.

It is important that you see not just whether the lens settings are correct for exposure but what aperture and shutter speed is set on the camera or lens. Both settings must be seen at the same time. Whether the settings are in the finder or somewhere else on the camera body or lens is not too important, but both must be at the same place. Having to look for the shutter speed in the finder and for the aperture on the lens is unacceptable.

If you override the meter readings or meter manually, it is desirable to see whether lens settings are set for the metered value or for planned overexposure or underexposure.

Unfortunately, with the added automation and all indications in finders, photographers seem to pay less attention to using aperture and shutter speed for creating images. They are set for exposure only. This is not the way to create image. From this point of view, a metering system that is not coupled to camera body is almost preferable, and it still exists on medium format cameras. The meter prism simply shows the EV that provides correct exposure. The reading is then set on the lens. It is one additional operation; otherwise there is no disadvantage. It might have the benefit of the photographer's paying more attention in selecting the most effective aperture and shutter speed combination.

A meter reading through the lens on an SLR camera is made with the lens wide open, so the meter must know the maximum aperture of the lens on the camera. This used to be, and still is on some cameras, a manual operation. The meter has an aperture knob, which must be set to the maximum aperture of the lens and must be changed when switching to a lens with another aperture. It is an additional operation that one can easily forget. On modern systems, the meter, even if it is in the prism rather than the camera itself, is coupled to the lens, so the meter is always set correctly and changes automatically when switching lenses. When using a $2\times$ teleextender, the meter must be set for the maximum aperture of the lens less the two f stops. For example, when a teleextender is combined with a 150 mm f4 lens, the combination becomes a 300 mm f8. The meter must be set for f8.

All meters also must be set for the ASA film sensitivity. This again can be a manual operation, requiring manual changing when switching film or film magazines. Because films are changed less often than lenses, it is not as serious an operation but still something one must remember.

Modern cameras have changed this too. The interchangeable film magazine is set for the correct ASA. It then sets the meter automatically when the magazine is attached to the camera.

Aperture or Shutter Speed Priority

Built-in metering systems provide the opportunity to preset either the aperture or the shutter speed. For the amateur, shutter speed priority is considered preferable. The shutter speed can be set at a relatively high speed, perhaps 1/125, for reducing the danger of fuzzy pictures due to camera shake. An amateur is usually not concerned with depth of field, so the aperture setting is unimportant. For more serious photography, aperture and shutter speed must be selected carefully. The photographer must decide whether a specific shutter speed is important for the effectiveness of the final image. This applies whenever photographing moving subjects—not just sports action but anything that moves—and panning with the camera.

In many other cases, it is the depth of field, the background or foreground sharpness, that is important, so the aperture determines the desired results. Frequently, compromise is needed—for instance, when the shutter speed for the required depth of field becomes too long for hand-held work and a tripod is not available.

Exposure automation has advantages and simplifies photography in many cases. The extent of automation, however, is not as important as the photographer's knowledge of when and how to use it to determine easily and quickly all the necessary image controls: aperture, shutter speed, distance, and depth of field.

Using the Built-in Meter

A built-in meter does not provide correct exposure automatically and does not necessarily provide more accurate exposure than a separate meter. Built-in meters, like separate meters, provide correct lens settings only if used properly.

All built-in meters are reflected light meters. They measure the light reflected off the area or subject that is being photographed, and they have all the same faults of any reflected hand-held meter.

You can make the same mistake as with any other reflected light meter. You must consider everything that is discussed here for reflected meter readings and make the same adjustments as when using any separate reflected meter.

Measuring Light Levels

There are two basic methods of measuring light levels for photographic purposes.

Incident Reading.   In incident reading, the meter measures the light falling on the subject. The cell of the meter is usually covered with a domelike

The reading on an incident meter *(A)* is affected only by the amount of light *(X)* falling on the subject.

diffusion disc. Many hand-held reflected light meters can be used for measuring incident light by sliding or attaching a diffusion disc over the cell. The meter is held in front of the subject with the cell facing toward the camera or sometimes facing in a direction between the camera and the main light.

Reflected Reading.   In the second method, the meter measures the light reflected from the subject; it measures the brightness of the subject as the lens sees it. The meter reading therefore depends on two factors: the amount of light that falls on the subject and the amount of flight reflected back from the subject. A light subject gives a higher reading than a dark subject even though they are lit in the same way. A reflected light meter is pointed at the subject from the direction the picture is taken. Meters built into cameras are reflected types.

Hand-held Reflected Light Meters.   Hand-held reflected light meters come in two basic types. The ordinary type has a measuring angle that is approximately equal to the standard lens on the camera. The second type is the spot meter. It has a narrow measuring angle of a few degrees only and measures a small area determined by looking through a finder in the meter. The two therefore differ not in the way the light is measured but in the area that is measured. Combination meters also exist.

A reflected meter reading (B) depends on the amount of light falling on the subject (X) *and* the amount reflected off the subject (Y).

With a spot meter, you can measure one specific small area, or several areas within a scene, from the camera position, obviously an advantage. On the other hand, you can make serious exposure mistakes by measuring the wrong spot within a scene. Spot measuring requires a more thorough knowledge of light measuring than a regular meter.

Some meters offer a choice of reflected or incident readings. They are fine for the photographer who may fall into the habit of measuring everything both ways, comparing the values, and compromising between the two. It is not a recommended approach and is usually practiced only by photographers who do not understand light and exposure.

Lens Settings for Correct Exposure

Lens settings for correct exposure are determined only by the amount of light that falls on the subject. The lens settings therefore should be the same whether you photograph a white or yellow subject or one that is black, dark brown, green, blue, or red. This statement is so important to light measuring that I will repeat it in a slightly different way: As long as the same amount of light falls on the subject, lens settings must be the

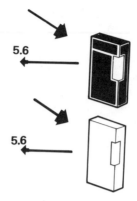

If the same amount of light falls on the subject, the lens settings are the same regardless of whether the subject is white, black, gray, or any other color.

same regardless of the color or reflectance value of the subject. Consequently, measuring the light that falls on the subject should provide the correct exposure regardless of what you photograph.

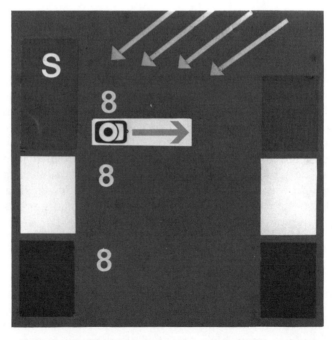

An incident meter held in front of gray, white, and black subjects illuminated by the same light shows the same lens settings, and these settings record the subjects as gray, white, and black.

Incident Light Measuring

The meter reading is affected only by the light falling on the subject, unaffected by the tone, color, or reflectance of the subject. In other words, the incident meter measures exactly what determines the correct lens settings. This should be the logical and preferred method. Incident metering is unquestionably the easiest method, the one most likely to provide the correct lens settings under most subject and lighting conditions. If you have used this method or if you have such a meter, by all means use it. The readings are not necessarily more accurate, but correct aperture and shutter speed are obtained in the simplest possible way, and metering mistakes are reduced or eliminated.

Reflected Light Measuring

Reflected light readings depend on how much light is reflected back from the subject. A reflected light meter reading is high for white or yellow subjects, low for black or dark brown, and somewhere in between the two for green, blue, and red. Which is correct?

The green is most likely to be correct because green reflects about 18° of light. A reflected light meter, separate or built-in, is adjusted for

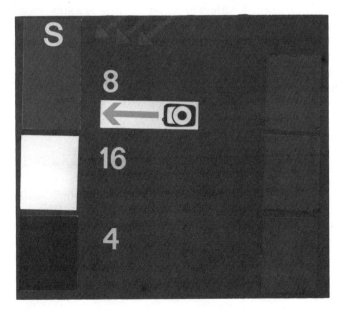

A reflected light meter gives different readings when pointed at gray, white, and black. Only the 18 percent gray reading is correct and will record gray as gray. If the lens settings from the white and black are used, they will record both as gray, not as white and black.

an 18° reflectance and thus assumes that the light it measures is reflected off an 18° reflectance subject. Its reading is correct only when you measure an 18° reflectance. If the measured subject reflects more or less, you must make the necessary adjustment. If you do not, neither the black nor the white subject is recorded as black or white; both are recorded as gray. Before you take the reading off a reflected light meter, ask yourself if you have measured something that reflects about 18% of the light. If so, use the reading.

Surprisingly, most ordinary scenes reflect about 18% of the light that falls on them; so you need to correct only rarely. Some typical 18° reflectance subjects are green fields and trees, brown earth, fall foliage, blue skies, and suntanned faces. If the reflected meter reading is taken off a brighter subject that reflects more than 18%, open the lens and set it at an aperture one or two steps larger ($f8$ instead of $f11$; EV 10 instead of 11). Some typical subjects requiring such an adjustment are: fog, 1 EV number or f stop; sand, 1 1/2; snow, 1 1/2 to 2; white flesh tones, 1; overcast skies, 2; reading off the palm of the hand, 1.

For subjects that reflect much less than 18%, close down the lens or use a higher EV number. For example, a blackboard, 2 f stops; black flesh tones, 1–1 1/2.

It seems to confuse many photographers that the aperture must be opened when reading bright subjects and closed for dark ones. Consider the following example. A reflected meter reading of a subject with an 18% reflectance is 1/250 sec and $f11$. A reading off a white subject would be 1/250 sec at $f22$. To bring it to the correct 18% reflectance reading, open the aperture two f stops from $f22$ to $f11$. A reading off a black subject would be lower, perhaps 1/250 sec at $f5.6$. The necessary correction means closing the aperture down to $f11$.

Spotmeters

A spotmeter is often considered the most sophisticated and thus the best and most accurate of all the meters. Accurate it can be, if the photographer knows what to do with it; it is also the most inaccurate in the hands of photographers who do not understand how meters work.

A spotmeter is a reflected light meter with a measuring angle of a few degrees only. It thus measures only the light reflected from the tiny area seen in its finder, and that is where the problem, or its advantage, comes in.

The spotmeter reading is correct only if the tiny area at which it is pointed reflects about 18 percent of light. Since the area is so small, it is easy to make mistakes, pointing the meter at an area brighter or darker. A spotmeter must be carefully aimed; the reflectance of the spot area must be carefully analyzed. You must furthermore carefully analyze whether it measures highlight or shadow areas.

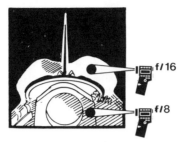

A spotmeter is a reflected light meter with a very narrow measuring angle compared to a regular meter that measures an area about the size covered by the standard lens. The spotmeter reading depends on the reflectance of the spot it is pointed at. The reading can easily vary four, five, or more stops.

Clearly the spotmeter is not an instrument for a casual snapshooter. The mistakes that can be made are far greater than with any other type of meter that averages out the reflectance from various subject areas. In the hands of the expert, it is a great instrument and has great advantages, especially in close-up photography, in distant shots with telephoto lenses, back-lit scenes, or other situations with great contrast. The small measuring area also makes it especially suited to measuring contrast ranges or lighting ratios.

GRAY CARD

A gray card, available in camera stores, can assure more accurate readings with reflected light meters as they allow measuring something that reflects 18 percent all the time. Hold the gray card in front of the subject and take

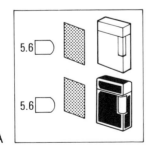

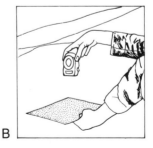

Instead of measuring the light reflected off the subject, you can measure the light reflected off an 18 percent gray card. The reading is then the same whether the card is held in front of light or dark subjects *(A)*. When photographing scenery, especially snow or sand, the easiest way to get a perfect reflected light reading is by holding the gray card parallel with the ground and pointing the meter straight down at it *(B)*.

a reflected meter reading from its 18 percent reflectance instead of a subject of unknown reflectance. The gray card reading should be the same as an incident light reading. Basically the gray card is held in the same place and direction as an incident meter would be—in front of the subject—so that the same light that falls on the subject falls on the gray card. Hold the meter not more than 20 cm (8 in.) from the card so it measures only the gray area. With a built-in meter, hold the camera in front of the card so nothing but the gray card is visible in the finder. With the standard lens, it must be as close as 6 in. Do not allow the shadow of your camera, hand, or meter to affect the reading. The purpose of the gray card is simply to eliminate the different reflected meter readings that you obtain from white, black, green, red, and yellow subjects. It gives the lens setting for 18 percent reflectance.

Although the gray card is an additional item to carry, it is highly recommended. It has provided extremely satisfactory results and has solved many exposure problems without extensive bracketing.

Gray Card as a Color Test

The gray card is of known color and can be photographed together with the subject to check how the light source matches the film. More important, a gray card included in one of the images on negative color film can be valuable or even necessary to the laboratory for printing. Without a subject of known color value in the negative, the laboratory is somewhat at a loss to know what the colors in the print should be. In portraits, flesh tones are the basis for colors. In images that do not include people, the insertion of a gray card in one of the negatives taken in one location is practically a necessity. It is especially important when pictures are taken under anything but standard lighting, such as fluorescent lights or on overcast days.

White Side of the Gray Card

The rear side of the gray card is a specific white that reflects 90 percent of the light and can be used for reflected light meter readings.

In low light levels, the light reflected from the gray side may be too weak to give a meter reading, or the reading will be at the extreme low end of the scale. In such situations, take the reflected meter reading off the white side, which reflects five times as much light. Compensate for the higher reflectance by setting the reflected exposure meter for a film sensitivity five times lower than the film in the camera; for example, set at 20 ASA if the camera is loaded with 100 ASA film. Hold the card as described, and take the reading off the white side. Use the lens settings as shown on the meter. Do not forget to reset the ASA index on the meter when the gray side of the card is used again.

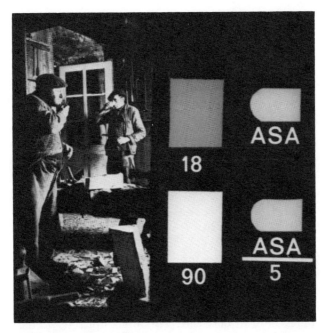

You can read the white side of the gray card and set the meter to one-fifth the ASA rating of the film. This is the correct adjustment because the white side reflects 90 percent of the light compared to 18 percent for the gray side.

PALM READINGS

The palm of the hand is frequently recommended as a substitute for a gray card. Hold your hand in front of the subject, as you would a gray card, and take the meter reading from about 5 cm (2 in.) away. The palm of the hand is a good substitute because its reflectance is practically the same for everybody at all times. The principle is sound, but most palms reflect more than 18 percent. When taking palm readings, therefore, set the lens one EV value, or one f stop, lower (open the lens one stop).

FLESH TONE READINGS

A common method of determining exposure when photographing people is through a close-up reading off the flesh tones. Although the flesh tones should be presented properly, such a reading can be correct only if the skin tone reflects 18 percent, which a suntanned face or body does. It cannot be correct for white or black skin tones, which need an adjustment as does any other subject. For white skin tones, open the lens one f stop. For black skin tones, close the lens one or one and a half f stops or EV numbers.

Close-up readings of skin tones with a reflected meter are not necessarily correct. White skin tones are one stop lighter than gray cards; black skin tones are one to two stops darker. Use a gray card to obtain correct readings for all flesh tones.

WHAT TO EXPOSE FOR

Up to now we have examined how to obtain correct exposure for subjects of different brightness and colors. Usually some areas in a picture receive more light than others; some subjects are in bright light and some in the shade. Which area should be exposed for: the shaded areas, the lighted areas, or somewhere in between? This does not refer to dark- and light-colored subjects but to the amount of light falling on these dark and light subjects. The logical thought might be to set the lens somewhere between the reading of the lighted and shaded areas. If the contrast is not too great, the result is probably acceptable but never the best. Negatives exposed in this way lack printable shadow details, and slides unquestionably have washed-out highlights. The method I use with all subjects, in all lighting situations, and photographed on all film materials is to base exposure for transparency films on the lighted areas and those for color or black-and-white negative films on the shaded areas where detail is desired. This method determines where and how to hold the exposure meter. For negative material, the incident meter is held in front of the shaded area of the subject with the cell pointing toward the camera. A reflected meter, a camera with a built-in meter, is pointed at the shaded area of the subject or at a gray card held in the shaded area.

For transparency film, an incident meter is held in the lighted part of the subject, a reflected meter or a camera with meter, is pointed at the lighted area or at a gray card held in the lighted area. Transparencies exposed in this way lack shadow detail, but this is not usually objectionable and always overshadowed by the rich color saturation. Washed-out highlights are objectionable in slides and movie scenes.

With front-lit subjects, hold the incident meter with the cell pointing toward the camera and hold a gray card facing the camera. With a side-lit subject outdoors or in the studio, point the incident meter cell halfway between the main light and the camera and hold the gray card so that the gray side faces halfway between the main light and the camera.

For photographing documents, lay the gray card flat on the artwork or hold the incident meter on top of the copy. The reading is correct whether you photograph black line work on white paper or white copy on black or any other color cardboard. The same approach—placing the gray card flat on the ground—is excellent for most scenic outdoor photography, especially when photographing bright areas, water surfaces, snow-covered fields, or sandy areas, such as deserts or beaches. The benefit of placing the gray card on the ground is that it makes no difference from which side the sunlight falls. Front, side, or back, the gray card reading is always the same. The reflected meter reading of the gray card is taken by pointing the meter straight down at the card.

A subject situation that requires careful metering. Hold a reflected meter close enough to the subject so the reading is based only on the subject and is not influenced by the dark background. With transparency film, measure the light falling on the lighted side (right) of the subject. With negative film, measure the light falling on the shaded (left) side of the subject. In either case (negative or slide film), point a reflected meter at an 18 percent reflectance part of the subject (the suntanned face) or hold a gray card in front of the lighted or shaded side of the face. Do not take a reflected meter reading off the white dress or open the aperture one stop more than indicated on the meter.

When using the method of shadow reading for negative material and highlight reading for transparency material, it is best to use the ASA rating recommended by the film manufacturers and to develop black-and-white films according to the manufacturer's instruction. There is no need to underexpose slides or overexpose negatives.

Photographic films and papers cannot cover contrast ranges beyond a certain point far below what we can see. If details are to be recorded on negative film in both shadow and highlight areas, the difference in the meter reading between the two should not exceed five f stops, and the selected lens setting must be between the two. Transparencies, however, always look best when exposed for the lighted areas. If details are necessary in shaded areas, cut the contrast down with fill-in light.

With reflected light meters, it is important to ascertain that the cell receives light only from the area to be exposed for without being influenced by surrounding dark or light backgrounds. This is of utmost importance with white backgrounds in a studio or white overcast skies outdoors because even the slightest amount of light from these bright areas can swing the needle two to three EV numbers higher. When subjects are back lit, the meter must be held so that a light, or the sun, does not shine directly into the cell. If necessary, shade the cell from direct light with your hand or another object.

Exposure can be checked with the Polaroid film magazine. When evaluating the Polaroid test shot for exposure, keep in mind the film in the camera. With transparency film, it must show correct exposure in the lighted area. With negative film, the lens settings are correct when the Polaroid test shows details in the shaded areas. The print as a whole may well look too light since the lighted areas are overexposed.

BRACKETING

If you use the exposure meter as recommended, you should have satisfactory exposure in all negatives or slides. *Bracketing,* which means taking the images at two or more different lens settings, should not be necessary. There is nothing wrong with bracketing, but it uses a lot of film, especially if you bracket every shot.

Many times bracketing is impossible. When photographing action—sports, candids, anything that is not staged—there is no possibility for a second shot, so the first must be right. Bracketing is recommended when slides are made of subjects with extreme contrast. The technique is not so much for the purpose of good exposure but for producing the most effective image. Perfect exposure in such cases is not necessarily determined by technical considerations but may be a case of personal preference. A darker image may be effective because it is dramatic. Early morning shots of scenery or people may be more effective when colors are on the pastel side, creating a low-key effect. Since today's black-and-white and color films have good exposure latitude, I suggest bracketing in full stops. A difference in one-half f stop is hardly noticeable. One-half f stop bracketing, however, is still recommended for critical work on slide film.

SPECIAL EFFECTS ACCESSORIES

When accessories are placed in front of the lens or between lens and film, exposure of a separate or built-in meter may have to be adjusted. Accessories made from clear glass or plastic and covering the entire lens or image area do not require a change in exposure regardless of whether the reading is taken from a separate or built-in meter.

Among the nonabsorbing devices are close-up (Proxar) lenses, multiprisms, diffusion filters, star filters and other clear special effects filters, and clear gelatin.

Accessories made from colored glass or gelatin and covering the entire lens absorb light and need an increase in exposure when a separate meter is used. Built-in meter readings are correct with most filters because the light is measured through the filter.

There is another group of devices that are placed a few inches in front of the lens and cover only part of the image area. This group includes all types of vignettes, masks, and diffusion devices that soften only part of the image. Exposure is always based on the area seen through the device. These devices, especially black masks and vignettes, block off some of the light that reaches a built-in meter, so the built-in meter reading made through the mask is incorrect. The simplest way to obtain the correct reading is to take the meter reading without the mask or vignette and to use this setting for the exposure.

OTHER USES OF METERS AND GRAY CARDS

Exposure meters are ideal for determining ratios between main and fill lights, front lights and back lights, subject and background, and shaded and lighted areas. They are important or necessary to ensure even lighting distribution, especially when photographing interiors or documents. In all of these cases, use either an incident meter or a reflected meter with gray card. The gray or white side can be used because the two values are only being compared. When photographing documents, take readings in the center and all four corners.

Controlling Backgrounds

Measuring the light falling on the background and comparing it with the light falling on the main subject is especially important in color photography. The background appears on the film in the color observed visually only if it receives the same amount of light as the main subject that the exposure was made for. All backgrounds appear in their true color only with this 1:1 lighting ratio. The lighting ratio is checked with an incident meter by holding the meter in front of the main subject and in front of the background behind the subject. With a reflected meter, the reading is made from the gray card held in front of the main subject and the background.

Determining Lighting Ratios

Decide whether you want to determine the real ratio between main and fill light or the lighting ratio that the lights produce on the subjects. These are not the same because the fill light usually adds light to the side covered by the main light.

For checking the lighting ratio between main and fill, hold an incident meter in front of subject, pointing directly into the main and the fill light. With a reflected meter, take a reading off the gray card held in front of the subject facing directly toward the main light and a similar reading with the card facing directly toward the fill. To determine the lighting ratio on the subject, turn the main and fill lights on and aim an incident meter from the subject toward the lights so that the maximum meter reading is obtained, or take a reflected meter reading off the gray card turned in front of the subject so that the maximum reading is obtained. Then turn the main light off and take the second reading of the fill light with the incident meter pointing directly into the camera lens or with a reflected meter off the gray card facing the camera lens. The two readings give the true lighting ratio on the subject. The actual ratio is obtained from the difference between the two measurements in either the EV numbers or the f stops. Lighting ratios with multiple electronic flash setups are determined in the same way but with a flash meter.

An equal reading on both measurements means a 1:1 lighting ratio. A 2:1 ratio exists with a difference of one f stop or EV number; 3:1, with a one and one-half EV or f stop difference; 4:1, with a difference of two; and 8:1 if the difference is three f stops or EV numbers.

Lighting ratios can be determined without an exposure meter from the light-to-subject distance. If two identical lights, such as main and fill lights, are placed at equal distances, the lighting ratio is 2:1 (not 1:1 because the main light also lights the area covered by the fill light). For a 3:1 ratio, move the fill light 1.4 times farther away and another 1.4 times farther away for a 5:1 ratio.

SUBJECT BRIGHTNESS RANGE

Our eyes are capable of bridging tremendous brightness ranges, allowing us to see details in shadows and highlights beyond those that can be recorded on photographic materials. Films and papers have far greater limitations than the human eye.

The subject lighting range is the range between the different colors in the subject. The range is greatest when the subject has clear whites and black blacks. The subject brightness range is therefore predetermined by the subject and cannot be changed, at least not if the area is evenly lit with one light. It can be changed only by using separate light sources for different areas—for example, for the light and the dark areas, for subject and background.

The subject brightness combined with the lighting ratio is what is recorded on the film, and that is known as the *scene brightness range:*

scene brightness range = subject brightness × lighting ratio.

For example, if the subject brightness is 10:1 and the lighting ratio is 3:1, then the scene brightness range is 10 × 3 = 30:1.

The brightness range that can be recorded on color negative or black-and-white film is about 64:1, which is equivalent to six *f* stops. If details are desired and necessary in the shadows and highlights, the difference in a meter reading between the darkest and the brightest area should not exceed the six *f* stops. Although this range falls within the capability of the film, it must be remembered that the paper has greater limitations. Its range is only about 40:1, or five *f* stops. This is also the approximate range for transparency film.

For the entire range to be recorded satisfactorily on the film, exposures must be accurate to ensure that they fall within the film's latitude. If the exposure is too long, the whites and light grays start to fall together, and the highlight areas lack detail. If exposure is too low, the blacks and dark grays are no longer separated, and the shadows lack detail. In black and white, contrast can be controlled with lighting, film developing, different grades of enlarging paper, and paper development. In most color photography, the control is limited to lighting.

TYPICAL SUBJECTS AND MEASURING METHODS

General Scenes with Blue Skies.   A reflected meter reading of blue sky produces good results on slide film. Make certain that the meter reading is not influenced by white clouds. With negative film, measure the shaded area if detail is desired.

Sunsets and Sunrises.   The sky is usually the most important part of the image. Foregrounds are silhouetted. For slide film, take a reading of the sky, making certain that the sun does not shine directly into the meter cell. For negative film, measure areas where you want shadow detail, the ground, or the water surface perhaps.

Backlit-Scenery.   For transparency film, measure the light falling on the lighted area. For negative film, measure the light in the shaded area.

Pictures through Windows, Archways, and Other Frames.   The foreground, the arch, or the window frame is to be recorded as a silhouette, so exposure is based on the background area. Hold the reflected meter through the arch or window so that it measures only the background. The same method applies whenever a foreground is to be silhouetted.

Back-lit Portraits.   Sunlight is used only as an accent light or a hair light. Exposure therefore should be based on the light falling on the face. Take an incident reading with the meter held in front of the face or a reflected close-up reading of a gray card held in front of the face adjusting for skin tone. The same method applies to negative and transparency film.

Portraits with Window Light.   Lighting ratio is high with daylight falling on one side of the subject only. Reflectors may have to be considered to lighten the shaded side and bring the contrast range within the capability of the film. For slide film, measure the daylight falling on the lighted side of the face. For negative film, base the lens settings on the shaded side of the face or, if the contrast is too high, between the highlight and shadow readings.

Stage Shows.   Spotlight performers on stage are frequently in front of dark, dimly lit backgrounds. Exposure must be based on the lighted performers. Try to take a close-up meter reading. A spotmeter has a definite advantage because you can take a reading of the performers from a distance. With built-in meters, the reading can be made through a telelens, which will cover the lighted area only. Consult exposure charts, which are very satisfactory.

Fireworks.   Set the shutter on time or bulb, and keep the shutter open from the beginning to the end of the rocket display. Suggested apertures for this type of photography are ƒ16 for 400 ASA film; ƒ11 for 160 ASA; ƒ5.6 for 40 ASA; and ƒ8 for 25 ASA.

DOUBLE AND MULTIPLE EXPOSURES

Combining two, three, or more images on the same negative or transparency creates unusual images that are likely to attract attention because they create a sense of unreality. It requires some artistic sense to decide which images go together, how the lines, shapes, colors of the two images will combine together, and how two or more images can be arranged so that the combination is more effective and beautiful than each individual image. The two or more images need not be exposed on top of each other; they can be composed so that they fall next to each other, or the second image can be arranged so that it falls into an unexposed area of the first.

The large medium format ground-glass screen makes it easy to mark the screen for accurate positioning of the subjects in a double exposure. Rather than marking the screen, make the markings on tracing paper placed over the screen.

Superimposed Subjects

The double exposure can be a combination of two sharp, general images; the common case is in wedding photography, with the bride's and groom's hands combined with an image of the wedding ceremony. Few of these images, in my mind, are photographically beautiful even though they are salable and well liked by many brides.

Frequently the best effects are obtained if only one image has a well-defined subject while the other is a pattern of colors and/or shapes and acts as a background for the first. Beautiful images have been created with brick walls, clouds, reflections, flowers, burlap, or paintings as backgrounds. There is no rule that both images must be in sharp focus. Extremely interesting and unusual possibilities are obtained in color when at least one of the images is out of focus; it adds touches of color rather than a pattern to the image.

Two images exposed on the same area of the film result in overexposure if normal lens settings are used. Exposure must be decreased, to an aperture one and a half stops smaller than indicated on the meter for each image. Take a meter reading for each subject in the normal fashion. Set the lens one and a half EV numbers or apertures higher for both images. For example, if the meter reads EV 14 or ƒ8, set the lens at EV 15 1/2 or between $f11$ and $f16$. With this equal adjustment in the lens setting, each of the two images should be visible to the same degree, which may or may not be the most desirable effect. This rule applies for transparency and negative film. One of the two images can be made more or less visible compared to the other by changing exposure, underexposing one more than the other. The combinations that I have found to work well are:

Image I	Image II	Effect
½ stop under	2½ stops under	Image II hardly visible
1 stop under	2 stops under	Image II less pronounced
1½ stops under	1½ stops under	Both equal
2 stops under	1 stop under	Image I less pronounced
2½ stops under	½ stop under	Image I hardly visible

These figures are easy to remember as they always add up to 3 (1 1/2 + 1 1/2; 1 + 2; 1/2 + 2 1/2).

Three images superimpsed over each other are seldom effective because they are usually confusing, but if you want to try it, underexpose each by two f stops.

The image resulting from double or multiple exposures made in the camera can be seen only when recorded on film—not be looking through the viewfinder. Test exposures are therefore recommended if possible. Instant film material is most helpful, as the result can be seen while the camera is still set up, but it is not a reliable guide for exposure in this case. Polaroid color film has a lower exposure latitude than the regular color negative or transparency emulsions. A one and a half or two lower EV number or aperture results in a completely underexposed Polacolor image. Therefore, rather than underexposing one and a half stops, underexpose each image not more than one stop on Polacolor film. To say it in a different way, if a one stop or one EV number underexposure looks good on Polacolor, underexpose one and a half stops on the other emulsions.

Ghost Images

A figure appears as a ghost when the background is visible through the figure. You accomplish this by photographing the same area twice: once with the figure, once without, adjusting exposure as explained. It can be successful only if the camera remains absolutely stationary between the two exposures.

Superimposed Titles

Superimposing the title over a background scene is a common method of producing titles in films. The same method can be used for slide titles. It is nothing more than a camera-produced double exposure of title and background. In this case, however, the background subject is exposed normally—as it would be without the title. The white titling letters must be photographed against a totally black background, so dark that it does not record on the film. Ordinary black construction paper or matte boards are not really black, just a very dark gray. Satisfactory materials are black velvet or television board available in some art supply stores.

Corrrect exposure for the white letters is best determined by an incident meter, held above the letters with the cell pointing toward the camera, or a reflected light meter reading off a gray card placed over the letters. White letters are best as they stand out against any dark background color and they can also be burned in without looking washed out.

Multiple Images

Multiple images are double or multiple exposures where the images are not superimposed—for example, several firework displays recorded in different areas of the film, the sequence of a solar eclipse recorded with six or more images of the sun side by side, or the faces of a family recorded in different masked-out areas. In these cases, all or most of the second image or images fall onto a dark, unexposed area of the film, and exposure therefore need not be adjusted. Use the lens setting as for a normal image.

The success of such multiple images depends mainly on the proper and effective placement on the images within the film area. Some multiple image exposures require masking—for example, head and shoulder portraits of the family or different flowers or foods, combined in one image. Each image is photographed through a mask of the desired shape placed a few inches in front of the lens. The mask keeps the rest of the film area unexposed. The masks can be of any shape—round, oval, triangular, heart shaped, etc.

A bellows lens shade is an excellent accessory to hold the mask. Exposure for the masked-down subject is the same as it would be without the mask. With a built-in meter, take the reading before you add the mask.

Split-Screen Effects

Split-screen effects are multiple images not separated by dark areas but recorded next to each other, preferably without a dark or white dividing line. The split can be in any direction—horizontal, vertical, diagonal, etc.

While the first image is made, the rest of the image area is masked off. The mask is made from black paper or cardboard and placed a few inches in front of the lens. The distance depends on the focal length of the lens and the shooting aperture. The longer is the lens and the larger is the aperture, the farther away the mask must be. Since it is usually best to place masks relatively close to the lens, standard and wide angle lenses are practical. Place the mask in a holder—a bellows lens shade, for instance—close the diaphragm down to the shooting aperture with the manual stop-down control, and mark the split line on the ground glass. Setting the diaphragm to the shooting aperture is necessary because the sharpness of the dividing line changes and its position shifts. Since this effect requires markings on the ground glass, an SLR camera is necessary. Expose normally.

For the second exposure, place the mask so it covers the exposed area of the film. That is where the masking on the ground glass becomes important. If the dividing line is to be as unnoticeable as possible, the mask is placed so that it just reaches the dividing line. For a black dividing line, leave some space; for a white line, have some overlap.

Instead of splitting completely different images, the background image can be continuous with only the foreground changed. As an example, the same person can appear twice in the same image, on the right and left side of a tree. Since the background is to appear as a continuous image, any visible dividing line must be avoided; otherwise it may reveal the technique used. Plain, light backgrounds are not recomended for this purpose since the slightest variation in density becomes visible. Select a darker background with irregular patterns, such as tree trunks, fences, pieces of furniture, curtains, window panes, corners of buildings, horizons, or anything else that follows the dividing line.

Double Exposure or Sandwich

Double exposures and sandwiches are combinations of two or more images. Double exposures are made in the camera and sandwiches by copying two negatives or transparencies laid on top of one another. Although such images might look alike on the final print or when projected on the screen, there is a major difference, which largely determines which technique must be used.

On a double exposure produced in the camera, the second image is visible mainly in the darker areas of the first. It is less visible or not visible

If the camera offers film magazine interchangeability, the two images to be superimposed need not be made right after each other. The magazine with the first exposure can be removed before the film is advanced, and a second magazine can be attached. The first magazine with the first exposure can be reattached anytime later for the second exposure. This advantage can be very valuable, especially to wedding photographers. Many different effects can be created with double exposures. A color pattern is superimposed over a black statue against a blue sky (1). A side-lit close-up of a piece of burlap was recorded in the camera over a portrait (2). A ghost effect was created by photographing the same interior twice: once with and once without the person (3).

1

2

3

at all in light and completely white areas. When two images are sandwiched together, it is just the opposite. The second image is visible mostly in the light and clear areas of the first and hardly, or not at all, in the dark sections. For sandwiches, images with white or light areas work best. Double exposures require images with dark areas. Remember that in a slide, the dark areas of the subject are also dark, and the light areas are also light. On a negative, it is reversed: dark areas are light, light areas are dark. Fascinating and interesting results can be obtained by combining two or more images, and it is therefore worthwhile to examine combinations of slides in front of a light box.

Camera Operation

Most medium format cameras have the necessary controls for producing double exposures. There are differences in the way the controls are operated. The camera may have a lever or knob with two positions on the camera body or film magazine. In one position the film is advanced when the shutter is cocked; in the other it is not. The procedure is simple but requires that you ascertain constantly whether the control is in the right position. If it is accidentally moved or if you forget to move it back to normal after making a double exposure, all the images become superimposed without the photographer's being aware. On other cameras, double exposures can be made only by lifting the film magazine away from the camera body while the shutter is cocked. It is an additional operation but can be done quickly and easily. It eliminates accidental double exposures. In a third solution, a special button or control must be depressed while the shutter is cocked. The button eliminates the need for removing the film magazines and prevents accidental mistakes because the film advance is inoperative only when this button is depressed. Perfect registration of the images is necessary only in rare cases when the same subject is superimposed. This cannot be guaranteed when magazines need to be removed but can be the case if magazines fit on the camera body without play. Removing and attaching must be done carefully to avoid accidental movement of the camera. Interchangeable film magazines, on the other hand, offer an important advantage. The second exposure need not be made immediately after the first. The film magazine with the first exposure can be placed aside until needed for the second exposure while another film magazine is used in the meantime. This offers interesting and extremely valuable possibilities in every field of photography, especially weddings, which otherwise could be made only if two cameras were available.

A signal on the camera or magazine indicating whether the film is advanced is helpful. It is easy to forget things like this, and the photographer should not have to worry about it. This signal must give the right indication whether the magazine is on or off the camera.

CHAPTER 11

Electronic flash

Electronic flash has become the most popular artificial light source in photography. Portable flash units are small yet produce a large amount of light. The duration of the flash is very short and therefore freezes fast action and helps to eliminate unsharp images due to camera movement. The color temperature of electronic flash matches that of normal daylight, so the two can be combined for color photography.

FLASH SYNCHRONIZATION

The electronic flash must fire when the shutter is fully open; otherwise a completely or partially blank, or underexposed image results. On a modern focal plane shutter camera, the flash must fire after the first curtain has fully uncovered the film area and before the second curtain starts to move. This happens only up to a certain shutter speed, which is longer on medium format cameras than on 35s because the focal plane curtains have to travel over a larger area.

The flash unit must fire when a lens shutter is fully open. That is easier to accomplish. That is why lens shutters can be used with flash at all speeds up to 1/500 sec.

If your camera permits you to open the back or remove the film magazine so you can look straight through the lens and shutter, you have an easy way to check whether the electronic flash is accurately synchronized with the shutter. With lens shutters, set the diaphragm to its widest aperture and the camera at the shutter speed to be checked. Attach the synchronization cord to the PC flash socket. Point the camera with the flash unit connected to the lens or camera toward a light wall. Place your eye approximately 1 ft behind the rear of the camera and trip the shutter while looking through the back of the camera. If you see a perfect full circle, the flash is synchronized. If the flash is not visible at all or not through the fully open lens, the flash synchronization is off. For a complete check, test at all shutter speeds, including the top speed of 1/500 sec. This test is accurate and reliable, especially at the shortest shutter speed.

Check a focal plane shutter in the same way. The flash is synchronized with the focal plane shutter if you can see the flash over the entire film area. If you cannot see the flash at all or not through the full frame, flash synchronization is off. For a complete check, test at all the synchronized shutter speeds. This test is accurate.

PORTABLE FLASH UNITS

Camera Flash Connection

A portable flash unit can be connected to the camera with a hot shoe or cable. A hot shoe makes the connection to the flash when the latter is slid into the shoe. Cameras with a hot shoe also have a synchronization cable connection, which provides versatility in placing the flash unit.

The flash can be mounted on the camera or a bracket held separately or mounted on a separate stand away from the camera, for which extension cables of up to about 10 m (30 ft) are available. It is possible to fire two or three flash units simultaneously by attaching a multiple connector (with two or three synchronization cable connectors) to the camera or lens and a synchronization cable from each connector to each flash unit.

Slave Units

Off-the-camera flash units can also be fired by *slave units*, small, light-sensing devices that trigger a flash unit in response to light from another flash. Slave units eliminate the need for cable connections between camera and flash. One small flash, mounted on the camera, can fire one or any other number of flash units off the camera as long as each is equipped with its own slave. The light-sensing eye of the slave must point toward the triggering flash and must also receive sufficient light to energize the slave.

The light from the flash must be considerably above the level of the ambient light. A slave that may work well in a relatively dark location may not work in a well-lit stadium.

The flash on the camera need not be used for lighting the subject at all but just for firing the slave unit or units. Alternatively, the arrangement could be with the camera flash as the main light and also firing a hair or accent light, or the camera unit can be the fill light and also fire the main light.

Synchronization Cable Polarity

Synchronization cables can usually be attached to portable flash units in one way only so there is no problem about polarity. Flash cables used on studio units, however, may have plugs that can be connected either way. For safety's sake and to avoid possible damage to the synchronization contacts in the camera, the cable should be connected so the grounded contact on the flash unit connects to the shutter contact that is grounded to the camera body. This can be checked as follows. Attach the cable to the power pack and camera. Touch any exposed metal part on the lamp head or light stand with an exposed metal part of the camera. If the light does not flash, polarity is correct. If the light flashes, reverse the cable.

FLASH FIRING FAILURES

Probably the most annoying occurrence in photography is when flash pictures are made and the flash does not fire. Everyone in front of the camera is aware that the photographer goofed.

Try to avoid flash failures. If they do happen, make sure you know where and what to check. There may be quite a few reasons for malfunctioning. Most flash units have an on-off switch, which should be checked. While you look at the flash unit, check whether the ready light is on. If it is not, there may be no batteries in the unit or the batteries may be dead or very weak. The battery contact may be poor, perhaps corroded, or an AC unit may not be plugged in. Look at the lens or camera to make certain the flash synchronization lever is at X, or the shutter speed is set within its synchronization capability. On some cameras, the flash will fire only then. Synchronization cables can become disconnected from the contact on the camera or lens or from the connection on the flash.

PC coaxial plugs are not good electrical connections. If one feels too loose, gently squeeze it with pliers into an oval shape, thereby making a firm connection at least on two sides. Take care, though; more often the center contact fails to connect. If the synchronization terminal on the lens appears to be loose, replace the terminal. If the flash is used a lot, the insulation in the terminal may wear out, permitting drain on a flash unit's capacitor. Try another cable if available.

If nothing helps, the fault may be in the shutter, which then needs a specialist to repair it.

READY LIGHT

The ready light indicates when the capacitor is charged and thus when the camera can be released again. If a picture is made before the ready light is on, the flash will not fire or will fire with less than the full amount of light, a frequent reason for underexposure.

On professional units, especially the studio types, it can be assumed that the ready light does not come on until the capacitor is totally charged. On many amateur units, this is not so since manufacturers try to shorten the recycle time for sales reasons, and the ready light comes on when the capacitor is only about 70 percent charged, which may be good enough for amateur snapshots. If flashed at that moment, however, pictures may be as much as one stop underexposed when working manually. To ensure perfect results with such units, it is recommended to wait 50 percent longer than the recycling time.

If the ready light takes 30 sec or more to light up, the batteries are probably exhausted.

FLASH UNIT SIZE

The size of a flash unit is determined mainly by the power source, which in turn determines the brightness of the flash and the number of flashes per charge. A small camera-mounted flash is fine if you work mainly within about 5 m (17 ft) of your subject, but it will not give sufficient light to photograph a banquet hall or factory interior, especially when the required depth of field means small apertures.

BATTERIES

Flash units can be powered by regular penlight batteries. The manganese-alkaline types provide more flashes and faster recycling.

Rechargeable nickel-cadmium batteries are the choice of the working photographer who uses flash frequently. They can be recharged a great number of times and, if used frequently, are more economical than regular penlight batteries. Some rechargeable nickel-cadmium flash units require charging times of 6 to 12 hrs, while others recharge fully in an hour or less. This rapid recharging is valuable when flash units may have to be used unexpectedly.

AC-powered units, limited to indoor use, usually consist of separate lamp heads and power pack. The lamp heads are usually mounted on light stands together with reflectors or umbrellas.

LIGHT OUTPUT AND GUIDE NUMBERS

The amount of light produced by a flash is rated in effective candle power seconds (ECPS) or beam candle power seconds (BCPS). Both measure the *light output*, the brightness and duration of an electronic flash unit. BCPS measures the center of the beam of light. ECPS measures the light output over the complete angle of illumination.

Instead of BCPS, the brightness of most portable units is indicated in more photographic terms, that is, as a guide number, which is the product of the lens aperture and distance needed for correct exposure.

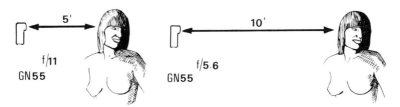

To decide the correct aperture for a flash photograph, divide the guide number into the distance between the flash and subject. For example, if the guide number (GN) is 55 and the distance 5 ft, the correct aperture is $f11$ (55 − 5 = 11). With same GN but at twice the distance, the correct aperture would be $f5.6$ (55 − 10 = 5.5). On manual, the flash duration is always the same.

The guide number for any flash unit varies with the film. Most companies quote the guide number for 100 ASA (21 DIN) film.

If the guide number for a certain film sensitivity is not available, you can determine it easily from the guide number of a lower or higher exposure index rating as follows. For an ASA rating twice as high (or the DIN rating three points higher), multiply the guide number by 1.4; for example, if the guide number for 200 ASA film is 110, then the guide number for 400 ASA is 110 × 1.4 = 154. Divide by 1.4 for an ASA rating of half (or a DIN value three points lower); for example, if the guide number for 21 DIN is 42, the guide number for 18 DIN is 42 ÷ 1.4 = 30.

COVERING POWER

Guide numbers do not tell the entire story about the performance of a flash unit. When a beam of light is controlled by reflectors or lenses, as on all flash units, the brightness at a certain distance depends on the size of the area over which the light is spread. Because wide angle lenses are frequently used indoors, covering power is an important consideration. Select a unit that covers the angle of your lens. If not available, as is the case for extreme wide angles, consider incident or bounced flash, multiple flash, or bare bulbs.

Although two flash units may have the same BCPS (beam candle power second) power, they may have different guide numbers. This is because the flash with the lower number spreads the light over a larger area. The area coverage of a flash unit must therefore be considered in any exposure calculation.

DETERMINING APERTURE

On a manual unit or an automatic unit set to manual, the correct aperture depends on the flash-to-subject distance, which is where the guide number comes in. To obtain the correct aperture, divide the guide number into the flash-to-subject distance. (Guide numbers are given either in feet or in meters, and you choose the same units.) For example, if the guide number is 110 and the subject is 10 ft away, the correct aperture is 110 ÷ 10 = ƒ11.

Instead of determining aperture from guide numbers, you can calculate the flash distance for any aperture. For example, to use ƒ11 with a guide number of 88, the correct flash distance is 88 ÷ 11 = 8 ft. With today's flash units, these calculations are no longer necessary because all come with charts.

Guide numbers for amateur flash units are established on the assumption that flash pictures are taken in average-sized rooms with light-colored walls and ceilings that reflect a certain amount of light. If flash pictures are taken in large halls or in dark rooms, a somewhat larger aperture may be necessary.

POWER RATIO

Many modern portable flash units include a capability that has been found in studio units for years: variable power output, the thyristor concept applied to manual operation. By changing a switch to 1/2, 1/4, 1/8, or perhaps up to 1/64, the amount of light is reduced to 50 percent, to 25 percent, or frequently down to 1.6 percent. This reduction in light output is accomplished by shortening the flash duration. When at full power the flash may be on for 1/1000 sec, it flashes for only 1/64,000 sec at the 1/64 setting. One obvious advantage is that you know the flash duration, so if you want to freeze fast motions, use the 1/16, 1/32, or 1/64 setting. Even if the instruction book only specifies the duration at full power, you can determine the others easily; 1/2 is 1/2, and 1/4 is 1/4.

Serious photographers are not limited to one aperture for each distance and film sensitivity. They can match the flash to a certain aperture that produces the desired depth of field, or vice-versa. This is extremely helpful when combining flash and daylight.

With two power ratio units, lighting ratios can be set with the power ratio switch. The shortened recycling time is another highly appreciated benefit of power ratio. When the unit is set at less than full power, only a fraction of the stored energy is used up. Thus, it takes a shorter time to refill the capacitor. Instead of having to wait 6 to 8 sec, the ready light goes on again in a second or less. At the 1/32 or 1/64 sec setting, it may even remain lit because it recycles so fast. It fires every time a motor-driven camera takes a picture.

To refill a partially emptied capacitor also requires less power from the batteries. Instead of getting perhaps sixty flashes, the same battery or batteries give several hundred—perhaps even more than a thousand at 1/64.

FILTERS

All electronic flash units produce a daylight-type lighting with a deca-mired value around 18 DM (5600 K). There are some variations among makes. Many units produce pleasing colors on daylight film without the need for filters. Others produce colors that might be considered somewhat on the cool, bluish side. Warmer results can be obtained with an R1.5, an 81A, or an 81B color balance filter.

SHUTTER SPEED

Electronic flash duration is shorter than 1/500 sec, so the shutter speed has no effect on flash exposures. The correct exposure depends only on the lens aperture. That explains why one hears so often that shutter speeds are unimportant in flash photography. As far as flash exposure is concerned, yes; as far as the image recorded on the film, however, no. The shutter speed does not affect the image in any way if you use electronic flash in a completely dark place—a place where it is the only light source. But rarely are pictures taken in a completely dark place. Wherever you use it—in the house, office, school, store, restaurant, gymnasium, or out-

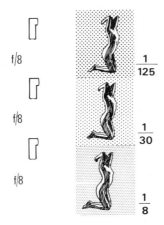

With an electronic flash, the exposure is determined only by the aperture. The shutter speed has no effect as long as it is within the synchronization range of the camera. If the electronic flash is the only light source in the room, the image on the film is also the same.

A

When flash is used in any location with ambient light (usually the case), shutter selection is very important. The shutter speed will determine how much of the ambient light is recorded on the film. For example, at an aperture of ƒ8 (A), a shutter speed of 1/125 sec will record very little background detail, whereas one of 1/8 sec will give a much lighter background.

doors—there is other light: daylight, tungsten, or fluorescent. As soon as there is another light source, shutter speeds become important because the shutter speed now determines the exposure for the ambient light. It determines the brightness of the surrounding areas—the living room, the church interior, the outdoors. If you have been wondering why room interiors were so dark in your flash pictures, why people were surrounded by darkness, you now know the answer: the shutter speed was too short, thus underexposing the interior. At a longer shutter speed, the natural light in the room becomes part of the picture; a living room looks like a living room. At 1/30 sec or perhaps even 1/8 sec, the flash exposure remains the same, but the ambient light is also recorded on the film. The flash then becomes almost the secondary rather than the main light. The effect is especially beautiful and natural with incandescent lights, which produce a much warmer color than the flash. Using longer exposures is most effective when the flash is off the camera and used as a sidelight.

B

On the camera, the flash also throws light and shadows on the background, somewhat destroying the natural feeling.

With a hand-held camera, you need to keep the camera steady, so you may have to use a tripod to go down to 1/15 sec or 1/8 sec and make the room lighting part of the photograph.

GHOST IMAGES

Shutter speeds are an important consideration when photographing fast-moving subjects, such as indoor sports. To freeze action, you do just the opposite: record only the exposure from the flash, not the ambient light. The latter produces what is known as a *ghost image*: an image that overlaps the sharp flash image, but only partially, because the subject (the ice skater, the dancer) has moved. You actually have a double exposure of the sharp flash shot and the unsharp available light picture. The total effect is unsharpness, with unwanted shadows, streaks, and ghost effects. In well-lit rooms such as sports arenas or gymnasiums, a secondary ghost image may be recorded even at the relatively short shutter speed of 1/60 sec and on relatively slow 64 ASA films. For this type of photography, full flash

A

When photographing with flash in a well-lit location, always the case with sports, a high shutter speed is needed to eliminate the image created by the existing light. This secondary ghost image is the reason for the unsharpness and the shadows along the skater's body, photographed at 1/60 sec (A). At 1/500 sec, the existing light will not register on the film, resulting in a much sharper image without the ghost effect (B).

synchronization up to 1/500 sec is a prime requirement. It is the only way to eliminate ghost images.

MODELING LIGHTS

AC-powered studio units are usually equipped with modeling lights that allow you to see the lighting effect on the subject. When lamp heads of different ratings are used, the brightness of the modeling lights must be changed proportionately to see the lighting ratio and effect. Because the modeling lights stay on when the flash exposure is made, they should not be too bright; otherwise they register on the film as a secondary (ghost) image or as a slight change in exposure and color. The effect can be avoided by using shorter speeds (1/125–1/500 sec) or by turning off the lights.

AUTOMATIC FLASH

Because the flash-to-subject distance determines the aperture setting on the lens, every change in flash distance requires a change in the lens

B

setting. This adjustment is eliminated by using an automatic flash unit, which is equipped with a sensor pointing in the same direction as the flash head. The sensor picks up the light reflected from the subject, just as a reflected light meter does. As soon as the sensor receives the correct amount of light for the aperture setting, it turns off the flash.

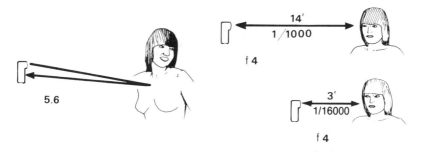

On automatic flash units, a sensor in the flash measures the light as it is reflected from the subject and switches off the unit when it has received the correct amount of light for the set aperture. The duration of the flash is therefore determined not only by the aperture but by the flash-to-subject distance. For example, at an aperture of ƒ4, the flash may be on for 1/1000 sec if the subject is 14 ft away but only for 1/16,000 sec if the subject is 3 ft away.

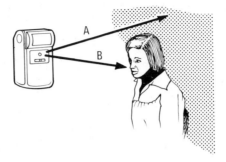

The sensor of an automatic flash unit calculates the duration of the flash from the amount of light reflected back to it from the central area. Thus, if the main subject is not positioned in the center, the exposure will be based on the background areas (A). With the main subject in the center, the exposure will be correct (B).

Automatic units are convenient because they eliminate calculations and possible mistakes but mainly eliminate changing the aperture. Everything within a certain distance range indicated on the flash unit can be photographed with the same diaphragm opening. The correct aperture depends on the film sensitivity and is again found on the chart. But contrary to general belief, changing to a faster film does not increase the range of the flash; it only permits photographing at a smaller aperture. To increase the range, the unit should be used on manual. With the less

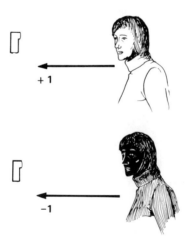

Another problem when using an automatic flash is the amount of light reflected by the subject. For example, a lighter-than-average subject reflects more than the average amount of light and will therefore be slightly underexposed; opening the diaphragm one stop may compensate. Conversely, a dark subject will reflect less light to the sensor and keep the flash on too long; closing the diaphragm one stop will give the correct exposure.

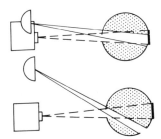

Using on-camera flash when photographing people often produces pink eye, which is caused by reflection of the flash light off the back of the blood-filled retina *(top)*. You can avoid this problem by placing the flash farther from the camera so that the retina is shaded *(bottom)*.

expensive automatic units, you must use one specific aperture for each film sensitivity. There is no choice of depth of field. Serious photographers should consider a unit that offers a choice of three or more apertures. Automatic units also offer a manual mode where the sensor is inoperative.

Automatic units provide surprisingly accurate exposures within the distance range indicated on the flash unit. But as with exposure meters, perfect results are not obtained automatically at all times. You must pay attention to a few points.

The sensor must aim at the main subject, not at something closer or farther away (a background wall, for instance). The main subject also must be sufficiently large in size to be read by the sensor. Furthermore, keep in mind that the sensor reads reflected light, and the reading is affected by the reflectance of the subject. Exposure is most accurate when the subject reflects about 18 percent of the light. A bright subject reflecting more light shuts the flash off too soon, resulting in underexposure; compensate by opening the aperture one-half to one stop. A dark subject keeps the flash on too long, causing overexposure; compensate by closing the aperture one-half to one stop.

Automatic units have also a tendency to overexpose subjects nearer than about 1 m (3 ft) because the flash duration is extremely short and the slightest delay from the sensor may keep it on longer than necessary. An aperture one stop smaller than recommended therefore may be advised for close-ups. A film test at various distances may be advisable.

ENERGY-SAVING CIRCUITS

Most recent flash units have energy-saving circuits, which means that the moment proper exposure is obtained, a switch in the thyristor circuit closes so that the remaining power can no longer escape from the capacitor.

The principle is the same as with power ratio, except it is in the automatic mode; power ratio is manual. In automatic, the closer the flash is to the subject, the shorter is the flash duration and the quicker the switch in the thyristor circuit closes to prevent the rest of the power from escaping. Just as in power ratio, the shortened flash duration reduces the recycling time and increases the number of exposures from a battery, but it is the flash-to-subject distance that determines all these facts. If the recycling time is short enough, it can be used with motor-driven cameras.

FLASH EXPOSURE

Correct exposure for flash pictures can be obtained by (1) using the flash in the automatic mode, (2) setting the lens apertures based on the chart on portable flash units, or (3) setting them according to the readings on a flash meter.

Flash Meters

These are usually incident meters. They are held in front of the subject, measuring the light that falls on the subject. The exposure readings are very reliable and unaffected by the color and brightness of the subject. Practically all professionals use these meters when working with electronic flash in the studio—not only for correct exposure but also for checking lighting ratios, measuring, and comparing the amount of light falling on the subject and the background.

TTL Metering for Electronic Flash

TTL metering for electronic flash is a standard feature in the top line of 35 mm cameras. It exists also in the medium format field and will undoubtedly be found in additional future models. TTL is an automatic system for electronic flash exposure. The sensor, which in a conventional auto flash system is on the flash gun, is in the camera body aimed at the film surface. The light reflected off the film surface is measured, and the flash duration is cut off when enough light has struck the film for proper exposure. Thus, camera and electronic flash gun must be mated to each other with matching electrical contacts (dedicated is the common term). Dedicated flash units for particular cameras can come from the camera manufacturers or from independent flash manufacturers.

A TTL sensing system for electronic flash has the same advantages as a TTL system for other light sources. Since the light is measured at the film plane, it automatically takes into account light lost through lens, extension tubes, bellows, or filters. The meter also measures only the area covered by the lens, especially valuable when using longer lenses. It prevents many errors that can occur if a conventional sensor picks up a foreground object or looks past the subject into the background. It also provides the advantage of conventional automatic flash units. Within range limits, the flash system allows free aperture selection. Small apertures can be used to increase depth of field in close-up photography; large apertures can be used for long-range flash or can be set for fast recycling.

TTL metering simplifies flash operation. Conventional manual flash demands that you set the correct aperture on the lens; TTL flash will cover you within its range limits, and a viewfinder light may warn if flash exposure was incorrect.

A dedicated flash unit may mount directly on the camera using a hot shoe for connection, or it may be separate, using a dedicated connecting cord.

Dedicated flash has been automated to such an extent on 35 mm cameras that it may even select the shutter speed, likely the highest X synchronization speed, automatically. This is unquestionably a disadvantage for serious work when slower shutter speeds for additional background detail are better. If this is of value to you, try to find a unit that lets you override this automation. Just like any other automation—exposure or focus—in the hands of the professional and serious amateur, the TTL automatic flash should never be a replacement but a complement. Use automation when it offers benefits or simplifies. You do it yourself the conventional way to produce specific results.

Ring Lights

Lighting without any shadows on the subject is obtained when light of equal intensity reaches the subject from all directions. All shadows then cancel each other out. Such lighting can be produced by a large umbrella or reflector placed close enough to surround the subject. A tent is a popular method to accomplish this result in commerical photography. The object or objects are placed inside this tent made from white translucent material with the light sources placed outside. The ring light is another solution to surround a small subject with light. A ring light is a round flash tube that can be mounted over the camera lens. The subject is lit evenly from all sides but only when the flash-to-subject distance is within a certain range—not too far and also not too close.

When the ring light is far away, it becomes almost as directional as an ordinary flash unit. There is no reason for not using the ring light at longer distances, but do not expect shadowless illumination. Actually a ring light is not completely shadowless at close distances; a slightly dark halo can be seen around the subject.

The ring light is made for all close-up work when flat, shadowless lighting of three-dimensional subjects is desired. It is extremely popular in medical photography. The greatest value of the ring light comes when photographing the inside of radios, television sets, and other machinery where it is practically impossible to light every corner and eliminate disturbing shadows in any other way.

Makroflash Units

Makroflash units offer another solution for flash in close-up photography. They consist of a bracket that is mounted on the front of the lens holding two compact flash units close to the lens. When they are used on both sides of the lens, they can produce an almost shadowless light and thus can be used instead of a ring flash. A makroflash unit can also provide many other lighting effects by moving the flash units to different positions, equipping one with neutral density filters or wide screen adapters, or using one flash head only. Combined with a camera with TTL flash metering, you can have automatic flash in close-up photography compensating for extension and filter factors automatically.

INDIRECT AND BOUNCED FLASH

Indirect flash, with the light reflected off umbrellas, reflectors, walls, or ceilings rather than directly on the subject, produces a soft overall light. The light illuminates the subject from various angles and therefore reduces or eliminates harsh, sharp shadows.

White or silvered umbrellas offer the simplest, most portable solution for indirect flash illumination. Flash unit and umbrella are mounted together, with the flash tube pointing at the center of the umbrella. The umbrella is folded when not in use. The softness of the lighting produced by umbrellas and any other reflectors is directly related to their size and distance. The larger is the umbrella or reflector, the larger is the spread of light. Close to the subject, the light from the umbrella or reflector reaches the subject from different angles, producing an almost shadowless light. The same umbrella or reflector far from the subject becomes more a point source of light, producing stronger shadows, almost like direct flash.

For the softest light, use the largest-sized umbrella, positioned close to the subject. A soft lighting similar to umbrella lighting can be obtained with portrait studio lights. They have a large reflector (50–60 cm, 20–25 in.), shaped almost like an umbrella, behind the flash tube; in front of the tube is another small reflector. All the light reaching the subject is reflected off the large reflecting surface.

Reflectors serve the same purpose as umbrellas except that they are flat instead of in a curved umbrella shape. Some reflectors can be folded for easy transport. Reflectors may be nothing more than sheets of cardboard or the foldable types made commercially. Flat reflectors can also be used outdoors for reflecting sunlight into the shaded areas of a subject.

The softness and direction of the lighting are also determined by the type of reflecting surface. White reflectors, white fabrics, or cardboard produce the softest illumination but reflect the least amount of light and need to be close to the subject. Silver and gold reflectors are readily available or can be made from crumpled aluminum foil. They reflect a large amount of light, but it is a rather directional and harsh light. Gold produces a very warm light, which can be desirable when photographing people in the shade of green trees or to add warm reflections to a product.

The soft box, which has become a popular light source in portrait photography, is nothing more than a flash head with a large diffusion screen in front of it. The diffusion screen, usually made from a whiter, translucent fabric, is approximately 60 cm (2 ft) square, so the light no longer comes from a point light source. The lighting effect is practically the same as from an umbrella, but the soft box is more compact and requires less working space.

Walls and ceilings in a room can be used to bounce flash. Ceilings are satisfactory for long and group shots but not for portraits. Illuminating people from above is not very flattering; it produces shadows under the eyes and little light in the eyes, especially when the light comes from a steep angle.

Bounced lighting can be improved by adding some direct light. Point the flash head toward the ceiling as for bounced light, but attach a small piece of paper (about 10 x 10 cm, 4 in. square) to the top of the flash unit. A small amount of light is then reflected off the paper and may be just enough to fill the shadows in the eyes. Some new flash units incorporate this principle.

Bounced wall and ceiling light can be combined by pointing the flash into a corner of a room. The softest light comes from a wall behind the camera. It is like a shadowless front light.

With bounced flash, the flash-to-subject distance is the total distance the flash travels, from camera to ceiling or wall, plus the distance from ceiling or wall to subject. Furthermore, some light is absorbed by the wall or ceiling. For white ceilings or walls, set the aperture two stops larger than indicated on the chart. Test exposures are recommended.

Some flash units come with diffusion filters, which can be placed in front of the flash tube. A diffusion filter can spread the light over a larger area, but it can produce a softer illumination only if the filter is much larger in diameter than the flash head. If the ceiling is low, a diffusion filter over the flash head throws somewhat more light on the ceiling, thereby softening the effect of direct flash. With bounced light, the diffusion filter scatters light over a wider area of the wall or ceiling, creating a softer and more even lighting.

AUTOMATIC FLASH UNITS IN INDIRECT LIGHT

You can use automatic flash units on automatic with bounced lighting as long as the sensor points at the subject. On many portable flash units, the flash head alone can be swiveled either up and down, or sideways, or both. The sensor remains pointing at the center of the viewing area. You can aim the camera-mounted flash anywhere; the straight, forward-looking sensor always measures the light reflected into the lens.

When the flash is taken off the camera and used as a side light, an umbrella light, the sensor on the flash goes too. For such cases, a remote sensor is available for many units. It works like the sensor in a flash unit but is a separate accessory. The sensor is mounted on the camera and again measures the light reflected into the lens regardless of how and where the flash unit is used. The remote sensor actually works like a flash meter held at the camera but is connected to the flash unit to turn it off as soon as the sensor receives the correct amount of light.

If a remote sensor is not available, use the off-the-camera flash unit on manual.

A

A 1:1 lighting ratio between the sunlit background and the flash fill is fine for a publicity photograph (A). Reducing the flash by one stop without changing the exposure for daylight, results in a pictorially better image, with the sunlight becoming the dominant light source (B).

COMBINING FLASH AND DAYLIGHT

Electronic flash is an ideal light source to combine with daylight because its color temperature matches sunlight closely. It can therefore be used in black-and-white and color photography.

In many cases electronic flash can help make better or more effective daylight pictures. Outdoor portraits, fashion shots, publicity pictures, and family snapshots are beautiful when the sunlight is used as a back light or strong side light, but the contrast between highlights and shadows is likely to call for a fill-in light in the shaded areas. Another example is when photographing sunsets or sunrises; exposure is based on the sky, and foreground subjects are then silhouetted. Flash can be used to light them.

Daylight from a window is useful for informal indoor portraits but is directional. The shaded side of the face may need fill-in light to bring the contrast to a pleasing, acceptable level. Fill-in light is necessary when room interiors are photographed toward windows to show the room interior and the view outside the window.

Flash is used as fill-in light, but flash can also be used outdoors as

B

a main light. In flat overcast lighting, the flash can take the place of the missing sun. Flash can also be used as an accent light, to add highlights, and to produce a hair light in portraits that may be missing on an overcast day or when photographing in the shade.

For filling in shaded areas when photographing people, consider the smallest shoe mount unit available. You need very little light since the flash is seldom more than 3 m (10 ft) from the subject and outdoor portraits are usually made at large lens apertures to blur out backgrounds. In all cases, the effectiveness of the image depends on the lighting ratio between the daylight and the flash, which is the result of flash placement, choice of lens aperture, and shutter speed. The results can be evaluated only after the image is recorded on film. A Polaroid film magazine is a helpful accessory.

FILL-IN AUTOMATIC FLASH

A flash unit can be used in the automatic mode when the main subject that is to be filled in with flash is in the center of the frame and is large enough to reflect the light into the sensor and there is no direct light shining into the sensor.

Proceed by setting the flash for the film sensitivity and check what aperture must be used or what apertures are usable with a unit that gives a choice, keeping the flash-to-subject distance in mind. Take a normal meter reading of the area lit by the ambient light that must be properly exposed: the background in an outdoor portrait, the daylight outside the window in an indoor-outdoor situation, or the existing light inside a room. Check on the meter all the possible aperture–shutter speed combinations that produce correct exposure. Most of the time you have a wide choice, from the lens being wide open to the diaphragm being completely closed down. Which combination to use now depends on several factors:

1.   The shutter speed must be within the synchronization range of your camera.
2.   If your flash unit must be used at one specific aperture, you have no choice. If it must be at $f5.6$ for the film sensitivity, you must shoot at $f5.6$. Hopefully, the correct shutter speed is then within the synchronization range. If it is not, you are out of luck.
3.   If your flash unit gives a choice of several apertures, select the combination that is best for depth of field but that is also opposite a shutter speed that is within the synchronization range of your shutter. If the choice for instance is between $f5.6$ and 1/250 sec, $f8$ and 1/125 sec, and $f11$ and 1/60 sec, select the last if the shutter synchronizes only up to 1/60 sec but use $f5.6$ and 1/250 sec if the background is to be blurred and the shutter synchronizes up to that speed. Obviously lens shutters and flash units with a choice give more freedom and wider possibilities.

CHANGING THE LIGHTING RATIO WITH AUTOMATIC FLASH

The aperture–shutter speed combination selected above provides a 1:1 lighting ratio; that is correct exposure for the existing light and equal exposure for the flash-lit area. You have two choices to make the flash exposure lighter or darker. The simpler requires changing the ASA setting on the flash. With 100 ASA film in the camera, setting the dial to 200 ASA should make the flash exposure one stop darker. Because aperture and shutter speed are the same, exposure for the surrounding area remains also the same. You can also leave the flash alone but change aperture and shutter speed. If ƒ5.6 and 1/125 sec produced a 1:1 ratio, ƒ8 and 1/60 sec makes the flash exposure one stop darker. The smaller aperture under-exposes the flash by one stop; the larger speed brings the existing light exposure up to the same level.

If you want to make the surrounding area lighter or darker without changing the exposure for the flash, change the shutter speed only. If ƒ8 and 1/30 sec produced a 1:1 ratio, ƒ8 and 1/60 sec darkens the background by one stop. The flash exposure is not changed since the lens was left at ƒ8.

FILL-IN MANUAL FLASH

While automatic flash is simple and produces the desired results in many cases, it sets limitations, especially when changing lighting ratios. It can be completely unreliable in back light when the sun shines into the sensor. These are two good reasons to recommend using manual flash or setting the automatic unit to manual mode. On manual, the sensor is inoperative. The setting on the flash unit controls the flash. Manual also gives greater freedom in placement of the flash and greater possibilities in changing lighting ratios, especially if the unit has power ratio and is used with lens shutters where all shutter speeds are usable.

Correct aperture, shutter speed, and flash distance can be determined in various ways:

1. Determine how far the flash is from the subject. You can read this off the focusing scale on the lens when the subject is in focus and the flash is on the camera.
2. Read on the flash dial the lens aperture that gives correct exposure at this distance, just as you do when using the flash on manual or power ratio, and set the aperture on the lens.
3. Take a meter reading of the daylight or ambient light that should be exposed properly. Use whatever exposure meter you normally use: incident, reflected, spot, or built into the camera. If you photograph an interior with windows, take a reflected meter reading through the window. When photographing people outdoors, take a reading of the daylight falling on the background behind the subject. Read for the sky when the subject is photographed against the sky.

4. Read on the meter the shutter speed that is opposite the aperture selected for the flash, and set the shutter speed on the camera.

It might happen that the shutter speed shown on the meter is higher than the maximum synchronization speed on your camera. If so, place the flash closer to the subject; the flash may have to come off the camera. With power ratio, increase the output so you can use a smaller aperture and consequently a longer shutter speed that will synchronize with the flash. This combination should provide a good 1:1 ratio in all cases where the ambient source and the flash source strike the subject from opposite directions (the sun backlighting the subject and people inside a room, for instance). If a larger amount of ambient light strikes the subject from the same side as the flash, you may want to close the aperture one-half stop.

You can also proceed the opposite way: set aperture and shutter speed first for the ambient light and then adjust the flash for the set aperture:

1. Take a standard meter reading of the daylit area that should be exposed properly, and set the desired aperture and shutter speed combination as you normally would, but select a combination that is within your camera's synchronization capability.
2. Find out from the chart on the flash unit or its guide number what distance is necessary for correct exposure at the selected aperture. Set the flash at this distance and shoot.

With power ratio, the configuration is even simpler:

1. Take a meter reading of the daylight or ambient light and set the desired aperture and shutter speed as described above.
2. Determine the actual flash-to-subject distance.
3. Move the power ratio lever until the flash-to-subject distance is opposite the selected aperture on the flash dial.

CHANGING EXPOSURE

Regardless of what flash you use—automatic, manual, power ratio—the background is always made darker with a shorter shutter speed and brighter with a longer speed.

The exposure for the flash portion can be changed in three ways:

1. With power ratio, change the power ratio setting. If 1/4 sec gives a 1:1

Electronic flash used on an overcast day (A) as a side light can substitute for the sun and add life and contrast to the image (B).

A

B

ratio, move it to 1/8 sec. It makes the flash exposure one stop darker, giving approximately a 1:3 ratio.

2. You can move the flash closer or farther away (from 8 ft to 11 ft),which is equal to one f stop. (Multiply the distance 1.4 times for a one stop change.

3. Change aperture and shutter speed. Close the aperture to make the flash exposure darker; open the aperture to make it lighter. This, however, also changes the exposure for the daylight. The daylight exposure is brought back to what it was by changing the shutter speed also.

Use combinations of the two that provide the same exposure for the daylight. For example, if f4 at 1/60 sec gives the 1:1 lighting ratio, f5.6 at 1/30 sec gives the same exposure for the daylight but makes the flash portion one stop darker.

FLASH AS AN ACCENT LIGHT

Electronic flash need not be employed as a fill light only. It can also become the main or accent light, opening many new possibilities to make outdoor pictures better or different. It works beautifully on overcast days where the soft daylight then serves as the fill-in. You can place a highlight on a leaf or flower, add a hair light to a portrait, or put an accent light on a product or still-life. Just as sunlight as a front light is flat and uninteresting, so is flash when used as a main or accent light. Take the flash off the camera and place it to produce a strong side, overhead, or back light. Aperture and shutter speed and flash-to-subject distance are determined as explained. If the flash is the main light, expose properly for the flash. Set the shutter speed so the rest of the image is slightly darker.

If the flash is used as an accent light, a hair light, or a back light to outline the subject with a rim of light, the flash level can be considerably more than the level of ambient light. Set the aperture and shutter to give correct exposure without the flash. Now put the flash at about one-half the distance indicated on the flash unit for the aperture on the lens. This will overexpose the accented area, as you do in a studio with a rim light. With power ratio, set the dial at least one notch higher (to 1/2 instead of 1/4).

Striking and fascinating effects can be obtained by combining daylight with colored flash. Transparent papers or gelatins of any color can be placed over the flash head. The flash can be positioned to serve as a main or an accent light. I have photographed tombstones in a cemetery and white birches this way against the sky at dusk. I used two flash units covered with different colored gelatins, lighting one tombstone or tree in one color and the one next to it in a different color. Aperture and shutter speeds are determined as for white flash, but keep in mind that the color filters absorb some of the light, and the flash must therefore be closer than the chart indicates or the lens aperture must be larger. Distances and aperture can be determined accurately with a flash meter.

CHAPTER 12

Filters and the image

There are five basic reasons for using filters: to obtain 'correct' color rendition on color film or correct gray tones on black-and-white film; to enhance color images or change gray tones in black and white; to create special effects and moods; to reduce the amount of light reaching the film; and to protect the lens.

FILTERS AS LENS PROTECTION

Lenses are the most expensive components in a camera system. They are also the components that are most easily damaged and probably the most expensive to repair. A simple way to protect the front element is with an optically plain piece of glass, which is easy to clean and relatively cheap to replace. A skylight, ultraviolet, or haze filter can serve this purpose. These filters do not change the colors or gray tones noticably and do not require a change in exposure.

Each lens should be equipped with a filter. It is too time-consuming to switch filters from one lens to another every time lenses are changed. Since the filter becomes a permanent part of the lens and all pictures are taken through this additional piece of glass, these filters must be made to the same degree of perfection as the lens. For color photography, use identical filters made by the same company to avoid possible differences in color rendition. A sunshade over the lens is essential when you use a filter. It is a further protection against possible mechanical damage and prevents snow or rain from falling on the lens element and creating a diffusion effect. This is especially true for a bellows lens shade because it can be extended quite a distance in front of the lens.

NEUTRAL DENSITY FILTERS

Neutral density filters, also called gray filters, are used in both black-and-white and color photography. Made from neutral gray-colored glass, their purpose is to reduce the amount of light reaching the film without chang-

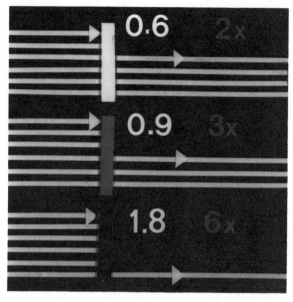

The amount of light absorbed by neutral density filters is indicated by density. 0.3 is equal to one *f* stop; 0.6 to two stops; 0.9 to three stops; and 1.8 to six stops.

ing the tonal rendition of the various colors. Neutral density filters come in different densities requiring the following compensating increases in exposure:

Density	Percentage Light Transmission	Increase in Exposure in Exposure Values or *f* stops
0.3	50	1
0.6	25	2
0.9	12	3
1.2	6	4
1.5	3	5
1.8	1.5	6

Neutral density filters can be combined. The increase in exposure is obtained by adding up the densities; for example, the 0.3 and 0.6 filters combined have a density of 0.9.

Neutral density filters can be used when high-speed films are used outdoors—for example, when the sunlight is too bright to permit photography at large apertures with shallow depths of field or at the slow shutter speeds necessary for blurred motion or zoom effects. Neutral density filters can also be used to compensate for different film sensitivities. The most valuable application in practical photography is when Polaroid material is used for test shots; the filters allow the same aperture and shutter speed to be used for both the final image and the test shot.

In black-and-white photography, color filters such as yellow, green, orange, or red can frequently be used instead of the neutral density type, as the change in the gray tones may not be objectionable and even beneficial.

FILTERS FOR BLACK-AND-WHITE PHOTOGRAPHY

In black-and-white photography, the various colors are recorded in a range of gray tones from white to black. Exactly how they are recorded depends on the type of film and light. Panchromatic films are sensitive to all colors and record subjects in a range of gray tones pretty much as we visualize them. There are, however, still cases where filters can improve the black-and-white images. For example, panachromatic films are still somewhat more sensitive to blue and therefore record blue lighter than we visualize

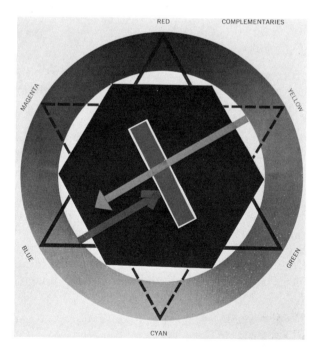

The color wheel makes it easy to determine how a color filter affects the recording of gray tones. Subjects that have the same color as the filter will be lighter. Those having a color on the opposite side of the wheel will be recorded darker. A yellow filter darkens blue skies.

it. A yellow-green filter corrects this and is recommended for outdoor scenes with blue skies.

A green filter lightens green somewhat, beautifying outdoor scenes with green fields and trees. It also produces good flesh tones in outdoor portraiture.

In tungsten light, red and green appear as the same gray tone; red, orange, and yellow appear lighter and skin tones and lips therefore somewhat pale. This can be improved with a blue (B-12) filter.

The main application of filters in black-and-white photography, however, is not for recording subjects in natural gray tones but for purposely darkening or lightening certain colors to emphasize, suppress, separate, increase, or reduce contrasts. You can lighten or darken any color. The color of the filter determines what happens to what color; the degree of color change is determined by the density of the filter. To lighten a color, use a filter of the same color or at least from the same side of the color wheel. To darken a color, select the color directly across the wheel or at least from the opposite side.

A yellow filter darkens colors from blue-green to violet. Green filters lighten green and darken purple and red. They can be used to lighten shaded green areas under trees.

COMBINING FILTERS

When color filters are combined with neutral density and polarizing filters, the effect of both shows up on the film: the neutral density filter decreases the light reaching the film, and the color filter changes the gray tones.

Two strong filters of the same color—for instance, two orange or two red filters—produce in black and white the same result as one filter. The explanation is simple. If one red filter already absorbs all the blue and green, a second red filter cannot do any more. It transmits less of the warm colors and requires a larger increase in exposure without altering the image. It makes even less sense to combine strong filters of completely different, complementary colors, such as an orange filter and a blue filter. The blue filter absorbs all or most colors at one end of the spectrum and the orange filter those at the other end, so little is left to form an image.

Combining two similarly colored pale filters, though, does double the effect in color or black and white.

EXPOSURE INCREASE

A filter absorbs light. With light-colored filters (UV, haze, and some light-balance and color-compensating types), the light loss is so small that it need not be considered for exposure determination. Darker filters, on the other hand, take away a sufficient amount of light to affect exposure. As a result, lens settings must be adjusted. With a built-in metering system, the light is measured through the filter, and the light loss is automatically compensated for. The meter readings are therefore correct for most filters. When light is measured with a separate meter, an adjustment must be made based on the information from the filter manufacturer..

Some companies give the necessary increases in filter factors, others in apertures. It is important to know which figure is on the chart because they are two different things. Simply multiply the shutter speed by the filter factor, or alter the f stop or EV setting by the aperture increase. For example, with a four times (or $+2$ stop) filter, change from EV 13 to EV 11 or from f11 to f5.6.

FILTER FACTORS AND f STOPS/EV

Filter factor	1.5	2	2.5	4	6	8	16	32	64
Increase in exposure in f stops or EV	½	1	1½	2	2½	3	4	5	6

There is still one other way in which you can compensate, especially if you use one filter most of the time. Divide the filter factor into the ASA rating of the film. For example, with an ASA rating of 200 and a filter factor of 8, the calculation is $200 \div 8 = 25$; i.e., the film sensitivity with the filter is 25 ASA. Set the meter at 25 ASA and use the meter reading directly.

HAZE PENETRATION: HAZE, UV, AND SKYLIGHT FILTERS

Haze and ultraviolet (UV) filters do not change colors noticeably. They do absorb UV rays. Most modern lenses, however, absorb UV light to a greater extent than the filter, so the haze or UV filters are of limited value. These modern glasses have reduced or eliminated the need for UV, skylight, and haze filters (except for lens protection). I suggest using an 81A or 81B (decamired R 1.5 or R 3) in cases where those filters used to be recommended. These filters can be used for a number of purposes:

Improving distance shots by reducing haze.

Eliminating the excessive UV radiation that exists at high altitudes and thus producing sharper images with more neutral colors.

Reducing the blue in shaded areas in outdoor scenes with a blue sky.

Producing warmer and more pleasing colors on overcast days.

Producing better colors when using electronic flash.

The best improvement in distant shots on color film is obtained with polarizing filters. They may not penetrate haze, but by eliminating reflections in the distance and in the air, they increase the contrast. They do so only, however, with the sun shining from the side. You will not see much, if any, improvement if you photograph into the sun (back light) or when the sun is directly behind you (straight front light). You may also want to add an 81A or 81B filter for a warmer rendition of the distant landscape.

In black-and-white photography, a yellow filter produces some improvement in distant shots, but orange and red filters are more effective. Complete or almost complete haze penetration can be obtained with a red filter combined with infrared film, but other colors are also changed; for instance, green appears as white.

COLOR QUALITY OF LIGHT

Color transparency films are manufactured for a specific color of the light source, and correct color can be obtained only if the color of the light matches that for which the film is balanced. The color quality of light is expressed as color temperature either in Kelvin or in decamired values. Kelvin and decamired values are directly related by the formula

$$\text{DM value} = \frac{100,000}{\text{Kelvin value}}.$$

COLOR TEMPERATURE OF TYPICAL LIGHT SOURCES

DM	Kelvin	Type of Light
8	12,500	Shade with clear blue sky
16	6,250	Overcast day
17	5,900	Electronic flash
18	5,600	Sunlight at noon
29	3,450	Photofloods
31	3,200	Tungsten lamps
34	2,900	100–200 W household lamps
36	2,800	40–75 W household lamps
54	1,850	Candlelight

The color films used in medium-format photography are matched to the following color temperature values:

Daylight type: 18 DM, 5600 K

Type B: 31 DM, 3200 K

Some light sources, such as sunlight at noon, photographic studio lights, and electronic flash, have known values as shown on the chart; they do not change appreciably, and actual measurement of the color temperature is not necessary. Other light sources, such as daylight early in the morning, late in the afternoon, or on overcast days, do not have an exactly known value. The light color can change within a few minutes without us being aware. Guessing is not good enough for an exact match. The color temperature must be measured with a color temperature meter.

Color temperature meters are held in front of the subject and measure the light falling on it. They read out in degrees Kelvin or decamireds so that you can select the necessary filter. The simpler meters measure only the red-blue values but are satisfactory for tungsten and daylight. For measuring fluorescent lights, unusual light sources, or light reflected off colored surfaces, the more expensive three-point meters that also measure green are necessary.

LIGHT BALANCE AND CONVERSION FILTERS

Light balance and conversion filters are used in color photography for matching the color quality of the illumination to that of the film or to obtain a warmer or cooler color rendition in the image. Light balance filters are used for minor adjustments, conversion filters for a more drastic change.

The filters that have a warming effect are the decamired red types, the 81 series light balance, and 85 conversion types; those with cooling effects are the decamired blue types, or the 82 series light balance and 80 conversion filters. The warming filters are used when the light is too blue for the film in the camera, the cooling filters when the light is too red.

In the Wratten filter series, the necessary filter can be determined only by a color-temperature meter or from a chart. There is no direct relationship between the color temperature of the light and the filter value. Also, a filter of a given value can effect a completely different change when the light is in the 3000 K range to when the light is in the 5000 K range. The Wratten filters necessary for the most common filter and light combinations are found in the chart shown here.

Film manufacturers usually indicate the loss of light caused by conversion filters by a lowering of the ASA rating. For example, a tungsten film rated at 125 ASA in tungsten light is shown as an 80 ASA film when used in daylight with a conversion filter. The film sensitivity has not really changed, but the sensitivity is lower in daylight because of the light absorbed by the filter. Do not compensate for the light loss twice by setting the meter on 80 ASA and also increasing the exposure by the factor shown on the filter.

When using a separate meter, either set the meter on 125 ASA and open the lens by the figure engraved on the filter, or set the meter at 80 ASA and use the setting on the meter without adjustment. Built-in meters must always be set on the film sensitivity for the original light source (125 ASA in the above example).

DECAMIRED FILTER SYSTEM

The decamired system, also referred to as the *photometric system*, can simplify the use of light balance and conversion filters. The required filter must always have a decamired value that is equal to the difference in the decamired values of the film and light source. For example, if the film is balanced for DM 31 and the light is DM 28, you need a decamired filter with a +3 DM value (31 − 28 = 3), which is a red filter (R3).

Various decamired filter values are obtained by combining filters of the same color—for example, a red 10.5 value is obtained by combining a Red 6, Red 3, and Red 1.5. With one set of decamired filters, you are able to match any light-film combination. Blue and red decamired filters are, however, not combined.

With light sources of known and fixed color values, color temperature meters are not necessary because the correct filter can be determined from the following chart.

FILTER VALUES REQUIRED IN VARIOUS CONDITIONS

Purpose	Decamired Filters	Wratten Filters
For a warmer rendition with some electronic flash units (some units produce a bluish light)	R 1.5	81A
Outdoor portraits in the shade (under a blue sky)	R 3	81B
On overcast days, in fog as a substitute for skylight filter	R 1.5 or R 3	81A or 81B
To reduce warm tones in early morning and late afternoon photography	B 3	82B
To use type A color film in daylight	R 12	85
To use type B color film in daylight	R 13.5	85B
To use daylight film with 3200 K light	B 13.5	80A
To use daylight film with 3400 K light	B 12	80B
To use type B film with 3400 K light	R 1.5	81A
To use type A film with 3200 K light	B 1.5	82A
With flash cubes on daylight film	B 1.5	82A
When using type B film with household lamps	B 3	82C

COLOR-COMPENSATING FILTERS

Color-compensating filters (CC filters) are used for changes in the overall color balance or for fine color corrections. They are available in six colors (yellow, magenta, cyan, red, green, and blue) and in different densities in each color, from about 0.05 to 0.50. These filters are most readily available in gelatin. One of their main applications is to compensate for variations in the color balance of professional films. The required filter is indicated in the film's instruction sheet. The filter matches colors even if the film emulsions come from different batches. Some other applications are when photographing through tinted windows, in underwater photography to compensate for the loss of red, and when photographing under fluorescent lights.

FLUORESCENT LIGHTS

Unlike sunlight or light from other incandescent sources, the light from a fluorescent tube is nowhere near evenly distributed through the spectrum, so the results with color film can be unpredictable (except with special color-matching tubes). Film and fluorescent tube manufacturers publish charts showing which color-compensating filters produce the most satisfactory results.

Instead of combinations of color-compensating filters, which are not always readily available, some simpler solutions exist. For example, with daylight fluorescent tubes, some of the new high-speed daylight color films produce fairly acceptable results without a filter. Also, with color negative films, some correction can be made at the printing stage. Special filters for fluorescent lights are also available—usually one filter for daylight film, another for type B. These are acceptable with some fluorescent tubes.

There are a few other problems associated with fluorescent tubes. The tubes vary somewhat among manufacturers, and their color changes with age and with voltage fluctuations. The color also changes during the warming-up period, and tubes should therefore be turned on at least 10 min before shooting time. Fluorescent tubes go on and off almost completely during each AC cycle, and the colors again change; the answer is to avoid short shutter speeds (1/125 sec or shorter).

POLARIZING FILTERS

Light that reaches our eyes or the camera lens directly is unpolarized; the light waves vibrate in all directions perpendicular to the light path. If such light reaches glass, water, or many other reflecting surfaces at an angle, between 30° and 40°, it becomes polarized; the consequent light waves vibrate in one direction only. Our eyes cannot see the difference, but, with a polarizing filter, we can determine whether light is polarized or unpolarized.

Polarizing filters are made from a material that changes natural into polarized light. The light that enters the polarizing filter vibrates in all directions; when it comes out on the other side, it is polarized and vibrates

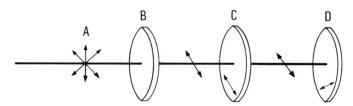

Natural, unpolarized light vibrates in all directions (A). As it passes through a polarizing filter (B), the light becomes polarized; it vibrates in one direction only. If this polarized light meets another polarizing filter (C) with its axis of polarization in the same direction as the first, the light can pass through. A polarizing filter with its axis of polarization at right angles (D) to the first will absorb all the light. This arrangement is called cross-polarization.

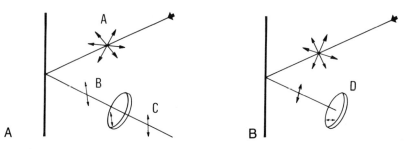

When natural, unpolarized light is reflected by a surface, it becomes polarized and vibrates in one direction only. In this state, it can pass through a polarizing filter with an axis of polarization in line with the light (A) but not through one at right angles to this position (B). In the latter case, reflections are eliminated.

in one direction only. A second polarizing filter placed behind the first will transmit the polarized light coming from the first filter if their axes of polarization are in the same direction. Turned through 90°, the second filter will absorb the light, so no, or very little, light is transmitted. We have what is known as cross-polarization.

Polarizers have one advantage over other filters: you can see the effect in the SLR finder or by simply holding and turning the polarizer

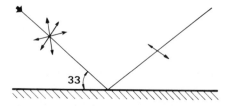

Reflected light is polarized only if it hits the surface at a certain angle—between 30° and 40°. Maximum polarization on glass is at 33° and on water at 35°.

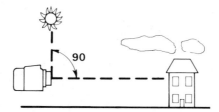

Maximum polarization (darkening of the sky) is obtained when the sun is to the side. With front or back light, the polarizing filter has no effect.

in front of your eyes. You know beforehand whether it improves the shot. You can also see whether the light is polarized.

If the light is not polarized, rotating the polarizing filter does not change anything. Looking through the filter, therefore, is an easy way to determine whether and which light is polarized and which is natural. If the object changes while rotating the filter, the light reflected off that surface is completely or partially polarized; if the object does not change, the light is regular unpolarized light.

Light from tungsten lights or electronic flash can be polarized by placing a polarizing filter over the light source. A polarizing filter over the lens then eliminates practically all reflections, at all angles, from all materials. This procedure is necessary to eliminate reflections on bare metal. It is also highly recommended when copying.

FILTERS FOR INFRARED PHOTOGRAPHY

Filters are used in infrared photography to absorb blue and UV light so that only the deep red and the infrared rays reach the film. A filter used for this purpose should absorb wavelengths shorter than about 600 μm.

For scientific purposes, filters absorbing all light below 700 μm are suggested. Two filters recommended for color work are Kodak 12 and 15. For black-and-white work, a deep red filter is recommended. For experimental and creative work, any filter can be used; yellow, red, green, blue, purple, and violet filters produce beautiful and unusual color effects with many subjects.

PARTIAL FILTERING

Filters can be positioned in front of the lens so that only part of the image receives filtered light. This may be used to improve an image or to create a special effect. Neutral density filters can be used to darken some areas, color filters to change colors in some areas, while other areas are unfiltered.

A polarizing filter can eliminate or reduce reflections but only when the subject with the reflecting surface (the store window, in this case) is photographed from an angle.

Filters that are clear over half of their area and neutral gray or colored over the other half are readily available. They must be square and mounted in a square filter holder so they can be moved vertically or horizontally. I use 3 in. gelatin filters for this purpose in combination with a bellows lens shade. The slot at the rear of the shade is ideal for sliding the gelatin in front of the lens as far as necessary, and the bellows shades the filter from direct light.

When positioning the filter, you must view the ground-glass image at the aperture that will be used or, even better, determine the aperture that produces the desired results while manually opening and closing the diaphragm. The sharpness of the dividing line between the filtered and nonfiltered area depends on the aperture. At large apertures, the line is very blurred; at small apertures, it becomes rather sharp and distinct. When the visual dividing line between the filtered and nonfiltered areas is also sharp, such as a horizon over a water surface, the small apertures are preferred—you do not want the sky colors to flow over into the water. In other cases, when the dividing line is a wide, dark area, a large aperture may be preferred. The position of the dividing line also changes as the diaphragm is closed down.

Partial filters reduce the amount of light falling on part of the film, leaving the rest undisturbed. What exposure changes should be made? If the filter darkens or changes the color over the main subject area, the filter factor must be considered. More often, the filter is used to darken or change the color over a secondary area such as the sky, in which case the filter factor is not considered. The main area—the landscape, the water, and the beach below the sky—is not affected by the filter, and so the lens setting is the same with or without filter. The lens settings are based on the regular meter reading of the unchanged area. With a built-in meter, therefore, take the meter reading and set the lens before positioning the filter.

DIFFUSION FILTERS

Diffusion filters are used to add a soft, poetic feeling to images or to suppress undesirable details. This is especially useful when photographing people where the diffusion filter makes blemishes and skin imperfections less visible, giving a more flattering appearance to people and reducing the necessary amount of retouching. Only a slight diffusion is necessary for this purpose.

Good diffusion filters do not produce out-of-focus images but images with diffused outlines where the highlights bleed into the shaded areas. The images can be beautiful in the flat lighting of an overcast or foggy day or in umbrella lighting in the studio. The effect can be very striking on back-lighted subjects or scenes where the diffusion filter creates a sort of a halo effect around every highlight in the scene or subject. The diffusion

Soft-focus filters bleed the highlights into the shaded areas. A good soft-focus filter does this without creating unsharpness. Notice the sharpness on the embroidery (the color shot).

effect can be distracting if the halo is unnatural (for example, in studio portraits against dark backgrounds).

Diffusion effects can be created in many different ways: with home-made gadgets such as black nylon stockings, with vaseline on glass, with clear acetate and diffusion lenses, and with diffusion filters.

Besides the effect they produce, diffusion devices vary in one major respect: with some, the lens aperture determines the degree of softness. It decreases as the lens is stopped down. The lens then must be set at a specific aperture to obtain a specific softness. With others, the aperture has no effect. I prefer this type because I feel the lens aperture should be set for depth of field. Some diffusion devices can be combined; others cannot.

LENS ATTACHMENTS FOR SPECIAL EFFECTS

Multiprisms are glass lens attachments with three to six or perhaps even more different prismatic surfaces. Each prism produces its own image of the subject; the result is multiple images on the film. The arrangement of the images depends on the design of the multiprism. It can be parallel, circular, or any other arrangement.

The effect of multiprisms depends on the aperture and, to some extent, on the focal length of the lens. Consequently, evaluate the results carefully on the ground glass with the diaphragm manually closed down to different apertures. At large apertures, the images overlap considerably. At smaller apertures, the images are more separated and distinct. Shorter focal length lenses produce more overlapping; longer lenses produce more separation by spreading the images into the corners. Also check the multiprism effect at different distances. Longer distances separate the images more. The effect with a long lens from a long distance is different from that with a short focal length lens from a closer distance, even though both may cover the same area.

Color prism. Multiprisms are also available with each field in a different color. Each image is recorded in a different color on color film. This offers extremely interesting possibilities with the prism stationary and even more when rotating during exposure so that the various colors blend into each other. White subjects usually produce the best effects.

Star filters and cross-screens. Used with the right subject on the proper occasion, a star-like pattern can be striking in both photographs and films. It enhances the feeling of beauty and glitter and should therefore be used when these moods are to be created. As star filters show their effect only in highlights, images must be framed to include such highlights (for example, lighted chandeliers, stage lights, candles, nightlights, sunlight bouncing off water). Star filters come in different versions producing four, six, or eight star patterns, two of which can be combined and rotated against each other.

Fog filters. A misty, atmospheric haze effect, very similar to fog, can be obtained with a fog filter placed in front of the lens. These usually come in different densities. The lighting in the scene must be of the type existing on a foggy day: soft and without shadows or highlights.

Diffraction gratings have thousands of microscopic grooves on their surface, which act like prisms breaking white light up into all the colors of the spectrum. The arrangement of the grooves determines the color pattern, which can be in one direction or symmetrical surrounding each light source. A bright light source shining directly on the diffraction filter is necessary. The effect can be made still more beautiful when combined with a diffusion filter.

QUALITY OF FILTERS

Filters used with high-quality lenses for critical photography must be made to the same quality standards as the lenses. This is especially important when filters are used all the time or when they are combined with long focal length lenses.

A filter that is not perfectly optically flat may have the effect of a very weak lens element. It may decrease image quality and make it impossible to focus the lens at infinity. The quality of filters becomes still more important when filters are combined. With deep orange and red filters, the best quality in black and white is obtained with so-called apochromatic lenses, which are well corrected for the red and perhaps even the infrared.

FILTER POSITION

With some lenses, filters can be placed inside the lens rather than at the front. This is common in fish-eye lenses where a filter in front of the lens would cut into the field of view. In such lenses, the filter is usually part of the optical design, which means the lens has been designed to produce the best sharpness with the filter or clear glass in the lens.

COATING AND MULTICOATING

Filters should be coated when used on a coated lens. Multicoating of a filter is of questionable value from a practical point of view but will not do any harm.

FILTER MAINTENANCE

Most filters are made from glass and are cleaned like lens surfaces by blowing or brushing off dust first and then cleaning with lens tissue and lens cleaner if necessary. Avoid unnecessary brushing and cleaning. Place a lens cap over a filter on the lens. Store filters in a plastic case. Some filters, especially diffusion types, may be made of clear plastic, and you should therefore never use lens cleaner or any other chemical solvent for cleaning. A soft brush or blower will remove dust. Grease or fingermarks are removed with a soft polishing cloth, if necessary, after breathing on the surface.

CHAPTER **13**

Motor drives

Motor drives are no longer an accessory to a manually wound camera; they have become a standard part of the camera body. The medium format has not stayed far behind. Motor-driven cameras have been available since the 1960s, and motor drives are now available as accessories for the major SLR medium format cameras. They also have become part of the camera body.

Motor drives originally were an afterthought to the camera. The camera was designed first as a manual winding camera; the motor drive came later as an accessory.

Today, cameras and motor drives are usually developed at the same time. Motor-driven operation is considered when developing the camera mechanism. As a result, it will likely be a more reliable, lasting piece of equipment.

MOTORS VERSUS WINDERS

The main function of a motor is to advance the film automatically after each picture. A motor that does nothing more than that is frequently referred to as an *autowinder*. In a more sophisticated version, the auto-winder might also wind the roll film to frame 1 and wind up the paper trailer after the last frame has been shot. If motorized film advance is all you expect, an autowinder serves the purpose. A true motor drive, on the other hand, can provide additional helpful possibilities, such as remote and sequence photography and multiple camera operation.

The convenience of electric film advance is somewhat suppressed by the need for a battery or set of batteries and additional components. A battery in good condition must be available. On an important assignment or when the motor drive is used extensively, a spare battery should be carried along..

Motors can go bad, but the likelihood that something will happen to the motor is not greater than on any other camera and lens component.

If the motor drive is an accessory, both problems can be overcome by removing the motor and operating the camera manually. Some cameras with built-in motors also allow operating the camera manually in an emergency, perhaps in a limited mode. Although this capability is appreciated in an emergency, the likelihood that it would be needed is too small for this to become a major factor in choosing a motor-driven camera. The possibilities offered by the motor drive should come first.

MOTOR-DRIVE BENEFITS AND APPLICATIONS

Sequence Operation

Shooting sequences of images at a fast rate is the first application of a motor drive that usually comes to mind. This can be extremely valuable in action, sports, and scientific studies. If this is your main reason for considering a motor drive, however, first determine what speed may be necessary in your application and then read camera specification sheets because most medium format cameras do not provide the speed of several frames per second that is offered by 35s. Most medium format cameras operate more in the neighborhood of one frame per second. Although a higher rate is necessary in some cases—the finish in a horse race or a 100 yard dash—one frame per second is often satisfactory. Not too many actions change sufficiently within 1/4 sec. At the 1 sec rate, you can capture the different actions without wasting too much film.

Shooting Readiness

More important than sequence operation is the fact that the motorized camera is always ready for shooting. You can shoot a second picture a moment after a picture is made. You can shoot that second or third image without even having to remove your eye from the finder, whether you work hand held or from a tripod. When photographing people, especially children, the best expression often appears just after the picture was snapped, perhaps as a sign of relief. This expression lasts for a moment— never long enough to capture it with manual film advance but long enough for a second push on the release of the motor drive.

Simplicity of Operation

Camera operation, which is now reduced to pressing the release, can be done with one hand, useful when the other may have to be used for holding on, holding a flash or other accessory, directing people, or shading the lens or eyes.

Automatic electric film advance is smooth, with little danger that a mounted camera will move out of position between shots. It is not easy to advance the film manually without moving a mounted camera, an annoyance, especially in close-up photography. The slightest shift in the camera requires realignment and perhaps even refocusing. A motor simplifies photography with the camera mounted on a copy stand or over a microscope.

Remote Operation

Remote camera operation has applications in just about every field of photography. It is useful or necessary when it is dangerous or impossible to be near the camera. That is the way the most striking images of space lift-offs at Cape Canaveral are done. Cameras can be set up much closer than the 3 mi minimum distance for photographers. Remote operation is frequently used in aerial applications with the camera built into the aircraft. Remote operation, however, is not limited to such special applications. It can be helpful in portrait, fashion, pet, and child photography.

Successful people photography means directing the people, whether they are professional models or nonprofessionals. Although this can be

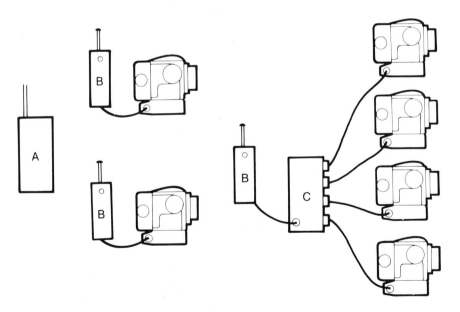

Wireless remote operation by means of radio or infrared is possible with motor drives. More than one camera can be operated in this fashion from one transmitter (A) either by attaching a separate receiver (B) to each camera or connecting the receiver to a multiple camera coupler (C).

done from behind the camera, it is often easier when you are close to the subject. With a motor drive, you can be close to the people, watch their expressions, direct, play with a child, and snap the shutter when everything is right. You need to return to the camera only to change film and lens settings.

A motor-driven camera can be set up to photograph a wedding ceremony from a location where a photographer is not allowed or from where it provides a different view from the camera that the photographer is using hand held in the aisle. One photographer can actually operate two cameras: one hand held and the other set on a tripod somewhere else.

A good motor-driven camera also allows electric camera operation with the camera in the prereleased mode (mirror locked up) without having to lock up the mirror manually before each exposure. This is almost a must when operated remotely.

Remote Operation with Cable   Remote operation can be done in many ways. Cables provide the simplest and least expensive method. The necessary cables may be readily available from the camera manufacturer or can be made up from the type of wire recommended by the manufacturer. If the releasing is done electrically, as it probably is, closing the contact between the two wires with a simple switch is all that is necessary. If the remote socket on the camera has more than two contacts, find out which two release the camera. Some of the other contacts are undoubtedly used for charging the batteries. You also need to find out how long the release cord can be. There is undoubtedly a limit because the wires cause a loss in the signal. The limit may be a few feet or several hundred. The distance can be increased by amplifying the signal. Such amplifiers are readily available from some camera manufacturers.

Wireless Remote Operation   The triggering source can also be a radio signal, a sound signal, a light signal, or infrared. The signal is produced by a transmitter and picked up by a receiver on or close to the camera and connected to the remote release socket. Some slide projectors can be operated in the same way. With light signals, the receiver must see the signal on the transmitter. With radio waves, this is not necessary. A camera can be outside a building and the operator inside. There is a limit to how far one can go with all signals. Wireless remote operation offers wonderful opportunities, especially outdoors (in wildlife photography, for instance). Basically any radio equipment designed for such purposes can be used if it complies with the law. Some radio units work on a specific FM wavelength; others have a choice of frequency bands. The distance range depends on the location and weather. Different channel frequencies are necessary if other equipment in the same area is controlled by radio or if another photographer is also using a radio release in the vicinity.

Two or more cameras can be operated from one transmitter if the receivers on all cameras work in the same frequency. If multiple cameras are within relatively short distances, it is not necessary to equip each with a radio receiver. Instead one radio receiver can be connected to two or more cameras.

Having radio-controlled cameras triggered by spurious signals is their main problem. The use of FM makes the equipment rather insensitive to external interference. Airplanes are a typical source of such interference. Radio signals are not used as much today because of the interference.

THE INTERVALOMETER

An *intervalometer* is in principle nothing more than a timing device that gives an impulse at regular intervals (set on a dial) to trigger a camera or other device. Intervalometers for cameras are made by many different companies. Many are specifically for motion picture cameras because movie cameras are more often used for this type of work, called time-lapse studies. This does not mean that they are not usable for motor-driven still cameras. Check their signal specifications. Most intervalometers need power for the timer and thus are limited in their use to locations where power is available. If that is a problem, you should be able to find a battery-operated intervalometer or one that uses the batteries in the camera as a power source. One intervalometer can operate more than one camera.

MULTIPLE CAMERA OPERATION

Multiple camera operation (taking simultaneous pictures at exactly the same moment with more than one camera) has interesting possibilities and important applications in many fields of photography. It usually involves recording unique events or happenings where the photographer has only one opportunity to capture a particular image on film and no time to change film, lenses, or camera angles. It could be the finish of a horse race or 100 yard dash, the take-off on a ski jump, or almost any other sports action. You can record the event as a color transparency and a black-and-white print by loading one camera with color slide film and the other with black and white. For an overall view and a close-up of the same action at the same moment, equip one camera with a normal or wide angle lens and another with a telephoto lens. Another application of multiple cameras is to record the action from two or more angles. For example, in a boxing match, actions can be recorded simultaneously from different angles.

Pairs of stereo pictures, even action shots, can be made easily with two motor-driven cameras. Recording simultaneous images on different film emulsions is also known as *multispectral photography* and is used mainly for investigating water pollution problems or diseases in fields and forests. The images on different films, including infrared, taken through

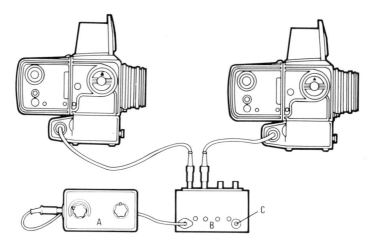

For multiple camera operation, motor-driven cameras can be connected to a coupler (B) so they fire simultaneously. They can be released manually with the release button on the coupler (C) and for time-lapse applications can be connected to an intervalometer so they fire at regular intervals set on the timer (A).

different color filters can show the scientist the source of the problem, which may not be possible from one image. Panoramic images that stretch across all screens in a multimedia show are taken with a set of cameras lined up so the areas match together accurately.

In all these cases, two or more motor-driven cameras are connected to one release. If the necessary release cable is not readily available, it can be made up easily by splitting the wire so the electrical signal goes to two or more release cables.

A splitter accessory called a *command unit* is also available for some cameras. Multiple camera photography can be successful only if all cameras fire. Should one fail, the entire undertaking may be a failure. A well-designed command unit can prevent such mistakes. A light next to each connecting socket indicates the firing, or nonfiring, of each camera. Although the various cameras connected to a common cable will fire at the same time, do not expect that one flash unit will be synchronized to all cameras. The electronic flash must be triggered by the shutter, not the release. The timing is critical, especially at higher shutter speeds. If multiple camera operation with flash synchronization is necessary, see whether it can be done at longer shutter speeds (1/8 to 1 sec), which precludes any other light in the room. Also make a test.

BATTERIES

Battery Operation

The battery or batteries that power the motor drive may be standard flashlight or a special type. The type to use is determined by the number of exposures that can be expected from a fully charged battery or set of batteries. That can vary from fewer than one hundred to a few thousand from a more expensive battery. The latter should be the choice of those working with motors extensively or shooting a lot of film in one session. Most batteries lose some capacity in cold weather so they should not be exposed to the cold longer than necessary. Remove them from the camera when not needed and store in a warm place. Those working in cold temperatures frequently should also consider the possibility of keeping the battery in warm surroundings while shooting, perhaps by inserting the battery not into the camera that is in the cold but in a separate battery compartment connected to the camera. The battery compartment can be kept in a vest pocket, in the car, or wrapped in a heat blanket. Not all cameras offer this possibility and the necessary accessories and cables. Batteries also lose some of the capacity if they are not used. Find out the so-called shelf life from the manufacturer.

Rechargeable Batteries

Most motor drives use rechargeable batteries or offer the choice of the rechargeable type. They are the logical choice when motor drives are used extensively. Such batteries can be recharged hundreds of times if properly cared for. Use only the charger that is recommended or specifically made for the battery. Never charge them longer than necessary. Overcharging is the most common cause of damage. A battery that has been overcharged loses some of its capacity and no longer provides the promised number of exposures. Excessive overcharging results in battery leakage or swelling, which can be dangerous. Unplug the charger after the correct time has elapsed, or connect it to a timer that automatically shuts it off after the set number of hours.

Charging Time

Battery manuals specify how long a completely discharged battery needs to be charged. If the battery is only partially discharged, charging time becomes a problem because there is no practical way to determine the condition of most rechargeable batteries. An instrument can show whether the battery has a charge but not how much.

The voltage in the batteries, especially the commonly used Nicads, does not drop gradually as in dry cell types. It remains at an almost even level until the end and then drops suddenly and fast, with little warning. A slowdown in the camera mechanism signifies that the battery is close to its end.

The state of charge and the required charging time can be determined only from the number of exposures taken. It is therefore recommended that you keep a record. The time is the total number of exposures compared to the charging time. Let us assume a fully charged battery is good for approximately 1000 exposures and the charging time for a discharged battery is 10 hrs. It needs a 1 hr charge for every 100 exposures (10 × 100 = 1000).

Rather than doing calculations, I suggest that each battery be used until the camera slows down—that is, until the battery is almost completely discharged. Then switch to a fully charged battery or set of batteries and use the second set to its end. While using the second one, recharge the first for its full time. This procedure is recommended not just for simplicity but to keep batteries in top working order.

If Nicad batteries are used up only partially and given a partial charge, they create a memory. They no longer give the number of exposures promised but only the number that corresponds to the partial charging time. For instance, if the battery is supposed to provide 1000 exposures but is used only to expose about 500 frames every time and recharged about half the recommended time, the battery after a while will give only 500 exposures and will never get back to its 1000 capacity.

If you want to discharge a battery without exposing film, attach a bulb with two connecting wires to either side of the battery (wire can be taped on) and wait until the light starts to fade.

AC OPERATION

If the camera is used indoors only, a motor-driven camera that can be operated from AC is a possibility. Then there is no need for a battery. The necessary accessory to change 110 V AC into the low-voltage DC required by the camera motor is readily available for some cameras. If it is not, a unit made for other accessories may be usable if it provides the correct DC voltage and current. Do not use such an accessory that is not made by the camera manufacturer without approval from the camera company or a reliable camera technician.

CHAPTER 14

Image quality

The image and image quality depend on the decisive moment: the moment when you press the camera release. Assuming that the lens and camera settings have been made properly, best sharpness can be obtained only if the camera is absolutely motionless from the moment the shutter opens until it closes.

HAND HELD OR TRIPOD

This is one of the first decisions to be made. A fairly common opinion is that medium format cameras are made for tripod use. They are heavier than 35s. Some are so heavy that they cannot be carried too far or too long without becoming a burden. But that does not necessarily mean the need for a tripod. Most medium format cameras are still light enough to be carried around the neck, on a shoulder, or in a hand without becoming uncomfortable. These lighter-weight cameras are ideally suited for hand-held operation. Properly held and operated, they can be as steady as hand-held 35s.

Hand-held camera operation is particularly suggested when photographing from different heights and angles. A tripod does not preclude this but does restrict you. It is time-consuming to set up a tripod and change tripod height, even more time-consuming to move tripods around while investigating different camera angles, and often impossible to go down to low angles. As a result, tripod photographers tend to shoot everything from the same, most convenient camera height and never to investigate different possibilities. If you want or have to use a tripod, my suggested approach is to investigate first all the possible angles, lenses, and lens settings before placing the camera on the tripod. Move around the subject with a hand-held camera; view the scene from every angle, from different distances, and through different lenses; go down on the ground and view it from below; go as high as possible and look down. The tripod is not set up until you have thoroughly exhausted all possibilities and found the most effective camera position.

Hand-held Photography

Most medium format cameras can be used hand held down to the same slow shutter speeds that are acceptable on 35 mm cameras. Grips and handles are available for many cameras. It is worthwhile investigating and actually trying out these accessories under specific shooting conditions. Many photographers would never use a medium format camera without them, and others feel more comfortable with their hands on the camera body. A grip or handle does not necessarily improve camera steadiness; it may make camera holding more convenient and certainly allows more convenient camera carrying. Whether to use a grip is a personal decision.

Manufacturers usually suggest a specific way of holding the camera that works fine in most cases and with normal lenses. Do not feel that you have to follow the instruction manual for holding your camera. If you find a better way for some or all shots, use it. Frequently with telephoto lenses, you may hold the camera completely differently than for shorter lenses. A common practice is to place one hand around the lens barrel rather than both hands on the body.

Try different methods of holding the camera until you find the way that suits you. However you hold the camera, however, you need a firm foundation. Start by standing with your feet apart. Press your elbows into your body for additional bracing. Hold the camera with both hands and press it toward your face or chest. These are the most important support points. To hold something steady, you need two forces opposing each other: one pushing one way and the other the opposite way. The direction

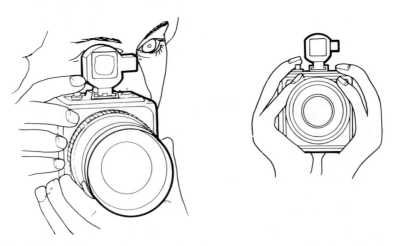

Cameras can be held in many ways. The manufacturer's suggested method works well in most cases, at least with normal lenses. With some cameras, both hands surrounding the camera body works well. With long lenses, it is frequently better to use one hand to steady the lens.

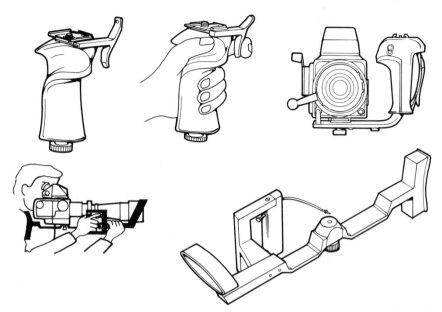

The shape and design of the medium format camera and personal preference determine whether to hold the camera with the hands directly on the camera body or with different types of grips or brackets.

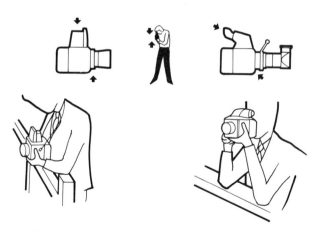

Best camera steadiness is obtained when two forces work against each other, such as the eye pressing the camera down or forward and the hand pressing it in the opposite direction. With the waist-level finder, the hands press the camera up, and the eye pushes it down. With prism finders, the hands push the camera back toward the face, and the eye pushes it forward. Always look for natural supports for the camera or your body.

Regardless of the finder used, you can obtain maximum camera steadiness by pressing the viewfinder eyepiece firmly against your eye. The eyepiece is the most important support for steadiness.

of the action depends on the viewfinder. With a waist-level finder, pull the camera up and push it down with your face, With a 90° or 45° view-finder, pull the camera diagonally up.

When shutter speeds become too long for steady hand-held photog-raphy, some kind of support is necessary. Before rushing for a mechanical camera support, investigate other methods of holding, such as leaning the body, head, or camera against a wall, post, or tree or resting the camera or your elbows on a suitable surface. Rather than placing the camera directly on the surface, try a beanbag, which shapes itself to the contours of the surface and camera, making it more difficult to move the camera. For low camera angles, lie on the ground and use your elbows as a support.

Holding the camera in the hand complicates communication with your subject. A tripod-mounted camera leaves you free to direct the people being photographed because your eye need not be glued to the viewfinder.

Tripods

Steadiness is the main but not the only reason for using a tripod. A mounted camera also leaves you free to move around and allows you to communicate more directly with your subjects. This is especially true with a motor drive. Once you have lined up a shot, you no longer need to look on the ground glass; you can look directly at the people and communicate with them. With a hand-held camera in front of your face, you lose contact with your subject; your hands are tied up and you actually talk into the camera, not to your subject.

CAMERA STEADINESS

Tripods and cable releases are excellent accessories for camera steadiness, but using either or even both is no assurance for best picture sharpness.

Two types of camera motion cause unsharpness: (1) motion or vibrations produced by the camera mechanism (2) and motion produced by the photographer. Motion produced by the photographer may be caused by not holding the camera steady in hand-held photography or by jarring the release, which can happen with hand-held or tripod-mounted cameras. Minimize this danger by depressing the release slowly and gently so you hardly know when the shutter clicks. With a tripod-mounted camera, use a cable release. It serves as a flexible link between you and the camera, absorbing whatever shake your finger might produce. A cable release is recommended whenever a camera support is used. It serves no purpose in hand-held photography.

Let us investigate the motion produced by the camera itself. Depressing the release on any SLR camera brings various camera functions into motion. The diaphragm closes down; the mirror lifts up; the shutter opens and closes. All camera manufacturers try to dampen these mechanical actions as much as possible, but they still can produce vibrations. These vibrations do not seem to affect picture sharpness in hand-held

When exposure times exceed 1 sec, the body and hands should not be in contact with the camera; a cable release should be used. For shorter times, steady the camera by pressing it firmly toward the ground with the hands and face.

photography; the body seems to absorb the effect. They do affect sharpness when the camera is mounted on a tripod or stand.

A camera on top of a heavy studio tripod is probably steady. On a lighter-weight tripod, the kind most often used on location, the tripod does not eliminate this camera-produced motion, especially when the center elevator is extended more than a few inches. The camera actually sits on a single post rather than a three-legged extension. It is prone to vibrate, as you can easily see when you tap the camera. A cable release does not in any way reduce these vibrations; in fact, camera motion is more likely eliminated by not using the cable. Hold the camera as firmly as you do in hand-held work. Lay your own weight on top of the camera, pressing the tripod and camera to the ground. Using this approach, which may be opposite from what you have been told, allows you to use light-weight tripods without suffering image unsharpness. This approach, however, works only with exposure times up to 1/2 or 1 sec. It does not apply for time exposures because you will not be able to keep your body steady long enough.

MIRROR LOCKUP

Most motions in an SLR camera are produced by the mirror and some by the lens aperture and shutter. Therefore it is logical to perform as many of these motion-producing functions as possible before the exposure is made. The camera feature that does this is the prerelease or mirror lock-up.

When the prerelease is depressed, the mirror lifts up, and all the other functions that need to be done before the shutter can make the exposure are performed. Now you can wait a second or two to let the camera settle down before you push the release.

The prerelease or mirror lockup is one of the most important features of an SLR camera. Do not buy an SLR that does not have it, and use it whenever you work from a tripod or camera stand. Use it also when making long time exposures with a cable release and on a motor-driven camera.

A prerelease or mirror lockup can serve another purpose: eliminating the time delay caused by lifting the mirror out of the way before the film can be exposed. This delay is short but nevertheless exists on SLR cameras. With the camera prereleased, the exposure is made the instant the release is depressed. In a lens shutter camera, the mirror lockup is likely to eliminate all possibilities for camera motion because the opening and closing of a lens shutter is extremely smooth. This is not necessarily the case on a focal plane shutter type. The abrupt stopping of the shutter curtain can cause vibration, and the first curtain in a modern camera stops while part of the film area is still being exposed, not afterward as often said. The second curtain stops afterward.

TRIPOD USE

Selecting a Tripod

Maximum camera steadiness would call for the largest, heaviest studio tripod mode, but tripods are taken in the field, so there must be a compromise between steadiness and portability.

A medium format camera does not necessarily require heavier gear than 35s. A relatively lightweight model can provide excellent steadiness if tripod and camera are used properly. Indeed more weight on top of the tripod increases steadiness. With long lenses, tripod size must be more seriously considered.

Besides being a solid stand, a tripod must be designed for fast, convenient operation so that working with it is a pleasure rather than a nuisance. The points that I recommend you look for are, in order of importance: steadiness; convenience of viewing and operating the camera; tripod head locks strong enough to hold any combination of equipment in all positions; ease of setting up; quick camera mounting and release; convenient adjustment of camera height and angle; portability; and the possibility of changing lenses and film magazine without having to remove the camera.

All tripods are made for what could be called normal shooting heights (5–6 ft). For photography from lower levels, some tripods are made so the legs can be spread beyond their normal position. Other tripods allow attachment of the camera to the bottom of the center post, or the centerpost can be inserted upside down so the camera is between the legs.

Center Post

The most solid, vibration-free camera support is obtained when the camera sits directly on top of three legs, not on top of a single post. From this

The steadiest position for a camera and tripod combination is when the camera rests directly on the three legs of the tripod and the center post is not extended. The center post should be used only for minor height adjustments; when extended too far, it is susceptible to vibration.

A

B

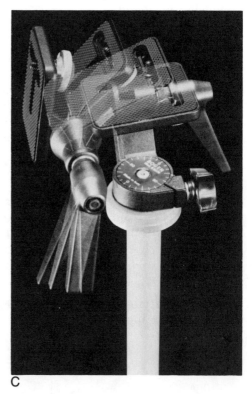

C

The tripod head used with a still camera should tilt forward as well as sideways. The two movements can be separate, controlled by separate locking levers (A) or a ball head that moves in all directions (B). The side tilt (C) is helpful for leveling the camera and turning the camera for vertical pictures. Courtesy Bogen Photo Corp.

point of view, a tripod without an elevating extension is best. The center post reduces camera steadiness when raised extensively and may nullify completely the advantage of a heavy tripod with good leg construction. On the other hand, an elevating extension is convenient for lowering or raising the camera, so try to compromise. Never consider the center post as part of the tripod height. Raise the tripod as high as possible or necessary with the three legs. Use the center post only for minor adjustments in the camera height.

Head

The tripod head must hold the camera without using excessive force on the locking levers, not only in a horizontal position but when tilted up or down with any of the lenses and accessories normally used. A head that allows the camera to be tilted up and down as well as 90° sideways for leveling without having to readjust the legs is preferred. The platform of the head should be large enough to hold the camera so it does not easily move when the camera controls are operated or when the film is advanced. Neither the platform nor any other part of the tripod must interfere with camera operation.

Coupling

Most tripods hold the camera on the platform by means of a screw from underneath the platform. Attaching and removing the camera can be inconvenient and time-consuming. The locking screw is not easy to reach and practically impossible to operate with gloves. Locking screws of this type can also be dangerous because they are made long to accept any type of camera. They can be forced into the camera body, causing damage to the inside of the camera. These problems are eliminated with a tripod coupling, which allows instant attachment and removal of the camera. The coupling is attached to the tripod and left there, becoming part of the tripod. The camera slides into the adapter plate, where it may be locked in some way. For removal, the camera slides right out.

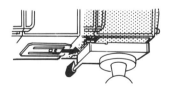

A tripod quick coupling permanently attached to the tripod head can save time when setting up a tripod shot. Slide the camera onto the accessory and lock it in place by turning the lever.

Screws

There are two standard types of tripod screw: the small so-called American and the larger European type. Practically all 35 mm and medium format cameras have the American type. But medium format cameras should have the larger type because it allows more solid fastening without worrying about wearing out the threads on the tripod or camera. Better professional tripods come either with both types or a reversible type. For other tripod types, the larger screw may be available.

OTHER CAMERA SUPPORTS

Tripods are not the only means of steadying a camera.

Camera clamps can be attached to almost anything: doors, tables, trees, window panes, railings, chairs. Although they are basically made for 35 mm cameras, they can be used with the medium format. To eliminate all possibility of camera-induced motion when the exposure time does not exceed 1 sec, hold the clamp-mounted camera with both hands with your eye pressed firmly against the camera body.

Table tripods are miniature tripods that hold the camera a few inches above the supporting surface. They can be placed on tables, cars, rocks, and so forth. Placed on the ground, they are good accessories for low angle photography, especially of flowers and other nature subjects. Maximum camera steadiness at shutter speeds less than 1 sec depends on how the camera is held.

Monopods

Excellent camera steadiness can be obtained with a *monopod*, which is easier to carry and quicker to set up than a tripod. A monopod may not guarantee sharp images at 1 sec but it is possible to obtain sharp results

The steadiest position for a monopod is when it forms the third leg of a tripod with the photographer's two legs, and the camera is pushed firmly against the face. In this position, the two forces oppose each other, which is not the case when the monopod is vertical.

down to 1/4 sec. Considering its convenience in carrying, serving as a walking stick during a hike, and the short time required to set up, it is well worth considering. Most photographers keep the monopod straight up, although that is not the best solution for camera steadiness. The monopod is free to move sideways in all directions. It is better to move its foot 2 or 3 ft forward and tilt it toward you; in this way, it forms the third leg of a tripod, with your own legs as the other two. You can obtain a steady grip with your eye pressed against the viewfinder, elbows pressed against your body, and either both hands on the camera or one hand on the camera and the other on top of the monopod. Pull the camera and monopod toward your face and press the outfit forward into the ground with your viewing eye. Direct releasing without a cable is preferable.

CHAPTER 15

Special medium format capabilities

The medium format has established itself as a well-liked film size for professionals. Photographers are trying to use these cameras for more and more of their work, including applications where view cameras have been the standard. As a result, these cameras have been made more adaptable through special accessories and built-in features.

BUILT-IN BELLOWS

Bellows, long popular accessories for close-up photography, are built into some medium format cameras. Instead of the lens being mounted into the camera body, it goes on a board that is coupled to the camera with a bellows. The built-in bellows is not just for close-up photography; it becomes the focusing mechanism for all photography from infinity down to a certain close focusing limit. The minimum focusing distance is considerably closer with all lenses than equivalent lenses mounted on a camera body. This can be a great advantage not only in close-up photography but when working with longer lenses in almost any other field of photography.

Lenses are interchangeable just as on the camera body. The minimum area coverage and the magnification depend on the focusing range of the lens. A built-in bellows does not extend as far as a bellows accessory but can still provide all the needed close-up possibilities with shorter focal length lenses. On the other hand, since it is part of the camera, it is always there, ready to be used, and does not need to be removed for shooting at long distances. Working with such a camera is somewhat like working with a view camera. All focusing is done by extending the bellows more or less. Such cameras tend to be somewhat larger but still portable. The camera-lens connection is not as rigid, thus requiring somewhat more careful handling and operation so the optical relationship is not disturbed.

EXTENDED DEPTH-OF-FIELD CONTROL

Since a bellows is a flexible camera-lens connection, it offers the camera designer the possibility of building in tilt capabilities that otherwise are limited to view cameras. The lens board is connected to the camera body in such a way that it can be tilted up or down almost 10°—not as much as a view camera but more than enough for extended depth-of-field control, which is what it is used for.

This tilt control is based on what is known as the Scheimpflug principle. Depth of field is normally determined only by lens aperture and area covered. With an inclined subject plane, lens tilt can be used to increase the depth remarkably.

An inclined plane exists when the subjects at the bottom of the picture are much closer than those on top, or vice-versa, or the subjects on the left side are much closer than those on the right, or vice-versa. This can happen when a camera is tilted upward to photograph a building from top to bottom, when tilted downward to photograph objects laid out on a table (a dinner arrangement), when photographing a row of houses

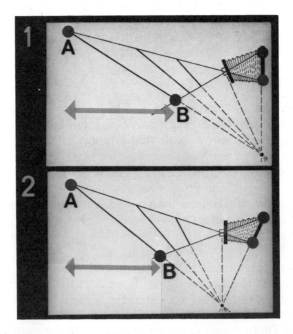

A lens photographing a subject from an oblique angle produces the maximum depth of field when a line extended from the lens meets at the same point as the two lines extended from the film plane and the subject. This control can be done with the lens board (1) or the film holder (2). A bellows between camera body and lens on some medium format cameras allows a limited amount of lens tilt for increased depth of field.

along one side of a street, or when photographing a banquet hall from a somewhat higher camera angle. The subjects on an inclined plane will be recorded on an inclined image plane. The subjects on one side that will be farther away will be recorded closer to the lens than those on the other side. If the lens is focused for one side, the other will be out of focus. On a view camera, the film plane could be tilted so that the images on both sides fall on the film plane and thus are sharp at the same time.

The same kind of control can be obtained by tilting the lens. You can determine on a piece of paper exactly how much the lens needs to be tilted. Maximum depth of field is achieved when the lens is tilted so that a line extended from the plane of the lens meets at the common point of a line extended from the film plane and a line drawn through the average plane of the subject. The three lines meeting at one point conform to the Scheimpflug principle. Tilting the lens changes only depth of field. It does not correct verticals. If the lens tilting is only in one direction (for example, up and down), you can turn the camera and have the same control when more depth of field is necessary from left to right, or vice-versa.

When a lens is tilted, the film plane is no longer in the center of its optical axis. The lens therefore must have the additional covering power to record off-center images with satisfactory quality and without objectionable loss of light.

Although the proper lens tilt can be determined accurately on paper, in actual photography it is done visually. With the camera set up, tilt the lens following imaginary subject and film plane lines. Then check the image on the ground glass and make the fine adjustment until best sharpness exists from top to bottom or sideways.

Lens tilt not only allows greater depth of field without stopping down the lens excessively, thus allowing shorter shutter speeds, but allows photography, especially at closer distances, where even the smallest lens aperture could not provide the necessary range of sharpness.

MEDIUM FORMAT VIEW CAMERA

Medium format photography can be combined with view cameras. The most common way to combine the two is by means of a roll film adapter made by the view camera manufacturer. The adapter attaches to the rear of the camera instead of a sheetfilm holder. The image is focused on the view camera's ground glass before the roll film holder is attached. A mask shows the area covered on the smaller medium format film. The camera is operated in the usual fashion, using the shutter in the view camera lens.

Another solution offered by some view camera manufacturers is by means of a camera adapter board. The board goes in place of the ground-glass back and has an adapter that fits the lens mount of the camera. The camera body is attached to the rear of the view camera. Viewing and

A medium format camera body with film magazine can also be attached to the rear of a view camera. It combines swing and tilt capability with the use of roll film. You can use the shutter in the view camera lens or the focal plane shutter if the camera has one.

focusing are on the ground glass of the medium format camera. If the camera has interchangeable film magazines, any magazine can be used. The film is advanced with the regular winding knob or the camera's motor-drive. With a focal plane shutter camera, you can use the shutter in the camera after opening the view camera lens shutter or use the shutter in the view camera lens after the focal plane shutter is opened. The latter gives flash synchronization at all shutter speeds. With a lens shutter medium format camera, open the rear curtain and then make the exposure with the shutter in the view camera lens. Combining the medium format with a view camera provides the advantages of the smaller medium format negative or transparency and lower cost while maintaining all the view camera capabilities. It allows you to use the swings and tilts to produce a 2 1/4 in. square or 4 1/2 × 6 cm transparency ready for projection.

The bellows offers excellent close-up possibilities and most important, you can use all the view camera controls, swings, and tilts. Shooting may be somewhat faster because advancing the film in a roll film adapter is faster and more convenient than changing the sheetfilm holder. Attaching a camera with an electric film advance actually results in a motor-driven view camera.

To appreciate the value of producing a medium format image on a view camera, we must understand how the various view camera controls are used to improve an image. Extending the bellows allows close focusing

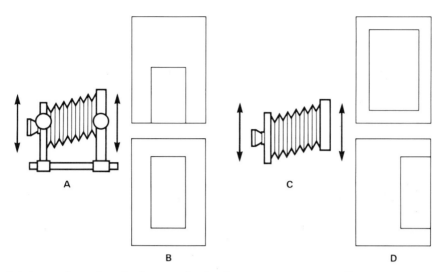

Raising or lowering the front or back of a view camera (A) allows moving the image on the ground glass up or down while maintaining parallel lines (B). A lateral shift of the front or back (C) does the same but in a horizontal plane (D).

without the need of attaching accessories. Tilting the lens board moves the plane of sharp focus so it coincides with the principal plane of the subject. It is used to control depth of field based on the Scheimpflug principle. The lens board can be tilted in the horizontal or vertical plane. The tilting back can be used for the same purpose instead of the front. Tilting the lens, however, is preferable.

The rising or falling front allows moving the image on the ground glass up or down without having to tilt the camera. The rising or falling back does the same, and the two actions can be combined.

The front or rear horizontal shift (swing) allows moving the image sideways without having to turn the camera.

The tilting front and back is used mostly to make the film plane parallel to the subject plane when the camera is tilted up or down. It eliminates the keystone effect, which happens when the camera is tilted up or down, and straightens out the verticals. Vertical lines are straight and parallel whenever the film plane is parallel to the subject—the building, for instance.

The horizontal swing is used like the tilting front and back but in the horizontal plane. A wall can be photographed with straight horizontals, for example, even though the camera is at an angle to the wall. A perspective control system also has been introduced in a 2 1/4 in. slide projector. The controls in the lens and illuminator system allow for moving the projected image up and down on the screen without tilting the projector. The slide thus remains parallel to the screen, eliminating the keystone effect.

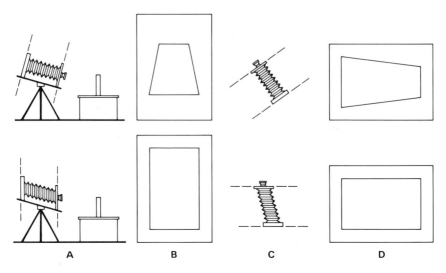

Tilting the front and/or back (A) allows straightening the vertical plane when the camera is tilted (C). Swinging the front or back (C) changes converging horizontal lines into parallel lines when the camera is photographing the subject from an oblique angle (D).

PERSPECTIVE CONTROL LENS

View cameras provide medium format photography with image control but only by sacrificing portability. Perspective control (PC) lenses attached to a regular medium format camera combine the two. PC lenses have been available for 35 mm cameras for some time. They are now entering the medium format field and still are somewhat difficult to find. A PC lens has the standard controls, focusing and diaphragm ring, and shutter speeds if equipped with a shutter. It can be used for ordinary photography just like any other lens of the same focal length.

The lens mount is constructed so part of the lens can be moved up or down parallel to the film plane. This allows the same possibilities as a rising and falling front: moving the image on the film plane without tilting the camera. You can photograph a tall building without tilting the camera. The entire control is built into the lens mount, an elaborate design requiring great precision in manufacturing.

With the camera turned sideways, the same perspective control is possible on a horizontal plane. A square cabinet remains square even when photographed at an angle from a corner.

The control limits in the lens are undoubtedly less than those in a view camera but undoubtedly more than sufficient for most applications.

A PC lens must be optically designed to cover a much larger area than the medium format negative. It must actually be designed for a larger negative size. If this were not the case, image sharpness and illumination in the camera would drop off drastically when the PC control is used. This consideration is another reason for the high cost of a high-quality PC lens. If you use the controls often enough, the price is justified. You can do most work with a compact camera, perhaps even hand held, where otherwise studio equipment would be necessary.

A PC lens may have a built-in tilt control that allows depth-of-field control based on the Scheimpflug principle. With the camera turned sideways, the same control exists; a wall can be in focus from close to far even when photographed from an angle. This control is built into the lens mount.

CHAPTER 16

Close-up photography

LENSES

Macrolenses (lenses that focus from infinity down to inches), which have become very popular in 35 mm, do not exist for medium format cameras. The longer focal lengths of the medium format camera require longer focusing travel, making macrolens mounts difficult to design and manufacture. Some medium format cameras have built-in bellows that serve the same purpose.

Most or all close-up work can be done by extending the bellows to the proper length. No special instructions for close-up photography are necessary with such a camera except what is in the camera's instructional manual. If the bellows extension is not long enough for particular purposes, the same close-up accessories described for cameras without bellows can be used.

If close-up photography is a prime objective, the medium format camera with bellows deserves serious consideration, provided the other features meet your requirements. The same close-up possibilities can be obtained on other medium format SLR cameras with interchangeable lenses and accessories.

Close-up accessories are easy to use and do not complicate operations or require calculations. The same type of accessories are available for all medium format SLR systems. The choice of accessory depends on the size of the area to be covered and the focal length of the lens.

Choice of Lenses

The lenses behave exactly as they do at longer distances.

The camera-to-subject distance determines the perspective. Different focal length lenses cover different background areas even if the main subject is recorded at an identical size. Longer focal length lenses blur backgrounds more than shorter ones. Different focal length lenses can cover the same area from different distances.

For working on a copy stand, a shorter lens is preferable or necessary to keep the camera on the steadier lower end of the camera post, while some subjects, such as surgery, timid insects, or dangerous activities like welding, call for a longer shooting distance and thus a longer focal length lens.

As far as focal length is concerned, all lenses are usable, but lenses standard and longer (from 70 mm up on medium format cameras) are likely to produce better image quality. Wide angle lenses on SLR cameras are of the retrofocus type. They are good at long distances but suffer a loss of quality at close distances even without accessories. Used even closer with accessories, the loss is even greater. The retrofocus types with floating lens element are better than the ordinary type. If the wide angle, on the other hand, is the only lens that produces the desired results, use it. I have taken close-ups of flowers with a 30 mm fish-eye combined with a short extension tube. Closing down the aperture can compensate partially or completely for the loss of quality.

REVERSING LENSES

Close-up pictures are often taken with the front of the lens toward the film and the rear toward the subject, just the opposite from the way it is usually positioned. This is because when the image is larger than the object, many lenses work better that way.

Normally the subject is much farther from the lens than is the film. The closer you photograph, the shorter the subject distance and the longer the image distance, until at life-sized magnification they are equal. Image distances are longer than subject distances when the magnification becomes greater than $1\times$, and this is the only time when reversing lenses can improve the image. Whether this is necessary or even advisable, however, also depends on the design of the lens. Do not reverse the lenses unless the manufacturer instructs you to do so.

MAGNIFICATION

Everything in close-up photography revolves around magnification. Magnification indicates how much larger (or smaller) a subject is recorded on the film; it is the ratio in size between the actual subject and its image recorded on the film. You can measure the image on the focusing screen after sliding off the viewfinder. A more practical way is to base it on the area coverage. We know the dimension of the film format—55 mm for both sides of the 2 1/4 in. square or the longer side of 4 1/4 × 6 cm, or

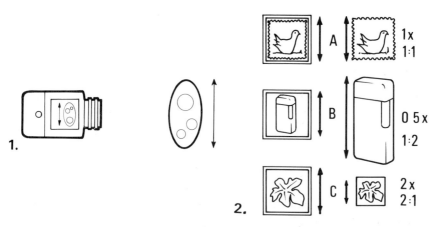

1.

2.

Magnification is the relationship between the size of the actual subject and the size of its image as recorded on the film or seen on the ground-glass screen of the camera *(1)*. Because the size of the subject is usually known in close-up photography, magnification can be determined quickly by relating the subject size to negative size *(2)*. For example, if the subject is about the same size as the negative, there is 1:1 magnification *(A)*; when the subject is twice as large *(B)*, there is 0.5 or 1:2 magnification; and when the negative is filled with a small subject half as large as the negative *(C)*, there is 2 times or 2:1 magnification.

40 mm for super slides and the shorter side of 4 1/2 × 6 cm. You can calculate magnification by dividing the negative side into the width or length of the area covered. If you can cover an area 220 mm wide, the magnification is 55 ÷ 220 = 0.25 or 1:4.

Life-sized or 1:1 magnification exists when the area that we cover is equal to the film format—55 × 55 mm for the 2 1/4 in. square. It is more than life sized when a smaller area than the format is covered—for instance, when filling the 2 1/4 in. negative with a small 27 mm square area, the magnification is 55 ÷ 27 = 2 or 2:1.

PROXAR OR CLOSE-UP LENSES

Proxar or close-up lenses are positive lenses that are mounted in front of the camera lens like a filter and should be as near the front element as possible. Proxars can be used with almost any focal length lens and also with zoom lenses. They allow closer focusing and must be removed for shooting long shots. Most manufacturers indicate the strength of their close-up lenses in diopter power like eyeglass lenses; others engrave the focal length. Diopter is just another way of expressing the focal length of a lens. Diopter and meters are converted as follows:

$$\text{diopter} = \frac{1 \text{ m}}{\text{focal length}}$$

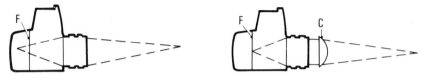

A subject that is closer to the lens than the minimum focusing distance of the lens forms its image behind the film plane (F). The addition of a Proxar lens (C) can bring the image onto the film plane.

$$\text{focal length} = \frac{1 \text{ m}}{\text{diopter}}.$$

Diopter strength is the focal length in meters divided into 1 m so 1 diopter equals a 1 m focal length.

The diopter power or focal length determines the subject distance at which the lens produces sharp images. With the lens on the camera set at infinity, a close-up lens always produces a sharp image when the subject distance, measured from the close-up lens, is equal to the focal length of the close-up lens.

The following distances thus apply:

Focal Length of Close-up Lens	Diopter Power	Subject Distance*	
2 m	+0.5	79 in.	2 m
1 m	+1	39½ in.	1 m
0.5 m	+2	19¾ in.	0.5 m
0.33 m	+3	13 in.	0.33 m
0.25 m	+4	10 in.	0.25 m

*Subject distances in this case are measured from the close-up lens, not from the film plane.

Although these distances apply for infinity setting on all lenses, the focusing ring on the lens need not be at infinity when taking the picture. You can use the focusing ring as you normally do for fine focusing and for shooting at closer distances.

Since adding a close-up lens means adding a lens element to a well-

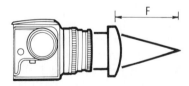

With the lens on the camera set to infinity, the correct subject distance measured from the Proxar lens is always equal to the focal length (F) of the Proxar lens.

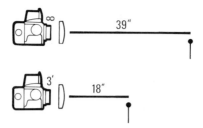

It is possible to photograph closer subjects by setting the camera lens to a closer distance. For example, with a camera lens set to infinity and a 1 diopter (1 m) close-up lens, the subject would be 1 m (39 in.) away from the camera; with the same close-up lens but with the 80 mm camera lens set to 3 ft, the subject would be 46 cm (18 in.) away.

corrected camera lens, quality on the edges suffers somewhat, depending on the power of the Proxar. Stopping down two to three f stops can restore quality. With lenses up to 0.5 m (+ 2 diopters), the loss of quality is rarely noticeable at the small apertures normally used in close-up work.

You can combine two Proxar lenses. The power of the combination is obtained by adding the two diopter strengths. For example, a + 1 and + 2 close-up lens adds up to a + 3 diopter lens with a focal length of 33 cm (13 in.). The more powerful lens (highest diopter rating, shortest focal length) should be placed closer to the camera lens.

Close-up lenses do not alter the exposure. You can use the lens settings obtained from your normal exposure meter.

Proxars are the easiest of the close-up accessories to use, but they are meant only for low magnification work—when it is necessary to go just a little closer than the focusing range of the lens. Strong close-up lenses (+ 4 to + 10 diopters) could be used for higher magnifications but with an obvious loss of quality.

PARTIAL CLOSE-UP LENSES

The medium format camera can also be used with a close-up lens that does not cover the entire area but only part, usually one-half. These types of lens are referred to as *split field* or *bifocal* lenses. They produce two different planes of focus—one at long distances, one close by. This opens up interesting possibilities: a sharp image of something very close to the camera and at the same time of something far away that could never be bridged by the depth of field.

The camera lens is set for the distance of the far subject. The close-up lens determines the distance of the close subject. This is, for instance, 50 cm (19 3/4 in.) for a + 2 diopter lens with the camera lens set at infinity. Two completely separate images are formed: a close-up image with its depth of field and a distant one with its own depth of field. Anything that is in between is out of focus and looks unnatural if it is obvious. It is therefore important to avoid such obviously blurred areas by careful framing and selection of camera angle. Frame the image so that areas that logically continue from fore to background, such as a field, a street, or a fence, are invisible.

Even if well composed, the images are seldom artistic. They are therefore better considered only in special fields of photography—for instance, when it is necessary to include data such as a number, a name, a time clock, a date, a title, or an instrument dial in the negative or transparency. The board with the data is photographed through the close-up lens and the rest of the image through the clear area. Even small data can be shown on the image in a large way if a strong close-up lens is used. Lighting for both must be equal so both are properly exposed on the film.

EXTENSION TUBES AND BELLOWS

Extension tubes and bellows are physically different but serve the same purpose in close-up photography. Both are mounted between camera and lens for the purpose of being able to move the lens farther away from the film plane. They are therefore an extension of the focusing ring. There are no additional optical components, just an increase in the lens-to-film distance. The longer is the tube or bellows with any particular focal length lens, the closer you can photograph and consequently the higher is the magnification.

The same extension tube or extension on the bellows gives different magnification with different focal length lenses: a higher magnification with shorter lenses, a lower magnification with longer ones. The necessary extension length with various lenses can be found on the charts included

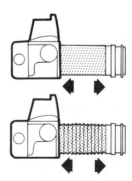

Extension tubes and bellows serve the same purpose: they move the lens farther away from the film plane. An extension tube and a bellows extended to the same length produce the same magnification and image.

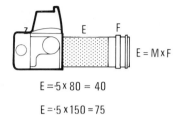

$$E = M \times F$$

$$E = \cdot 5 \times 80 = 40$$

$$E = \cdot 5 \times 150 = 75$$

The necessary length of an extension tube or bellows for a particular magnification can be determined easily from the formula $E = M \times F$, where E is the length of the tube or bellows, M the magnification, and F the focal length of the lens.

with the accessories. You can also determine the requirements from the following formula:

length of extension = focal length of lens × magnification.

For example, the extension necessary to obtain 0.5 times magnification with an 80 mm lens is 80 × 0.5 = 40 mm; and with a 120 mm lens, 120 × 0.5 = 60 mm. Knowing this relationship eliminates time-consuming experimenting, moving cameras, and adding and changing lenses and accessories to find out what area is covered.

From the same formula, you can determine the magnification:

$$\text{magnification} = \frac{\text{length of extension}}{\text{focal length of lens}}$$

With the lens set away from its infinity position, the distance the lens has been moved forward should be added to the length of the extension for accurate calculations. The formulas above are not scientifically accurate since they depend on the design of the lens, but they are sufficiently accurate for photographic purposes.

For high magnifications, bellows should be considered. To get the same extension, several tubes are necessary. For lower magnification, either accessory serves the purpose. Tubes are less expensive, but because they are fixed in length, two or three tubes may be necessary to cover a wide range of magnifications. Tubes are small and lightweight so even two or three are easy to carry. The bellows gives a wide choice and, more valuable, provides a convenient way of changing subject and image distance. Most good bellows have two adjusting knobs. Turning one moves the entire rig—camera, bellows, and lens—so the subject distance (the distance between lens and subject) changes. Turning the other mainly moves the camera. It changes the image distance (the distance between lens and film plane) and eliminates a constant moving of a tripod. Bellows usually also are made to hold accessories like a slide copying device.

Extension tubes can usually be added to the front of the bellows for longer extension. Modern bellows have coupling shafts so the lens mech-

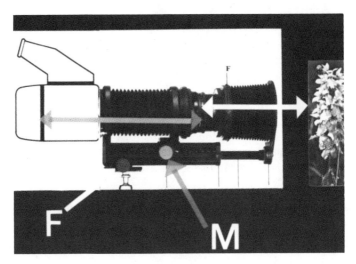

A good bellows offers the advantage of two controls. One *(F)* moves the entire camera-lens combination and thus changes the subject distance. The other *(M)* moves the film plane farther from the lens and thus changes the image distance.

anism is coupled to the camera. The diaphragm closes down automatically, and with shutter lenses, the shutter operates as it does without the bellows. You thus maintain the automatic operation. Older bellows required a double cable release, with one end of the release going into the lens and the other in the camera. Properly adjusted, it works fine. With shutter lenses, however, the shutter cocking after the picture is a separate operation.

PHOTOGRAPHING SUBJECTS LIFE SIZED

A subject is recorded life sized, in 1:1 magnification, when the area coverage of the subject is equal to the film format; the length of the extension needed is equal to the focal length of the lens (80 mm with an 80 mm lens, for example).

Adding an extension equal to focal length means increasing the lens-to-film distance (the image distance) to twice the focal length of the lens. Optical principles also tell us that 1:1 magnification is obtained when image distance equals subject distance. So the lens-to-subject distance is also twice the focal length of the lens and, adding it up, the subject-to-film distance is always equal to four times the focal length of the lens: 320 mm with 80 mm lens and 480 mm with 120 mm.

DEPTH OF FIELD

Depth of field in close-up photography is determined only by the area coverage (magnification) and the aperture (*f* stop) of the lens; not even

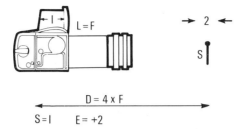

Life-sized magnification is always obtained when the length of the extension tube or bellows, L, is equal to the focal length, F, of the lens (L = F). The distance from the subject to the film plane, D, is equal to four times the focal length (D = 4 × F). The exposure increase, E, is always two f stops. The depth of field at f11 is about 2 mm.

the focal length of the lens influences depth of field. If tubes and bellows seem to produce less depth of field, it is not because of the accessory but because of the higher magnification. Since the area coverage or magnification is usually predetermined, depth of field can be increased or decreased only by opening or closing the aperture. Although depth of field is identical with different lenses, the sharpness beyond the limits of the depth of field falls off rapidly with a longer lens and more gradually with a shorter lens.

DEPTH OF FIELD AT VARIOUS
MAGNIFICATIONS

Magnification	Total Depth of Field in mm at f11*	
	A	B
0.1×	100	50
0.2×	30	15
0.3×	15	7
0.5×	6	3
0.8×	3	1½
1×	2	1
1.2×	1.5	0.7
1.5×	1	0.5
2×	0.8	0.4
3×	0.4	0.2

*About half of the depth of field is in front and half behind the set distance.
A: Circle of confusion 0.06 mm (1/400 in.).
B: Circle of confusion 0.03 mm (1/800 in.).

To determine the depth of field at other apertures, keep in mind that when you close the aperture two stops, the depth of field becomes about twice as large; by opening the aperture two stops, depth of field is cut down to about half.

The above figures clearly indicate the limited depth of field in close-up photography and stress the importance of extreme accuracy in focusing.

EXPOSURE

Correct exposure in close-up photography is no different from photography at long distances, but you ensure that the meter reading is taken off the small area recorded on the film, sometimes even off a smaller main subject within the area. A built-in meter does this and is therefore a great help. With a separate meter, it is often not so easy to hold the meter close enough to the subject without shading the subject or bumping into the camera. I suggest, therefore, that you consider a gray card reading, which gives a large area for a reflected meter reading and reflects the proper amount of light for correct exposure. The gray card is a good aid with all reflected meters, even in combination with a built-in meter.

A built-in meter has another advantage when close-up accessories are used: the meter reading is made through the accessory, so there is no need to consider extension factors. Whatever the meter says should be correct regardless of what lens and close-up accessories are used.

When extension tubes or bellows are used and the meter reading is made with a separate meter, the so-called exposure factor must be considered. This is necessary as the tubes and bellows move the lens farther

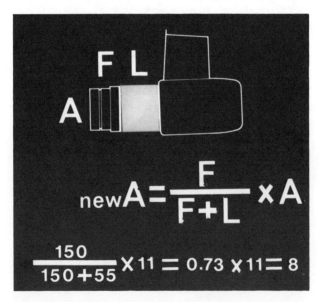

A formula to determine the correct aperture with a tube or bellows (new A) is shown here. F is the focal length of the lens, L the length of the tube or bellows, and A the aperture indicated on a separate light meter.

from the film plane and the light is spread over a larger area, with consequently less light reaching the film.

The exposure increase is based mainly on the ratio between focal length of lens and length of extension. Consequently, the increase can also be determined from a simple chart, as shown below, which applies to any camera. This chart is helpful when the close-up tables are not available.

EXPOSURE INCREASES

Extension ÷ focal length	Increase in Exposure in f Stops or EVs
⅒ to ⅕	½
¼ to ⅓	1
½	1½
1	2
1½	2½
2	3

For example, a 120 mm lens with bellows extension of 180 mm will need an increase in exposure of 2 1/2 f stops or 2 1/2 EV (180 ÷ 120 = 1 1/2).

THE CAMERA

The SLR concept with its accurate framing and focusing makes close-up photography easy. It eliminates parallax and provides a good focusing method—and focusing is critical to close-up work.

A motor-driven camera is even better. The motor-driven film advance eliminates the danger of moving the camera, which often happens when film must be advanced manually. In close-up photography, even a slight movement of the camera can be very inconvenient because it may require

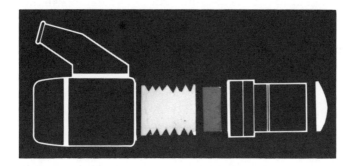

Close-up accessories can be combined. A Proxar in front of the lens can be added to a tube and bellows.

time-consuming resetting or refocusing. A tripod is recommended for most close-up work. The mirror lock must be used.

FOCUSING

In close-up photography, focusing is frequently made easier by moving the camera back and forth rather than turning the focusing ring until the subject is sharp on the ground glass. Try it especially with a hand-held camera. You can hold the camera with both hands in the most convenient fashion rather than holding the camera with one hand and using the other for operating the lens.

SLIDE COPYING

There can be many reasons why you may like to have a duplicate of a slide. The most important one that comes to mind is to protect against loss or damage to the original. A second reason is perhaps to have a duplicate in another size, perhaps a superslide from a 2 1/4 in. original. A third reason is to improve the original technically. A slightly under-exposed or overexposed slide can be copied lighter or darker to end up with a properly exposed duplicate. This correction works better with underexposed slides than overexposed ones, which lack color in the high-lights. Improvements in the color rendition can be made by placing color balance filters over the lens when the duplicate is made.

You can improve slides artistically by cropping or composing the duplicate differently from the original, as in enlarging negatives. Slide duplicating offers almost unlimited creative possibilities, such as radical changes in colors, changing colors over part of the slide by partial filtering, producing title slides, producing double and multiple exposures by duplicating two or more slides together.

Instead of producing a slide from a slide, you can make a black-and-white or color negative from the slide. The only difference in the procedure is the film loaded in the camera.

All this work can be done in laboratories, and for quantity production this is probably best. Best quality is obtained when the slide, illuminated by transmitted light, is photographed directly.

Slide Copying Setup

For extensive slide duplicating or the utmost in quality and versatility, use a special slide duplicating unit and a complete copying stand with light source and slide holder. All you need to do is attach the camera. Check to be sure the unit will take your camera. Some are made for 35 mm only or for 35 mm and small medium format cameras. The light source may be flash or tungsten or both. If duplicating quality is critical, check whether the unit allows flashing the film, a good way to cut contrast.

For occasional duping the most reliable and easiest-to-use slide duplicating setup is obtained when camera, lens, and slide holder are combined into one unit, which consists of a bellows, sunshade, and transparency copy holder. The transparency copy holder has a diffusion glass to spread the light evenly over the entire surface, so no additional diffusion device is necessary between light source and slide.

Holding the Transparencies

To maintain sharpness over the entire area, the slide must lay absolutely flat in the slide holder. The original must be free of dust, dirt, fingermarks, and other marks. To maintain contrast, the slide must be masked so no extraneous light reaches the lens.

If necessary, attach the slide to a cardboard frame that covers the entire diffusion glass area. The cardboard with slide attached is then inserted into the transparency copy holder. Glass-mounted $2\frac{1}{4}$ in. square transparencies can be copied in the glass provided the glasses are absolutely clean and newly mounted. (Dust particles are also copied.) The glasses of slides that have been mounted for some time are usually fogged up, reducing the brilliance, and should be removed.

Light Sources

Electronic flash and tungsten lights are recommended light sources. Place tungsten lamps of 3200 K (31 DM) or 3400 K (29 DM) or electronic flash units straight in front of the transparency holder, shining directly on the diffusion glass. The power of the light source and its distance from the slide determine exposure. A flash unit can be placed at any distance because it produces no heat, but I suggest leaving at least about 25 cm (10 in.) between slide and light to ensure even illumination. With flash you need another light source illuminating the slide for framing and focusing. The modeling light in a studio unit is excellent. Tungsten lamps, whether used for photography or for framing and focusing only, are best kept at a distance of 60 cm (2 ft) or more because of the heat.

Films

Daylight color film is used with electronic flash and tungsten film for tungsten lights. Make certain that the color temperature of the light and film match. Slide duplicating films are best for this purpose because their low contrast produces a result close to the original. These films are, however, not easy to find for medium format cameras.

Unless you intend to produce a very large quantity of duplicates, you will have to use regular color slide films. I have found they produce satisfactory copies if the original is of good quality. The best originals are those with a relatively low contrast. if you have a choice of color film, use the one with the lowest contrast.

To avoid an increase in contrast on black-and-white negatives, increase the exposure slightly and reduce the developing time.

Filters

The use of filters when copying slides follows the same rules and suggestions as for original photography. What you photograph is simply an image of the actual subject rather than the subject itself. If you normally use a slightly warming filter like 81A or CR 1.5 with your electronic flash unit, use the same filter for slide duplicating. You might also find after the first test that you prefer an even warmer rendition, so try the 81B or CR 3.

Exposure

Photographing a slide is like photographing the actual subject. Hold a light meter behind the slide so that it measures the picture area as the camera sees it, which is similar to pointing the meter at the actual scene.

A built-in meter is ideal for this purpose. It compensates for the neccessary increase in exposure. The reading on the meter therefore should be correct, and while test exposures should not be necessary, they are nevertheless recommended when copying for the first time. If you have a Polaroid back, use it. You can also use separate reflected light meters, but exposure must be increased due to bellows extension, which amounts to two EV or f stops for life-sized magnification. Set the lens to around f 11 for best results. If you need a long shutter speed, prerelease the camera to avoid any possible shake.

Double and Multiple Exposures

The copying procedure allows two or more slides to be combined into one image. Place the two slides together into the transparency copy holder. If both sides are to be sharp, place them emulsion toward emulsion. If one image is to be unsharp, separate the two original slides with a piece of glass and focus on the one that is to be sharp. Results can be seen and studied on the ground glass at the shooting aperture.

Copying Slides without Special Equipment

Copying slides means nothing more than taking a picture of a slide, so a special camera setup with bellows extension and transparency copy holder is not necessary. You can photograph the slide as you would a close-up picture of a small subject, but mount the transparency on a card with a suitable cutout and arrange for it to be evenly lit.

CHAPTER 17

Copying

Photographs of documents must have edge-to-edge sharpness, good contrast, even exposure over the entire image area, and true colors, if done in color.

CAMERA ALIGNMENT

The basic rule in copying is to square up the camera with the original. This means that the plane of the original and the film plane must be exactly parallel. The lens axis is then at right angles to both. Any deviation leads to a dimensional distortion of the image. This is disturbing even in simple copying work and totally unacceptable for precision copying, in photomechanical reproduction, when making printing plates, and especially in the production of masters for printed circuits.

The frequently used hit-or-miss method of visually examining whether the camera seems to point straight at the copy can never be sufficiently accurate, and better methods must be found. A spirit level on the camera ensures excellent horizontal positioning of the camera. If not built into the camera, it may be available as an accessory. A camera aligned with a spirit level will have the film plane reasonably accurately parallel to an original mounted on a wall, at least in one direction. If the object to be photographed has definite parallel lines—for instance, a picture frame—align the camera as carefully as possible so that the two horizontal lines of the frame are perfectly parallel to the horizontal edges of the viewing screen and the two vertical lines parallel to the vertical edges. The ground-glass screens with engraved vertical and horizontal lines (checked screen) simplify this alignment because the vertical and horizontal lines can be checked along each engraved line.

A simple, accurate, yet uncommon method involves a mirror that is placed on the copy while watching the reflected image. Obtain a small frameless mirror about 5–10 cm (2–4 in.) in size. Place the mirror as accurately as possible in the center of the subject. Set the camera at the correct distance from the subject, and adjust the focus to produce a sharp reflection of the camera. Move the camera in any direction until the mirror is centered on the ground-glass screen and the camera lens is reflected in the center of the mirror. The camera is now reasonably well centered above the copy with the film plane parallel to the copy.

FOCUSING

When camera and copy are aligned parallel to each other, focus the lens as accurately as possible. If the subject does not have fine details for precise focusing, place a substitute focusing target over the copy, such as a piece of paper with very fine detail (fine newsprint).

FILMS

The quality of the reproduction often depends on the brilliance of the copy. Brilliance is the result of contrast, resolving power, and graininess. Because graininess and resolving power are usually directly related, fine grain emulsions are highly recommended. Grain is more objectionable in copying than in photographing other subjects. Usually films of lower sensitivity are preferable because they have better definition and less grain.

If maximum contrast is desired in black and white, developing times should be increased by about 20 percent. For continuous-tone originals, regular black-and-white films of moderate contrast are best. They can also be used for line originals, but high-contrast films are better for this purpose. Technical Pan film rated at 100 ASA and developed in D 19 developer produces beautiful reversed, high contrast copy images. Photograph black copy on white and you obtain clear white copy against a deep black background. The images make beautiful transparencies especially when combined with colored gels in a glass slide mount.

For color images, the same color films are used as for all other color photography: daylight type for electronic flash, tungsten type for quartz lights.

LENSES

Maximum brilliance requires a clean camera lens of high resolving power, accurate focusing, a steady camera, and proper exposure and development. For the corner-to-corner sharpness required in copy work, I suggest closing down two or three stops with any lens.

FILTERS

When photographing in color, filters are necessary only for special effects or when the color temperature of the light source does not match that of the film. When photographing colored originals on black-and-white film, on the other hand, color filters are used to increase or reduce the contrast or to suppress or emphasize certain sections of the orig n al. A yellow filter can be of value when photographing old, yellowed originals because it will lighten the yellow background and thereby increase the contrast.

LIGHTING

In an emergency, copying can be done in daylight. The soft light of an overcast day is better than sunlight, which washes out dark areas. When working in color on an overcast day, measure the color of the light with a color temperature meter and use the necessary correction filters.

For serious copying, it is better to work under controllable artificial lighting, where you can select the type, color, position, and amount of light. Tungsten lights are best. You can use electronic flash, but this is less satisfactory because you cannot see the results.

Lighting must be even from corner to corner and without disturbing reflection. For smaller documents, you can use two identical lights. Place them at equal distance on two sides far enough away to cover the entire area and each at an angle of approximately 35°. For larger objects use four identical lights, two on each side. The best way to achieve even illumination is by tilting and moving each light separately until it lights the proper area while the other or others are turned off. The most even lighting is obtained when each light is aimed at the far side of the copy. Check the evenness of the lighting with an exposure meter. This flat, shadowless lighting is used in most cases because it suppresses surface detail and patterns.

When surface detail is to be shown—for instance, when photographing oil paintings where brushstrokes are an intergral part—a side light is necessary. One or two lights on the same side should be placed so low that the light beam just touches the surface, highlighting one side of the brushstrokes while the other is in shade. If necessary, a weak fill-in light can be placed on the other side to add some overall illumination without destroying the highlights and shadows.

When you work in color, be aware that surrounding areas (walls, ceilings, floors) may reflect light onto the original and change its color, particularly if the walls and ceilings are colored or have wood panels. Select a room with white or gray walls and ceilings, or shade the lights with barn doors or in some other way so their light falls only on the copy, not on walls and ceilings.

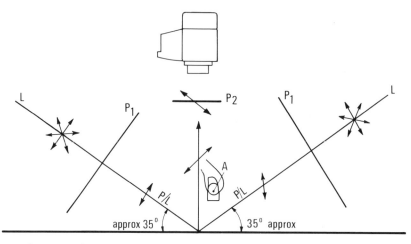

A simple set up for copying in polarized light consists of a copying stand or a sturdy tripod with the center post reversed so that the camera is held between the legs. Two lights *(L)*, one on the left and the other on the right, illuminate the copy from the same angle. The light from both lamps goes through the polarizing material *(P₁)*, which can be mounted in picture frames, so that the light falling on the copy is polarized. A polarizing filter *(P₂)* on the camera lens is turned to produce maximum contrast. Exposure is based on a meter reading *(A)* off a gray card placed on top of the copy.

Copying results can be improved, often dramatically, with polarized light, which eliminates or reduces reflection and produces images with higher contrast. Polarized light is recommended for photographing colored copy, shiny surfaces such as glossy photographs or pictures under glass, and charts on black backgrounds. Polarization makes the background really black instead of gray, and, even more valuable, faint pencil lines and other marks need not be erased because they disappear completely.

These improvements can be accomplished only if the light that reaches the copy is polarized and the polarizing filter on the camera lens is rotated for cross-polarization. Filters that are placed over tungsten light sources must be heat resistant, and such filters are expensive. A less expensive solution is to use sheets of polarizing material placed away from the lights. This is perfectly satisfactory as long as the filter sheet is large enough to encompass all the light reaching the object. My own setup consists of 14 × 17 in. sheets mounted in picture frames and placed on each side of the copy stand. If several lights are used, the polarizing filter between each light and the object must be polarized in the same direction. The filters are usually marked. If they are not, hold two on top of each other, and look through them while turning one; they are polarized in the same direction when most light goes through. The polarizing filters on the light sources and the one on the lens must be accurately adjusted with respect

A

B

Polarization in copying can improve the results drastically. With ordinary light (A), the same artwork (B) photographed with polarized light and a polarizing filter over the camera lens turned 90° to the axis of the polarizing filters over the light sources.

to each other for best results. Proceed as follows. First turn on one light with the polarizing filter in place. Put a shiny coin in the center of the copy and, while viewing through the camera, turn the polarizing filter on lens until the coin shows minimum reflections. Turn off the first light and turn on the second. Turn the polarizing material in front of the light until the coin shows minimum reflections (without touching filter on lens). Proceed the same way with the other lights if more than two are used. The 35° angle recommended for the light source is most efficient for polarization.

In some cases you may not want to eliminate surface reflections completely. For instance, when photographing oil paintings you expect to see some reflections on the brushstrokes. In such a situation, rotate the polarizing filter on the lens only to the point where the reflections are reduced to the desired level rather than eliminated completely.

EXPOSURE

With any type of copy, accurate exposure determination is obtained either by placing an incident meter in the center of the copy and measuring the light falling on the copy or, if flash is used, by holding the flash meter over the copy. With a reflected hand-held or built-in meter, place a gray card over the copy and measure the light reflected off the card. Make certain the meter measures only the gray card and none of the surrounding area, especially not when it is black or white.

If polarized light is used, the measurement is made with the polarizing filter over the lights. In addition, it is necessary to compensate for the polarizing filter on the lens if measurement is made with a separate meter.

COPY STAND

For copying large originals, a horizontal camera with the original mounted on a wall is best. For originals up to about 30 or 40 cm (12 × 16 in.), vertical copying is usually easier. If this work is done extensively, a special stand is recommended; it offers some conveniences, such as a firm support for the camera and a simple way of changing the distance between copy and camera, and it frequently has built-in lights. A sturdy tripod makes a good support for horizontal work and can also be used for vertical setups if the tripod head tilts 90°.

An even sturdier tripod setup results when the center column can be reversed so the camera sits between the tripod legs. The whole purpose of the setup is to eliminate the possibility of camera motion—a good case for prereleasing the camera.

FINAL PREPARATION

To ensure the best possible quality, turn off all room lights and close curtains or shades to keep out daylight. There should be no strong light in the room other than the lights used for the photography.

Check carefully that nothing from the room, the camera, the copy stand, or the photographer is reflected on the copy. This is especially important when glossy surfaces are photographed, such as pictures under glass and glossy photographs. Reflections must also be checked with flat copy because bright highlights, especially from the chrome parts of the camera, can be reflected. If this is the case, shade the reflecting part from the lights. Shading chrome cameras or lenses from the light is a good safeguard in any case. When checking for reflections, place your hand, arms, and eyes in exactly the place they will be because a white shirt, arms, sleeves, or jewelry can reflect light on the copy.

CHAPTER 18

Slides

Excellent medium formats for projection are the 2 1/4 in. square, 4 1/2 × 6 cm and superslides, and projectors and slide trays are readily available. On the other hand, 2 1/4 × 2 3/4 in., 6 × 7 cm, and 6 × 9 cm slides are not projection formats. They can be projected only on lantern slide projectors, which are difficult to locate. Slides in these formats, of course, could be cut down to the 2 1/4 square for projection.

Some laboratories return 2 1/4 in. square, 4 1/2 × 6 cm, and superslides in cardboard mounts ready for projection, but most do not, which is just as well if you plan to glass mount them.

SLIDE MOUNTING

Glass mounting is highly recommended. The film surface of all medium format slides is large. Popping caused by the heat in the projector cannot be avoided, and medium format slides pop more than 35s because of the larger film area. Glass mounts also ensure a more reliable slide transport. Medium format mounts are large, and damage to the cardboard mounts may give problems.

Glass mounts protect slides physically but will not prolong their life or prevent fading of the colors. For longest life, slides should be kept in a cool, dry place. For the least amount of fading, they should not be exposed to the bright projection light longer than necessary. They should be kept in the dark as much as possible, away especially from direct sunlight and fluorescent lights (a light box, for instance), both of which have large amounts of ultraviolet rays.

Glass Mounts

For a faultless slide transport, mounted slides must fit in the slide tray so they can move freely in it. The mount should have no rough edges or

2¼ in. slide mounts with pin registration have three registration pins on one side of the slide mount.

sharp corners. Plastic frames with rounded corners that slide or snap together are preferable to frames that must be taped together or metal frames that must be bent. The thickness of the mount is important. Thick mounts give problems in some projectors. Slide mounts for pin registering the medium format slides are available. Pin registration requires perforation holes in the film. Equipment to register 2 1/4 in. slides and punch the registration holes into slides made on 120 or 220 rollfilm is available.

Newton Rings

Glasses come plain or with coating to avoid *Newton* rings, rainbow-colored patterns caused by the contact of two extremely smooth surfaces: the film and the glass. Newton rings in slides are objectionable because they may be visible on the screen. This happens in light areas of the slide but rarely in darker areas.

Newton rings can be avoided by using anti-Newton glasses, which have a coating or etched pattern designed to prevent the rings. If only one side of the glass has this coating, the coated side must face the shiny base side of the film. If necessary, check the proper positioning of the glasses before mounting the slides. Hold the glass in such a way that a bright object is reflected on the glass. The reflection appears with a sharp outline on the uncoated side and very diffused on the coated side. The diffused side should face the base.

Newton rings can also be prevented by glass mounting slides as soon as they come back from the laboratory and before the heat from a projection lamp has the opportunity to dry out the film and cause a permanent curl.

If a slide must be permanently attached to the mount (for accurate registration or to avoid movement if it has been cut too small), attach it on one side only, never on two opposite sides, so the slide has the possibility of moving.

Condensation

Newton rings do not harm the slide itself; condensation or moisture can. When slides are stored in a place of high humidity, the film base soaks up the moisture from the air. The heat from the projection lamp causes the moisture to evaporate and settle between glass and film, eventually clouding the cover glass. The cloud is not obvious on the screen but will reduce brilliance and contrast. Avoid condensation by storing slides, mounted or unmounted, in areas of low humidity (not basements). In addition or especially when storage areas of higher humidity cannot be avoided, store the slides with a desiccant such as silica gel.

Moisture that has settled between slide and glass should be removed as soon as possible to avoid deforming the slide and perhaps resulting in the growth of fungus. Take the slide apart and let it dry out before remounting.

Cleaning the Glass

Most new glasses are factory cleaned and need nothing more than brushing off the dust. For cleaning used glasses with condensation, use either a glass cleaner or a solution of 1/4 cup ammonia (without soap) and a pint of water.

Identification

All medium format slides (except lantern slides) go into square mounts: standard 2 × 2 in. for superslides and 2 3/4 in. for 2 1/4 square in. and 4 1/2 × 6 cm. Square slide mounts fit in the slide trays in every way so it is not necessary to pay special attention to the positioning of the film frame in the mount. If slide sequences are changed and slides removed from the trays occasionally, it is wise to mark the slide frame with a dot in one corner or a band along one side, which can also serve to identify the content of a slide. Proper positioning is assured when the bands on all slides are visible on top or when all dots are visible in the same corner when glancing from the back of the tray.

SLIDE PROJECTORS

Superslides

Superslides can be projected in a standard 35 mm projector using standard 35 mm slide trays. Just like 35s, the slides can be in glass, cardboard, or plastic mounts, with eighty slides fitting the standard Kodak-type trays. Superslide projection therefore offers the same possibilities as with 35s, using all the standard dissolve, programming, and sound equipment. The only difference is that superslides are square, and their area is almost twice as large on the screen compared to 35 mm when projected from the same distance with the same lens. To determine the screen size, keep in mind that each side of the mounted superslide is 38 mm compared to 34 mm for the long side of a mounted 35 mm slide. The superslide thus requires a square screen that is 10 percent larger than the long side of the projected 35 mm slide. If a 35 mm slide fills a screen 72 × 50 in., the superslide needs one 80 × 80 in.

The projector's illumination and lens quality are important for optimum superslide quality. The illumination should have no objectionable or visible falloff out to corners. If it does, check another machine unless special condenser lenses for superslides are available. Many projection lenses are not of exceptional quality and barely give satisfactory sharpness out to the corners for the 35 mm slide, so they are not capable of producing satisfactory quality for the much larger superslide. A simple test can show whether the projection lens is acceptable. Focus the image from a glass-mounted slide in the center. If the corners are not sharp, see whether refocusing the lens brings the corner in focus. If it does, the projection lens is the problem. With a zoom lens, make the test at different focal lengths. If the lens that comes with the projector has such a quality problem, investigate professional projection lenses made by other companies. Some companies make special lenses for superslides. Also some manufacturers make flat field and curved field lenses. The latter take into account the curvature in a cardboard-mounted slide. Flat field lenses must be used for glass-mounted slides. Flat field lenses are also recommended for projecting cardboard-mounted superslides. The curvature of the larger film area is not uniform across the slide as it is on 35s and therefore cannot be corrected by a curved field lens. With flat field lenses, the slide can be inserted with the emulsion toward the lamp or lens.

While checking sharpness, also determine the amount of distortion. Make certain the outside lines of the projected slide are straight so the superslide is projected as a square, not a barrel. Curved lines are obvious and objectionable on a superslide.

2 1/4 in. Square and 4 1/2 × 6 cm Projection

2 1/4 in. squares and 4 1/2 × 6 cm slides are used in the same slide projectors and same slide trays and thus can be intermixed within a slide

presentation. Slide projectors are available though the choice is somewhat limited. You can choose among a projector that is completely manual, including the changing of slides; a projector that operates from slides in a tray but is still basically single slide projection; or a professional machine that allows you to do everything that can be done in 35 mm.

Single Slide Projection

Somewhat like projecting lantern slides, the 2 1/4 in. square slide is dropped into the holder, pushed in the light path, and removed on the other side where the second slide is inserted. This is suitable only for home projection and evaluating the effectiveness of the image by the photographer or client.

Single Slide Projection from Tray

The next move is the typical 2 1/4 in. square slide projector holding the slides in a tray. Some projectors on the market are made for the straight European slide tray holding thirty glass- or cardboard-mounted slides. The slides are moved in and out of the projector gate from the side, so in this respect they are not too different from the single slide unit. You can see the slide moving in and out on most—an unprofessional slide presentation unless the projector has a blackout curtain. With a curtain, the blackout is somewhat longer than on a gravity-feed 35 mm machine but certainly not objectionable considering the beauty of the 2 1/4 in. square slide.

These projectors have many advantages, however. Thirty slides can be projected from a tray; the slide change is operated by push button in forward and reverse. Slide changing is also possible from a remote cable. Focusing may be operated by push button rather than manually moving the lens.

If you plan to project cardboard-mounted slides, consider a machine with automatic focusing to compensate for the popping of the mounted slides. Even with this feature, you will still be aware of the popping, but at least the machine eliminates manual refocusing. This is unnecessary for glass-mounted slides. Some projectors also have a variable timer built in or as an accessory, helpful for projecting slides at regular intervals.

The price of such a projector is about that of a better model 35 mm. It is really designed for one-projector setups and is not readily adaptable to dissolve units and programmers. As expert should be able to rewire the machine, however, for this purpose. Even when rewired, however, a standard dissolve unit may not produce an even, professional-looking dissolve because the projection lamp and wattage are different from what is used in standard 35 mm projection for which the dissolve control is designed. A modification in the dissolve unit can overcome this last draw-back.

Professional 2 1/4 in. Slide Projection

A 2 1/4 in. square slide projector that can be considered professional from the point of view of features, suitability for multiple projection setups, and reliability of operation under the stringent requirements of multi-media presentations is available. In addition to remote forward, reverse, and focusing, the projector is built to work with the standard dissolve and programmers made for 35 mm. It thus provides all the possibilities for multiple projectors and multiimage presentations that are possible in 35 mm but can do it with the large 2 1/4 in. square or 4 1/2 × 6 cm format. The techniques for arranging and presenting the visual and audio part of such shows are identical. With a professional projector of this type, you can produce and arrange a multiimage presentation that is as sophisticated

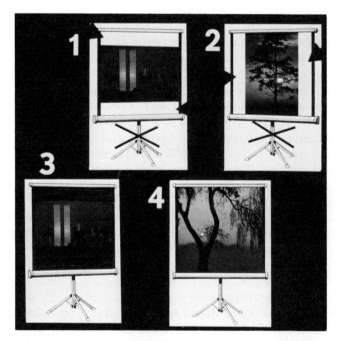

When mixing verticals and horizontals in a slide presentation, the horizontal leaves blank spaces on the top and bottom of the square screen (1). The verticals do the same on both sides (2). When working in a rectangular format, it is preferable to produce all slides as horizontals and then project them on a movie screen with each filling the entire horizontal format screen (3). Squares are the most effective for filling the entire square projection screen (4).

as anything done in 35 mm since the 2 1/4 in. square projector is controlled by the same programming equipment used in 35 mm. You can combine 2 1/4 in. square slides with 35 mm. For example, make a multiimage show using twelve 35 mm projectors, four 2 1/4 projectors, and one 16 mm motion picture projector. The 2 1/4 projectors are used mainly when presenting slides where quality is important, slides fill the entire screen, panoramas cover three or four screens, or slides remain on the screen for long periods.

For a multiimage presentation you must plan the production of the images. You must visualize the combination of the projected images and photograph them so they combine visually and effectively in the projected presentation. If you use multiple images on one or several screens, you must plan which images are to be combined and how and, equally important, which images are to follow one another. Many multiimage presentations are just a juxtaposition of images put together in a haphazard fashion without any relationship from one to the next. In multiimage presentations, you may also need to repeat the same image or similar images, so shoot multiple exposures to avoid the need for making duplicates. You will discover that you need to shoot many more slides than you would for a one or two projector show.

The large 2 1/4 in. square slides are perhaps most effective for less elaborate presentations using two or three slide projectors. No one should feel that such presentations, using only two projectors and one large screen, are ineffective, outdated, or unsophisticated. A two-projector show with the large 2 1/4 in. square slides can be more effective than an elaborate 35 mm multimedia presentation that throws hundreds or thousands of images in front of the audience. With a two-projector show, one does not need the elaborate equipment and knowledge required by multiple projector setups. Many simple two-projector programmers on the market are capable of producing cuts, dissolves, and flashes of various lengths and allow synchronizing the slide show to a sound track. A unit like this has dissolve rates from 1 to 8 sec or even longer, a flickering effect used for highlighting a slide or part of a slide, a reverse button, a freeze key that allows stopping a dissolve at any point during its sequence, and the possibility of turning either projector on or off without advancing the slide for superimpositions. It may also be programmed so each projector will move forward to any slide, not just the next one. The dissolve unit remembers where both trays are at all times.

There are, of course, limits to what can be done with two projectors. Double exposures are limited or impossible. Slides cannot be changed rapidly. You must wait until the slide in the projector is changed, which takes at least 1-1/2 or 2 sec—rather long for a modern visual presentation. These limitations are eliminated by the use of three projectors. Slides can be changed more rapidly. Double exposures can be made at any time.

Most dissolve units made for a two-projector show do not work with three projectors. Some dissolve and programming units are made for two or three projectors. Investigate these possibilities before deciding which route to take.

LEGIBILITY OF ARTWORK

Although a projected 2 1/4 in. square slide is much sharper than a 35 mm equivalent, that does not mean that letters and figures on the screen are easier to read or are readable from farther away. Legibility is determined mainly by the size of the lettering in relation to the viewing distance. To read a newspaper, even with perfect eyesight, you can be only a certain distance away. Improving the printing quality by using a higher-quality paper that makes the letters appear sharper does not, or does not appreciably, improve the legibility as long as the letters are the same size. The same is true with copy projected on a screen. Whatever copy, graphs, or artwork is projected on the screen must be easily readable even by the people sitting in the back row. Generally the screen used should be large enough so no one in the room sits farther away than eight times the height of the screen (40 ft for a 5 ft screen or 56 ft for a 7 ft size).

There is a simple way to determine legibility before you even photograph the artwork. View the artwork from a distance eight times longer than the height of the artwork that will be covered on the slide. If the artwork is 6 × 6 in., view it from 48 in. or 4 ft (6 × 8 = 48). You must be able to read the copy easily, assuming that your eyes allow you to see well at that distance with or without eyeglasses.

Once the artwork is readable from these viewing distances, it makes no difference how large or how small the slide is projected. Whatever the projected image size, make certain that no one sits farther away than eight times the image height. Conversely, once you know the size of the artwork, you can determine how large the letters and figures need to be by viewing the board from the correct distance. You will probably find that a good minimum size for letters is about one–twenty-fifth the height of the copy area. If the area to be photographed is 12 in. high, 1/2 in. lettters are easily readable. If the copy is only 3 in. high, keep the letters 1/8 in., about the size of regular typing. They can always be larger.

Since the medium format slide is large enough for direct viewing, you could judge legibility also by viewing the slide from eight times the slide size (from 17 to 18 in. for a 2 1/4 in. square, for example).

When you prepare the artwork, pay attention to a few points that make the copy not only readable but visually attractive:

- Lines, letters, and figures must stand out against the background.
- Contrast between copy and background is most important. Colored or white letters against a black background, as obtained on high contrast film, are especially good.
- Colors should be strong and attractive and harmonize with each other.

- Stay away from fancy types and lettering; use bold and simple types.
- Keep the artwork and information simple. Limit the amount of text, and reduce the information to what is absolutely necessary.
- Stay away from complex arrangements.
- Compose the information to the essential elements.

COMBINING SOUND AND SLIDES

With a professional projector-dissolve-programmer combination, a 2 1/4 in. slide-sound presentation can be as elaborate as anything that is done in 35 mm as far as the number of projectors or the combination of screen images and effects is concerned. Such a 2 1/4 in. multiimage show is produced like a 35 mm multiimage presentation. A number of books are available to help beginners.

Although such multiimage presentations can be and usually are effective, a simple two-projector show on one screen with one dissolve programmer can equal the attention-getting quality, if not impact, of the more complex show. Such a simple sound-slide show, however, must be carefully thought out, prepared, and presented to have the maximum visual impact. (The following thoughts are meant for newcomers to this field.)

There is a vast difference between presenting slides with personal comments and presenting them with a prepared, taped sound track. In the former, the presentation can be very informal. Slides can be left on the screen for a long time, as long as something interesting and entertaining can be said about them. Details presented on the slide can be pointed out; one can go back to a previous slide if desired or necessary; and perhaps most important, the presentation can be slower or faster or different each time depending on the purpose and the audience. In this type of presentation, the speaker remains the main element of the program; the visuals are just an accompaniment. The audience may expect nothing more than a visual conversation.

When the sound comes from a speaker connected to a tape recorder, the audience expects professionalism. They assume that the program was prepared with the same care and effort as anything that is projected on the television screen or the movie screen. They expect something as beautiful, interesting, entertaining, and fast paced as a prime-time television program. Today's audiences, both adults and children, have spent a good part of their time in front of the television screen and are conditioned to the pace of television commercials, which can get an entire story across in less than a minute. That is the pace to strive for in a slide presentation. Some say that such comparisons should not be made because of the difference of media. I do not agree. When people look at a screen and listen to recorded sound, their only concern is to see something interesting, entertaining, and beautiful, and they do not really care where it comes from: Super 8, 16 mm, 35 mm film, videotape, slides, or whatever else it might be. If this assumption is correct, the techniques and approaches that are used to make effective films and videotapes will also apply to producing effective sound-slide presentations. What are some of these principles that produce effective films, and how can these motion picture approaches be used for producing effective slide programs?

An effective opening. The television viewer usually decides during the first few minutes of a program whether to see the rest or change the channel. Consequently, what happens during the first few minutes of a program has an immense bearing on the audience's reaction to the presentation. How we open the presentation, what we expose our audience to during the first few minutes, is therefore of utmost importance and may determine the success or failure of a presentation. Do not start the slide presentation with ordinary images. Give the audience at the beginning something they have not seen before, something so visually striking that they want to see the rest. That is one reason why most programs today do not start with a long list of titles but with strong visual images. The titles follow later or at the end of the program.

Images determine success. Although a sound track can make the presentation more enjoyable and exciting to watch, it cannot turn a poor visual presentation into a good one. A poor, ineffective image is bad and distracting with or without sound. Good sound is important, but a slide program is a visual experience, and the visual image is still the most important part. Since you cannot rely on the sound to carry the show, use only slides that give this visual experience: slides that are technically and artistically perfect, slides that are worthwhile looking at and are necessary to carry the show.

Logical and effective flow of images. In many slide and multimedia presentations, images follow each other without any visual connection; sunrise shots are followed by images taken in full noon sunlight, and close-up shots of flowers are intermixed with long shots of sailboats. This is seldom done in films because filmmakers have been trained in finding ways so images follow each other visually in a logical and effective manner.

A slide presentation must be effective even without the sound track. If it is not, start by working with the slides alone; worry about the sound afterward. As a general rule, however, this is not the way to proceed. For an effective blend of sound and images, the two must be prepared together. Great sound films are not produced by adding a sound track to a film that was meant to be silent; the same is true for sound-slide shows. For sound presentations, images are combined differently; frequently different images are needed. It is best or necessary to plan the presentation before the slides are made. Decide before you go on a trip at least whether the slides will be combined into a sound-slide presentation and determine what the basic approach should be (people, architecture, beauty, problems, etc.). If all the slides are already made, you can try to make the best of the existing material, which probably will be a compromise.

Sequences

Most effective sound-slide presentations are made up of sequences of images rather than individual unrelated still pictures, another reason why planning must start before the images are made. It is also a main difference between the still photographer's and the moviemaker's approach to photography. Photographers usually think in terms of one image of a subject. Filmmakers have been taught in terms of sequences, photographing a subject from different angles and distances to end up in sequences of long, medium, and close-up shots. For successful sound-slide programs, think like a moviemaker and photograph everything in three, four, five, or even more different ways, making certain that each image is sufficiently different so it appears new to the audience. Usually just moving a little closer to the subject is not good enough. A change in distance should be combined with a change in angle.

This sequence approach also allows faster pacing, a more rapid change of images on the screen. Instead of boring the audience with a single long shot of a waterfall that remains on the screen for 30 sec (the time required to describe the view in the soundtrack), entertain the audience by seven different images, perhaps as follows:

long shot of mountains with waterfall in background, 6 sec.
long shot of entire waterfall, 4 sec.
medium shot of top of fall from side, 4 sec.
close-up of water falling over top, 3 sec.
medium shot of entire fall from side, 5 sec.
medium shot of bottom of fall, 4 sec.
close-up of water falling, 4 sec.

The visual approach to effective sound-slide presentations can be learned from films, not from photo galleries. Fast pacing is especially important for today's young audiences accustomed to quick cutting. Movie scenes 1 to 3 sec are long enough to be seen. Slides also need not stay longer on the screen.

Preplanning is necessary to ascertain that there is an image for everything described in the narration and that the image shows the described detail clearly, even to people sitting in the last row of an auditorium.

Variety

Next strive for variety. Anything that is repeated over and over becomes monotonous regardless how effective it might be the first time. This applies to both the visual and audio parts.

Visuals Vary the type of image as much as possible by intermixing long-distance images with close-ups, low angle shots with high angles, outdoor images with indoor types, candids with patterns, high-key with low-key lighting if the mood calls for it, and anything else that can be done with lighting, cameras, lenses, and accessories as long as it helps to tell the story effectively.

Sound Visual variety must be accompanied by variety in the sound track. Narration from beginning to end may be fine for an instructional program that has one purpose only—to teach—and the audience expects nothing more than to learn. And in a poetic presentation, nothing but music from beginning to end may be the perfect choice because the purpose may be just to enhance the beauty of the image. For most other presentations I would strive for variety in the sound track, as is done in most motion pictures. Intermix sequences with music with sequences with sound effects. Sound effects can be more effective than music because they enhance the feeling of presence, of being there instead of just looking at an image. This requires that the selected sound effects are sounds that actually exist in that location—church bells, bird sounds, foghorns, seagulls.

In voice sequences you can add variety by changing from narration to dialogue. Good examples are found in documentary films and television news programs where narration is frequently used to introduce a sequence and then a switch is made to dialogue of a person seen in the image.

Transition Scene change is one of the important elements in film planning. Intermix straight cuts with fades, dissolves, and wipes. Try to vary the change from slide to slide as much as possible. Do not use dissolves from beginning to end. Try intermixing dissolves with straight cuts, and vary the length of the dissolve, making it longer when a lazy, peaceful mood is to be conveyed, and shorter for faster-paced action.

Pace A good way to put your audience to sleep is to keep each slide on the screen for the same length of time so the audience can practically anticipate when the change will happen. This is another area where you can learn from the moviemakers and benefit by watching scene length in films. Moviemakers have learned that a monotonous rhythm has no place in a film; pacing (proper scene length) is an important element in film editing. Long scenes are mixed with short cuts; the longer ones are used to convey a quiet, peaceful mood and the shorter ones to speed up the pace.

Do the same in slide programs. Surprise the audience by changing images at an unexpected moment and by intermixing slides with longer screen time with slides changing every 1, 2, or 3 sec. Constant image change keeps the audience glued to their seats.

Narration

Narration is an important part of many slide presentations. Those in the audience like to know what they are seeing but do not like the narrator to say what is obvious from the image on the screen. "This is the Eiffel Tower" or "Here we're feeding the seagulls" are unnecessary comments. The visuals should carry the message; words should explain or elaborate on them.

A slide-tape show is not supposed to be an illustrated lecture, so keep the words conversational. The words on the script should be those you would use when talking face to face with your audience.

As you look at slides on the slide sorter, jot down a few words to suggest what you want to say. Then type the script, double-spacing the lines so that you can make changes easily. Project the slides and read the narration aloud. Do not be reluctant to change either the words or the slides.

Slide Change Timing   In narration or dialogue sequences, variety can be added by changing slides sometimes at the end of a sentence and sometimes in the middle. If images always change at the end of a sentence, the presentation becomes monotonous, and the words quickly sound like captions to the images rather than narration. Narrations should be used to bridge images—as a transition from one slide to the next, with the new image appearing at a precise word that acts as an introduction.

Slide changes in the middle of sentences are likely to result in a more continuous flow of writing rather than writing just for the purpose of describing an image. The best narration in many cases is the one that is interesting to listen to even without the image.

Music

Background music is meant to enhance the visual image so it must fit the mood, time, and location. As time, mood, and location change, background music must change too in style or in instruments. Background music adds to the visual image without the audience's usually being overly aware of it. So-called nondescriptive music (music one can listen to but neither dance nor sing to) is best.

Slides from various countries are frequently accompanied by typical native music, native instruments, and native sounds or tunes written for something associated with a story from the country, like "Never on Sunday" for Greece, "Zorba" for Turkey, and the *King and I* for Thailand. This technique may be satisfactory for some sequences—perhaps with images of people or places where the music actually might exist—but it is seldom effective with scenery. For that purpose, use the nondescriptive type that has the flavor of the country.

The sound track of the audiovisual presentation—its quality and components—is of paramount importance to the ultimate success or failure of the production. All the audio elements (music, narrative, sound effects, and silence) must mesh harmoniously to integrate the visual segments properly. Good music orchestrates the visual elements of a show much as a dancer follows choreography to create a ballet.

Prerecorded music is available through numerous music libraries. These libraries have thousands of pieces of music available on albums and tapes and through catalogs. The disadvantage is that you may have to sample hundreds of selections before choosing the best available music.

If you can afford original music, look for a composer who has produced in your particular medium and whose musical ideas are compatible with yours. Watch some productions he or she has scored.

Since sound and music are new to many photographers, it is worthwhile studying books describing composers and their work and listening to various styles and types of music. I recommend even more highly studying and evaluating films of all kinds, especially good documentaries, television commercials, and television news programs for inspiration for sound-slide programs. Their approach can be duplicated almost step for step with slides and will likely result in a prize-winning sound-slide presentation.

CHAPTER 19

Applications

Medium format cameras are excellent for just about every photographic application. The large negative size combined with camera portability is one reason. The extensive interchangeability of components combined with the wide range of accessories available for many camera models is another. The camera features and accessories used are determined not only by photographic technique but also by the photographer's personal approach and opinion on how the images should be recorded on the film. It is thus impossible to suggest exactly what type of camera, what camera features, and what camera accessories must be considered. But I can summarize what photographers have found helpful and useful for particular jobs.

WILDLIFE AND BIRD PHOTOGRAPHY

Long focal length lenses combined with an SLR camera is a must. A built-in meter can be used to determine the light level at distant areas. A motor drive is a great help, especially when following birds or animals. Black cameras and black lenses are less noticeable than the more reflective chrome-trimmed models. If you want the bird or animal to trigger the camera, a motor-driven camera that can be released from a distance is a necessity.

NATURE PHOTOGRAPHY

Nature photography can include anything from scenics to extreme close-ups, the latter usually forming a large portion of nature subjects. The necessary close-up features and accessories are listed in chapter 16.

Nature close-up photography frequently involves recording moving subjects. The setup time may be limited, and the nature photographer must be prepared to move fast. Hand-held close-up photography may be desirable or necessary. All close-up accessories, even bellows, can be used hand held.

CLOSE-UP PHOTOGRAPHY

The camera and accessory equipment are determined by the size of the area to be photographed. A bellows built into the camera eliminates the need for separate accessories. But it does not simplify close-up photography otherwise compared to working with a bellows as an accessory. SLR cameras are a must. Built-in light meters simplify exposure because they eliminate calculations for exposure factors. A mirror lockup is another must because exposure times are often fairly long. For the best quality, lenses that are designed especially for close-up photography should be used. Retrofocus wide angle types are not particularly recommended for this purpose.

HIGH MAGNIFICATION PHOTOGRAPHY

This includes magnification three times or higher (recording the subject at least three times larger than its actual size). For magnification up to approximately twenty-five times, special lenses like Luminars are easy to use in combination with a bellows between camera body and lens. For higher magnifications, the camera without lens can be mounted over a microscope. A light-tight connection between camera and eyepiece (microscope adapter) is necessary. A Polaroid film magazine is helpful in both cases to check the camera setup and to determine exposure. A mirror lockup is even more important than for general close-ups. A motor drive

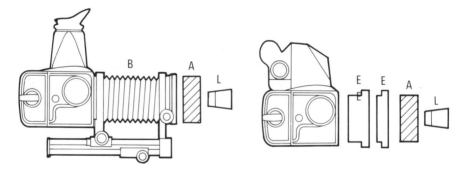

Special objectives for high-magnification photography from about three times to twenty-five times, such as the Luminars (L), can be used on SLR cameras with interchangeable lenses. The objective is mounted into a board (A) that fits into the bellows (B) or extension tube (E). The board is readily available for at least one 2¼ in. camera. The bellows is recommended; it offers a range of magnifications, as well as a convenient method of focusing.

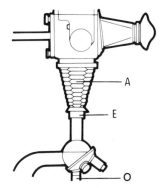

In photomicrography, the eyepiece (E) forms the image so no camera lens is used. The microscope adapter (A) holds the eyepiece and shields the camera from extraneous light. The eyepiece is dropped into the microscope adapter, and the adapter is then attached to the camera like a lens. The microscope objective is shown at O.

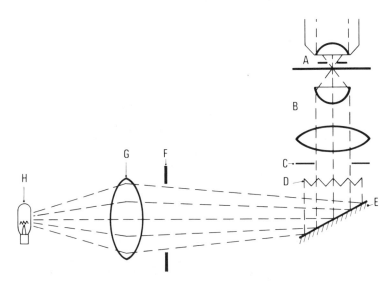

Proper illumination is the most important step to successful photomicrography. The recommended specimen illumination is obtained by first centering the lamp and then changing the distance between the lamp (H) and the condenser lens on the lamp until a sharp image of the filament is recorded on the back surface of the stopped-down substage diaphragm (C). The field diaphragm is stopped down (A), and the position of the substage condenser is adjusted (B) until a sharp image of the field diaphragm appears on the ground glass of the camera. The image of the field diaphragm is then recorded in the specimen plane. The field diaphragm is opened just enough so its image fills the entire diameter of the objective lens.

Example of the possibilities with high-magnification lenses. Slide 1 shows a two times magnification of a postage stamp and slide 2 a detail out of the stamp with a ten times magnification.

is very desirable because it avoids accidental moving of the camera while advancing the film to the next frame.

AERIAL PHOTOGRAPHY

Highly professional aerial photography, especially mapping, is done with special cameras using the 9 × 9 in. size. Medium format cameras, however, are an excellent choice, either with the camera built into the aircraft or with a hand-held camera. Brackets for mounting medium format cameras into the airplane are made by special companies. Motor drives and manually wound cameras are used by professionals. There are arguments about shutter speed. Some feel that 1/500 or 1/1000 sec is sufficient; others will insist and prove that a 1/2000 sec speed provides sharper results. Regardless of what side you are on, you certainly could not go wrong using the 1/2000 sec or 1/1000 sec shutter speed for any aerial applications. An SLR type is not necessary, but if it is used, it must have a prism or frame finder. The latter is preferred by many photographers. Interchangeable film magazines are a must, and a larger capacity 70 mm film magazine is very desirable because it reduces the number of magazine changes and allows use of infrared film. For multispectral photography, two to four motor-driven cameras are used. They must be connected to a camera release so all release at the same time.

Two medium format cameras on the market are specifically designed for mapping and other photogrammetric applications. One has interchangeable lenses, the other a wide angle type with a 90° diagonal angle of view, about the same as the angle of view on 9 × 9 in. mapping cameras. Both have a reseau plate, and the lenses are calibrated to the camera body.

ARCHITECTURAL PHOTOGRAPHY

Quality is vital, so the choice of lens is most important. Retrofocus-type wide angle lenses on an SLR model are fine, but for even better corner-to-corner sharpness and less distortion, one of the special medium format wide angle cameras equipped with an optically true wide angle type should be considered. A spirit level, built in or as an accessory, is necessary. PC (perspective control) lenses will allow even more extensive applications without the need to consider a view camera. A Polaroid back is highly desirable. It allows checking the evenness of illumination and lighting ratios and helps to find troublesome reflections.

PRESS PHOTOGRAPHY

Convenience and speed of shooting are most important. An SLR with a built-in motor is the best choice, but a good rangefinder type can be a close second. An instant return mirror on an SLR model is preferred. Motor drives are not as necessary as on 35 mm because medium format motor drives do not provide the shooting speed of several frames per second. Fast wide angle lenses and fast medium telephotos (100 to 150 mm focal length) are most helpful. Flash synchronization at all shutter speeds is very helpful or necessary in many applications. The camera should be rugged and solidly built. Interchangeable magazines allow easy switching to whatever film is best for the job.

WEDDING PHOTOGRAPHY

Since you carry the camera constantly for three or more hours, size, weight, and convenience of carrying must be the first consideration. Outside of this, almost any type of medium format camera is usable. Film format is the last consideration. Wedding photographs in an album or displayed any other way are equally beautiful as squares or rectangles. Equipment should be simple. Two lenses and perhaps a close-up accessory for photographing hand and ring shots are sufficient. A popular lens is a slight wide angle: 60 mm for 2 1/4 in. square and a medium telephoto, 150 mm for 2 1/4 in. square. Flash synchronization at all shutter speeds is important for sunlit outdoor shots. If the client wants double exposures, make sure the camera can do this work. A TLR camera or lens shutter SLR with mirror lockup provides the quietest operation.

CHILD PHOTOGRAPHY

One camera and one lens (a medium telephoto) are all that is necessary for indoor and outdoor work. The camera should be a motor drive with remote capability so you need not stand behind the camera. You can be next to the subject, where it is much easier to direct and get that precious expression so important in child photography.

FASHION AND BEAUTY PHOTOGRAPHY

Beauty photography is studio work and frequently means tight head shots and shots of hands and legs, all of which can be done with a regular portrait lens of around 150 mm. A relatively long telephoto—about 250 mm—is popular. Its longer shooting distance compresses perspective and brings out the elements that are important in beauty: the eyes, lips, and cheeks.

Fashion photography is almost equally divided between studio and location work. In the studio, it is often done from a tripod and on location from a tripod or hand held. Motor drives are very helpful; they allow shooting a second picture the moment the expression or pose changes.

Professional models are expensive, so speed of shooting without time-consuming film loading is essential. A popular lighting approach outdoors is fill-in flash with the sun being a side light or back light. A lens shutter with flash synchronization at all speeds is useful.

A good sunshade is essential in the studio because much of this work is done against white backgrounds. Image sharpness is a main requirement for magazine cover shots. This is a competitive business, and you cannot compromise in quality. The square is a popular format with art directors, but some photographers prefer to submit the 4 1/2 × 6 cm or 2 1/4 × 2 3/4 in. that conforms to the magazine cover, so the image must be used as submitted. A camera that gives a choice of the square and rectangle solves this problem. A Polaroid magazine allows the client or art director, who is usually present during the shooting, to see and approve the results.

PORTRAIT PHOTOGRAPHY

Portrait photography can be studio or location work and full-length, three-quarter, or head and shoulder shots. The camera and lens requirements are thus basically the same as for fashion photography. Portrait work, however, is best done from a tripod because it makes directing the non-professional easier. A prerelease mirror lockup must be used because exposure times are relatively long, especially in shaded locations out-doors, and fill-in flash is usually not used. There are two differences from fashion work: portrait work means negative film and extensive use of diffusion devices or soft focus lenses. The lens or soft focus accessory must create diffusion without throwing the image out of focus. If retouch-ing is done on the negative, the largest possible negative is helpful, but less important than other camera features.

SPORTS PHOTOGRAPHY

A professional with a press pass can do much sports photography with practically any medium format camera and even a standard lens. A tele-photo short enough for hand-held work (120–250 mm), however, is an advantage.

For the spectator who needs to photograph from the viewing stand, close-ups can be obtained only with long and very long telephotos. A monopod is a great help. Train yourself to follow moving actions hand held with long telephotos. A prism finder ensures that the SLR or TLR camera is moved in the right direction. A frame or sports finder accessory is even better for following moving subjects. There is another advantage to using such finders on SLR cameras: the cameras have a slight delay because the aperture has to close down, and the mirror has to lift up before the exposure is made. The delay could mean an unacceptable change in fast actions. You can eliminate it by prereleasing the camera. Once the mirror is out of the way, however, a frame or sports finder is necessary to frame the subject. There is some disagreement whether shutter speeds higher than 1/500 or 1/1000 sec are necessary, but you certainly could not go wrong shooting at 1/2000 sec if the camera has this shutter speed. Slow shutter speeds can be used to blur motion.

For professional results indoors, flash is necessary. To eliminate the ghost image caused by bright lights in an arena, shutter speed must be 1/500 sec. Flash synchronization at all shutter speeds is thus necessary.

MEDICAL PHOTOGRAPHY

Medical photography can by anything from photography of patients to copying and photomicroscopy. Much medical work involves slides for presentation in a 35 mm projector. A medium format camera that can shoot superslides would be a definite plus and can replace the need for a 35 mm camera.

COMMERCIAL PHOTOGRAPHY

Commercial clients are extremely critical, so high quality and consistency are foremost requirements. Lens quality, color rendition, good field coverage of lenses, film flatness, and shutter accuracy must be the primary camera requirements. A Polaroid film magazine is the best assurance for accomplishing the desired results. An SLR type is a definite choice.

A PC lens allows more extensive use of the medium format camera where a view camera might otherwise be necessary. A tilting lens used to increase depth of field is also helpful. It need not be a main requirement, however, because commercial photographers usually have access to a view camera that offers all the controls.

ULTRAVIOLET PHOTOGRAPHY

UV photography down to wavelenghs of about 320 μ can be done with regular glass lenses. For short-range UV work below this wavelength, a quartz lens must be used. Glass does not transmit short-range UV radiation. A quartz lens is available for at least one medium format camera. Black-and-white film is normally used because it shows everything the investigator wants to see and often does the work better than color film.

FLUORESCENT PHOTOGRAPHY

Subjects that fluoresce can be photographed with any camera and any lens because the fluorescent light is ordinary, visible light. A good UV filter should be placed over the lens. Daylight or tungsten color film can be used. Daylight film enhances the reds and tungsten type the blues.

INFRARED PHOTOGRAPHY

Infrared photography requires special film, which is readily available for a medium format camera only in 70 mm or sheetfilm. Special lenses are not necessary, but an apochromatic lens that is well corrected into the red and infrared range produces better results, especially in black-and-white infrared work. It also eliminates the need for a focusing adjustment required with black-and-white (not with color) infrared film. A red filter is used in black and white and an orange 12 or 15 for scientific work in color. For color experimenting, any filter can be tried.

VIDEO DISPLAYS

Until a few years ago, this application was limited to photographing regular television shows. It has increased tremendously in the last few years because of the extensive use of computer-enhanced imaging systems and the widened use of videotapes.

All video images, whether computer or camera generated, can be photographed using the same basic procedures. Any camera can be used with color or black-and-white film. A close-up accessory might be necessary to fill the frame with the television screen, though this depends on the size of the screen and the close-up focusing capability of the lens or camera.

A normal focal length lens is satisfactory, but a short telephoto is recommended because the required longer screen-to-camera distance makes the curvature of the television screen less noticeable. It also is likely to produce more even exposure over the entire screen area.

Just as for copying, the camera must be set up so its film plane is parallel to the screen. Careful visual evaluation should be good enough, but an accurate test can be made. With the monitor turned off and the room lights on, view through the finder; focus the lens on the camera reflected on the screen; and then move the camera until the monitor screen and the reflection of the camera are centered in the camera's finder.

Black-and-white or daylight color film of about 200 ASA should be used. An 81B (R-3) filter produces somewhat warmer, more pleasing colors on color film.

Exposure is determined with any separate or built-in reflected exposure meter, holding the meter close enough so it only measures the screen area. The reading on the meter is correct for regular television images. For video displays consisting of white or colored lines or data surrounded by large black backgrounds, the meter reading is based on the dark background, while the film should be exposed for the lines or data.

The aperture must be opened about two f stops more than indicated. Still better is to make test exposures, on Polaroid if possible.

Selection of shutter speed is important. Too short a speed shows up in uneven brightness caused by the scanning on the screen. Theoretically 1/30 sec should be satisfactory. To be safe, however, I suggest 1/15 sec or even 1/8 sec with lens shutters and 1/8 sec or, better, 1/4 sec with the focal plane type. These short shutter speeds may result in subject motion. Although it would be possible to pause videotapes to stop the action, the procedure is not recommended. The image quality and sharpness are normally better from a rolling tape. Computer displays or laser video disc displays, on the other hand, can be photographed in the stopped mode.

UNDERWATER PHOTOGRAPHY

Special medium format cameras for underwater work are not made, but underwater cases, both amateur and professional types, are available for various cameras. Wide angle lenses are used mostly because the higher refractive index of water cuts down the angle of view. Correction lenses are available for professional underwater housings. A motor drive simplifies operation underwater, and a large-capacity magazine reduces the frequency of coming to the surface for reloading.

SPACE PHOTOGRAPHY

Medium format cameras are the type used for most photographic work aboard the U.S. space shuttle. The cameras are the standard motor-driven types equipped with a 70 mm magazine for darkroom spool loading (not cassettes). (All magazines are loaded before the liftoff.)

Most photography is done hand held with 50 mm wide angle—100 mm standard and 250 mm telephoto. Satellite launchings are photographed in sequences of one frame per second with one or two mounted cameras. A medium format camera has also been placed in a satellite to photograph the shuttle from outside. It was operated remotely and wireless.

INDUSTRIAL PHOTOGRAPHY

The medium format camera is an ideal tool in the industrial field because industrial work can involve any type of photography from executive portraiture to commercial subjects and photomicroscopy. A versatile SLR type, with its extensive range of lenses and accessories, can meet any requirement.

A medium format camera is an excellent tool for industrial photographers whose work involves everything from portraiture, to action, to nuts and bolts close-ups. Photograph by Mike Fletcher.

OUTDOOR SCENERY

Most outdoor photography is at medium and long distances; thus just about any camera can serve the purpose. The choice of lenses is not so much determined by the photographic technique as by personal choice. The same landscape can be recorded in many different ways. Some photographers like to concentrate on patterns, lines, shapes, and small areas that require long lenses. Others like to enhance the space, the relationship between close and far, with wide angles. For a spectacular presentation of the outdoor space, a panoramic camera can be used.

A good lens shade and an R 1.5 or 81A filter when photographing shaded areas on color film are the only necessary items. Camera weight

Nature photography calls for the SLR camera type that allows accurate framing and focusing at all distances and with all lenses and close-up accessories. Photography by Ernst Wildi.

and ease of method of carrying are important considerations if much walking or hiking is to be done.

CREATIVE EXPERIMENTING

There are hundreds of ways to experiment with cameras and create images in black and white or color that are different from the way we see things with our eyes. For most experimenting, an SLR camera is a must. The rest of the equipment depends on the individual purpose. The more interchangeable components the camera has and the wider the choice of accessories, the greater are the possibilities. Almost regardless of what you try to do, a Polaroid magazine will be the most valuable accessory because it provides the only way to see the effect and results.

Most medium format cameras are excellent for special applications as well as for news and documentary coverage. Fast hand-held photography even with larger lenses is possible. The larger negative offers great possibilities to crop into the important part of the negative.

COPYING

Photographing documents requires the utmost in corner-to-corner quality. A flat field lens with high acutance and corrected to provide the best image quality at close distances is the best choice. Camera alignment so the film plane is parallel to the copy is vital.

CHAPTER 20

Maintaining equipment and materials

Keeping equipment clean is better than cleaning it. Keep all equipment away from dust and dirt whenever possible. Store each item in its case or box, and keep the cases clean by vacuuming them frequently. When a camera is stored or carried without a lens or magazine, the inside of the camera is completely exposed. Fit protective covers on the lens mount and the back, or store and carry them with lens and magazine attached.

CARRYING CASES

Cases are the best means to protect the camera equipment. For shipping equipment and placing it on planes in the baggage compartment, only metal or fiber shipping cases with partitions for the various items should be considered. Additional padding should be placed in each compartment so the items cannot move.

If only one camera is carried, an ever-ready case may be the choice. They are popular for 35 mm cameras but have never enjoyed the same popularity with medium format cameras. Medium format cameras are not so much carried around the neck as are 35s. Most photographers prefer to hang this camera over the shoulder or carry it with the neck strap or camera grip in the hand. An ever-ready case can offer protection to the camera, but the time-consuming process of opening and closing the case outweighs its advantage for many.

Larger shoulder cases that hold the camera and additional lenses and accessories are popular and practical. Try to find a case that holds all the items that you normally need and that holds the camera complete with the normally used items (lenses, lens shade, film magazines, viewfinder, etc.). It is too time-consuming and inconvenient to assemble camera components every time the camera is needed.

Consider the case that you normally carry not just for protecting the equipment but to make photography more enjoyable. It is easy to miss a shot because the necessary equipment cannot be found when needed in a hurry. The case should be arranged so each item can be stored in an orderly fashion and found instantly when needed. It is not likely that a case as it comes from the factory meets all requirements. Cases need to be a compromise since almost every photographer has a different assortment of cameras, lenses, and accessories. It is usually possible to move and add separators, partitions, straps, or whatever else may be necessary to have a neat arrangement.

The case may be a shoulder type or suitcase style. Suitcases must be placed down; shoulder cases may allow you to remove camera and lenses while hanging over the shoulder. You may want to consider both: a metal or fiber suitcase type to transport everything from location to location and a shoulder case to carry items for the next shot.

CLEANING THE CAMERA

Blow dust from small crevices with compressed air using a small syringe or a similar item. Take great care when dusting the mirror, viewing screen, or finders. Do not touch the focal plane curtains. Never use canned air; it is usually very cold and results in condensation, and the propellant agent may leave an oily residue. Cleaning the film magazines or film channel is most important. Focusing screens may be plastic or glass and need special treatment (see chapter 9).

Polaroid Film Magazine

The developing mechanism under the magazine should be cleaned with a damp cloth after each film pack has been used because chemical residue tends to accumulate on the rollers and may cause problems. If the magazine has a glass plate, clean it as you would a lens, especially when using negative-positive film. Dust marks on the negative may be very objectionable when the negative is enlarged.

Cleaning Lenses

All antireflection coatings are relatively hard but can be scratched by grit and other dirt on the lens surface. Before rubbing the surface of any lens with a tissue, blow away all loose particles of dust. Then use a soft brush, such as a special lens brush.

To remove a fingerprint, breathe on the surface and quickly wipe it with a soft tissue. Then check to see if the surface is thoroughly clean by breathing on it once again. If the fingerprint has gone, the condensation will form an even deposit without spots and will evaporate gradually and evenly. If the element is still dirty, repeat the process with a drop or two of lens cleaning fluid on a lens tissue. Never put the fluid directly on the lens as it may find its way into the lens mount. Use lens cleaning fluid sparingly.

Fungus

When camera equipment is used in tropical climates or where humidity is high, clouding of glass surfaces, lenses, prisms, and filters often occurs. This is caused by a microscopically fine network of fungi attacking the polished surface by etching its pattern into the glass. Removing the fungus does not solve the problem.

Fungi develops at humidities of 80 percent or more, but relative humidity decreases as the air temperature increases; therefore, humidity can be decreased by heating the air surrounding the camera equipment. For example, keep the camera in the sun or in circulating air; do not enclose it in an equipment bag or box without using a desiccant. Direct exposure to sunlight is very favorable. Do not store equipment in cupboards or drawers that are dark and without air circulation. Do not cover cameras and lenses with plastic bags or hoods, which limit air circulation. If possible, have a fan blowing air on the equipment.

Nutritive substances, grease, and dust can also help fungi to develop. It is of paramount importance that all equipment be cleaned thoroughly after use; especially fingerprints, grease, and dust must be removed from all glass surfaces. Pay special attention to lens mounts, eyepieces, mirrors, and the interior of the camera.

Humidity in small areas can be reduced with desiccants. Silica gel, usually in the form of small crystals in a dust-proof bag, is best for this purpose. Place the bag inside camera cases or containers, which should be airtight. Choose indicator gel that changes color from blue to pink when it reaches saturation point and needs regeneration. To regenerate, heat it at 120–150°C (250–300°F) for about 12 hrs.

Optical surfaces covered with a slight film of fungus should be cleaned not with alcohol but with a special fungus cleaner. It is applied with cotton, if necessary using a new piece of cotton each time. If fungus remains visible on the glass, return the equipment for service.

COLD WEATHER PHOTOGRAPHY

Photography in cold weather is not only unpleasant for the photographer but also brings up problems in camera and battery operation that do not exist at normal temperatures. To make the work pleasant, dress properly and wear gloves that allow you to operate all the important camera controls with gloves on.

Simplify camera operation as much as possible. Remove any unnecessary accessories that cannot be operated with gloves or add accessories that allow easier operation. Preload film magazines before you go in the cold if possible. Make certain that you have the ground-glass screens you want to use in the camera. Changing screens is impossible without removing gloves.

Mounting cameras on tripods with tripod screws can be a frustrating experience in the cold. You will appreciate a tripod coupling. Once you are out in the cold, avoid touching unpainted metal surfaces with ungloved hands or your face or lips because the skin will stick to the metal. Do not breathe on lenses; the condensation will freeze, perhaps instantly, and is very difficult to remove.

Condensation also occurs when cold equipment is brought into a warm room. This means that the chilled camera cannot be used indoors until its temperature equals that of the surroundings. A camera with condensation also cannot be taken out into the cold until the condensation has evaporated. If you do, the condensation will freeze. This can be very serious because condensation may also cover the camera and lens mechanism inside and may freeze up the entire camera and lens operation. Interior camera parts may also start to rust. It is possible to avoid this problem by placing the camera in an airtight plastic bag and squeezing out the air before entering a heated room from the cold.

Extreme cold causes leather and rubber to become brittle. A wax leather dressing of good quality should be rubbed into carrying cases and leather-covered cameras to prevent the absorption of moisture. Rubber should be eliminated whenever possible.

Equipment should be cool before it is taken out in a blizzard; otherwise the snow will melt when it hits the warm camera and lens and then freeze, covering the equipment with ice.

The viscosity of lubricants increases (lubricants thicken) as the temperature declines. Consequently in cold weather, the camera mechanism operates more sluggishly, and mechanical reaction time increases. Mechanical lens shutters are the first affected, with shutter speeds lengthening; for example, 1/4 sec becomes effectively 1/2 sec, especially if the lubricant in the lens and shutter is old and dirty. You will get better shutter operation if the lenses and shutters have been cleaned and lubricated recently. Another suggestion is to operate all the shutter speeds a few times with the magazine removed or without film in the camera, which may get the lubricant working. If the shutter speeds still appear too long, set the lens to a higher shutter speed. Electronically controlled shutters are less affected, but keep in mind that the opening and closing of the shutter is still a mechanical operation.

Camera and lens manufacturers do not publicize specific temperatures at which equipment is guaranteed to work because temperature is only one aspect that can affect operation. Others equally important are the wind-chill factor, humidity, the length of time equipment is exposed, and the amount of time that has elapsed since the equipment was cleaned and lubricated. The camera manufacturer or a qualified service station may be able to lubricate the camera and lenses with special cold weather lubricants. Although this measure is no guarantee against malfunctions, the use of special cold weather lubricants does reduce some risk factors. On return to normal conditions, it is imperative to relubricate the equipment with a standard lubricant; otherwise camera wear will be greatly accelerated since cold weather lubricants often have a low viscosity, are volatile, and quickly work their way out of the mechanism at ordinary temperatures.

All batteries lose efficiency at low temperatures, and fresh batteries may become too weak to operate the equipment after only a little use. Keep the batteries in a warm place, and do not put them into the camera until they are needed if that is possible and practical. Always carry a spare set and keep them warm (perhaps in a pocket) until they have to be used.

To avoid the effects of static electricity discharge with film and because it becomes brittle at very low temperatures, move the film slowly from frame to frame. Also move the film slowly up to frame 1 and when taking up the paper trailer at the end of the roll. Do not leave the film in the camera longer than necessary. It may dry out and break when it is used again. It is better to remove a partially exposed roll and reload the camera with a new roll when the camera is used again.

CARING FOR FILM

Photographic films are perishable products and must be treated and stored properly if they are to produce high-quality images. This applies especially to color materials.

All films have an expiration date printed on the box. You can expect that the quality will be satisfactory up to that time provided the film has been stored under the recommended conditions. With black-and-white films, temperature and humidity requirements are not very stringent, but no films should ever be exposed to high temperatures and humidities over extended periods.

When traveling, keep films out of glove compartments and in shaded areas, if possible in an insulated picnic bag or chest. Dry ice can be used to keep the film cool. Keep film in air-conditioned rooms whenever possible.

Amateur and Professional Films

Color shifts slightly as films mature. Amateur color films are manufactured so they produce correct color after they have been stored at room temperature for a certain time. This time has been established from surveys determining the average time a film lies on the dealer's shelf, before the customer actually uses it.

When you buy a roll of amateur film, you can never be certain how long and under what conditions it has been stored; thus color variations must be expected. Professional color films are made to give optimum quality results close to the time the film is manufactured. To maintain that quality, the films must be stored under refrigeration. A good temperature is 13°C (55°F) or lower. These films also must be protected from humidity—no problem as long as they are left in the foil package. Leave them in there as long as possible, taking them out of the foil only about 1/2 to 1 hr before they are used in order to bring them up to room temperature without condensation. Packages of sealed film that have not been opened can be placed back in the refrigerator or freezer for further storage.

Care after Exposure

Exposed color film should be processed as soon as possible. In warm weather, store the developed film in a refrigerator or an air-conditioned room until it can be shipped or delivered to a laboratory for developing. If such storage is not possible, silica gel should be added to a sealed film container when the humidity goes above 60 percent.

X-Rays

In addition to heat and humidity, fresh and exposed film can be damaged by X-rays and industrial gases, motor exhaust fumes, and vapors from paints, solvents, cleaners, and mothballs. Keep films away from X-rays, radium, or other radioactive materials.

The X-ray equipment used at airports is not likely to produce any visible effect on normal speed (up to 100 ASA) films during a one-time inspection, but multiple exposure of the same film to airport X-ray equipment is not advisable, especially since the dosage of X-rays of the machine varies from one country to another. Request hand inspection, especially with 1000 ASA film, which most security officials will honor if the inspection is easy.

Storing Photographs and Slides

Color films   All dyes undergo changes over extended periods of time. This applies to the dyes in color negative and transparency film. The causes are light, moisture, and heat. Faulty processing can also play a part in the deterioration. Before storing any photographic material, remove fingerprints, dirt, and dust, which can contain chemicals or fungus spores that might harm a photographic image. Store all color films in complete darkness when not in use. Color negatives are exposed to light mainly when viewing them on light boxes and during the printing process. Do not leave them on light boxes over long periods of time. Always use a heat-absorbing glass in the enlarger.

Transparencies   Transparencies are exposed to light when they are viewed and exposed to strong light and heat in the projector. Slides made on color films can be projected many times before a noticeable change takes place; nevertheless, originals should not be used for continuous projection. Use duplicates for this purpose so a damaged or faded slide can easily be replaced. A slide should not be left in the light and heat of the projector lamp for longer than 1 min. For setup purposes, especially when two or more projectors must be lined up, which can be time-consuming, use scrap slides or special registration slides rather than the slides that will be presented.

Metal is preferred over wood or plastic as a storage container material. A temperature of 21°C (70°F) and relative humidity not exceeding 40 percent is good for general storage.

Long-Term Storage

A temperature of − 18°C (0°F) and a relative humidity of 30 to 35 percent is excellent for negative and transparency films. Virtually no dye changes occur at these conditions. The films must be stored in special envelopes.

COLOR PRINTS

The dyes in color prints are equally affected by light, heat, and moisture, although the extent varies somewhat among color materials. What has been said about film also applies to color prints. Prints not in use should be stored in a dark place. Albums are good for easy access and long-term storage because they automatically provide dark storage. Keep the album at room temperature and normal humidity. Bookshelves are better than drawers, which are often contaminated. Check with the album manufacturer that all parts of the album are suitable for long-term storage. Temperature should be below 24°C (75°F) and relative humidity 50 percent or less. Prints for storage should be unmounted if possible. Sunlight or fluorescent lights produce fading in prints, so be prepared to make a new print after some years—no problem if the negative is stored properly. Do not make the lights stronger than necessary, and turn them on only when needed. Subdued incandescent illumination (regular roomlight) is best.

Cleaning

Light dust can be removed from color films with a clean, dry, camel's hair brush. Light fingerprints or oily smudges can be removed by applying film cleaner sparingly on a plush pad or wad of cotton. If you feel that your color films need protection from fingerprints, light scratches, and fungus growth, apply a film lacquer or equivalent as directed on the label. A lacquered surface is more readily cleaned. For detailed recommendations, consult the film or paper manufacturer.

Filing

Negatives and transparencies that are used often should be filed where they can be found easily. For storage purposes, roll films are best cut in strips of three or four and stored in individual sleeved envelopes. The strips are convenient to handle for viewing, printing, and enlarging.

Positive images can be identified and located more easily than negatives. For most photographers, therefore, the best filing method is done with proofsheets. Make a contact proofsheet from each roll and file the proofsheet together with the negatives in a ringbinder or filing cabinet. Because proofsheet and negatives are together, no special identification marks are needed on the negatives or sleeves.

Negatives can be stored according to subject, location, client, job number, department, year, or whatever else is useful. If you loan out a negative, keep a record, perhaps on the page of the missing negative. After you have used a negative, make certain it goes back in the right place. A misfiled negative may be as bad as one that is lost.

Strips of unmounted transparencies can be filed like negatives. Individual mounted slides are filed in properly identified negative envelopes.

You probably want to leave the cardboard- or glass-mounted slides that are used often in the same sequence as for projection, in the slide trays, or in storage boxes from where they can be switched instantly into the trays. Such boxes are available for 2 1/4 in. square slides. For slides that are never or seldom used for projection, plastic sheets are convenient. They hold twelve 2 1/4 in. square slides and fit into large ringbinders or filing cabinets. Being made of translucent plastic, the sheet is simply held in front of the light box.

Index

Acutance, 114
Aerial photography, 54, 64, 325
Angle of view, 103–105
Aperture, 108
 exposure and, 179–180
 flash and, 218
 numbers with, 179
Architectural photography, 54, 325
Area coverage, 106–108
Automatic flash, 222–225

Backgrounds
 exposure meters and, 201–202
 lenses and, 135–136
Barrel distortion, 123
Batteries
 flash, 216
 motor drive, 255, 260–262
Beattie cameras, 61
Beauty photography, 326–327
Bellows, 121, 275, 278, 288–290
Bird photography, 321
Black-and-white film, 77–80
 filters and, 241–242
 instant, 93
Blurred motion effect, 154
Bounced lighting, 228–229
Bracketing, 200–201
Brightness range, 202–203
Bronica cameras, 61

Cable remote operation, 258
Calumet cameras, 64
Camera clamps, 272
Camera types, 43–68
 panoramic, 56–58

press, 58
rangefinders, 52–53
single lens reflex (SLR), 43–49
studio, 59
twin lens reflex (TLR), 49–52
view, 58–59
wide angle, 54–56
Carrying cases, 335–336
Child photography, 326
Clamps, camera, 272
Cleaning and maintenance, 335–342
 camera cleaning, 336–337
 carrying cases, 335–336
 filters, 254
 glass slides, 309
 lenses, 336–337
 screens, 163
 viewfinders, 171
Clear glass screens, 162
Close-up photography, 283–297, 322
 camera used with, 293–294
 depth of field and, 290–292
 exposure in, 292–294
 extension tubes and bellows with,
  288–290
 focusing in, 294
 lenses for, 283–284
 magnification with, 284–285
 partial close-up lenses with, 287–288
 proxar lenses and, 285–287
 reversing lenses with, 284
 slide copying and, 294–297
 zoom lenses and, 127–128
Coatings
 filters, 254
 lenses, 118–119
Cold weather photography, 337–339
Color negative film, 80–82
Color prism, 253
Color transparency film, 82–83

Command unit, 260
Commercial photography, 328
Composing the image, 175–179
Conversion filters, 245
Copying, 299–305, 333
    camera alignment in, 299–300
    exposure in, 304
    filters in, 301
    final preparation in, 304–305
    focusing in, 300
    lenses used in, 300
    lighting in, 301–304
Copy stand, 304
Correction lenses with viewfinder
    added, 170–171
    built-in, 169–170
Covering power, 108
Creative experimenting, 332
Cropping, 19–20
    6 × 4.5 cm, 34–35
    6 × 9 cm, 39–40
Cross-screens, 253

Decamired filter system, 246–247
Depth of field, 144–147, 172–173
    close-up photography and, 290–292
    extended control of, 276–277
Diaphragm, 149
Diffraction gratings, 253
Diffusion filters, 251–252
Distortion, lens, 123–125
Double and multiple exposures, 204–211
    camera operation and, 210–211
    close-up photography and, 296
    ghost images in, 206
    sandwiches and, 208–211
    split-screen effects and, 207–208
    superimposed subjects in, 205–206
    superimposed titles in, 206–207

Electronic flash, *see* Flash
Enlarging
    black-and-white film, 80
    comparing formats for, 38
    2¼ × 2¼ in. square for, 29
Exacta cameras, 62
Exposure, 23, 179–211
    aperture and, 179–180
    bracketing and, 200–201
    close-up photography and, 292–293

copying and, 304
double and multiple, 204–211
estimating lens settings for, 183
film sensitivity and, 182–183
flash and, 226–228
flesh tone readings and, 197
gray card and, 195–196, 201–202
meters for, 184–195, 201–202
palm readings and, 197
shutter speed and, 180
special effects accessories for, 201
subject brightness range and, 202–203
typical subjects and measuring
    methods for, 203–204
Exposure meters, 184–195
    built-in measuring method with, 185–
    186
    cells with, 184
    incident light and, 193
    lens settings and, 191–192
    light levels with, 189–191
    reflected light and, 193–194
    shutter speed priority and, 189
    spotmeters and, 194–195
    transfering built-in reading with, 186–
    188
    TTL, 226–227
Exposure value (EV), 180–182
Extension tubes, 288–290

Fashion photography, 326–327
Fast lenses, 180
Fill-in automatic flash, 232
Fill-in manual flash, 233–234
Film, 77–100
    black-and-white, 77–80
    caring for, 339–341
    changing, 20–21
    color negative, 80–82
    color transparency, 82–83
    copying and, 300
    exposure and sensitivity of, 182–183,
    188
    instant, 21, 88–95
    loading, 94–99
    magazine interchangeability and, 20–
    21
    operating signals with, 99–100
    roll, 83–87
    sheetfilm, 87–88
    sizes of, *see* Sizes
Film roll, 83–87

long roll, 85–87
120 roll, 84
220 roll, 84–85
Filters, 239–254
  black-and-white photography with,
    241–242
  close-up photography and, 296
  coating of, 254
  color negative film and, 81–82
  color quality of light and, 244–245
  combining, 242
  copying and, 301
  decamired system, 246–247
  diffusion, 251–252
  exposure increase and, 242–243
  flash use and, 219
  fluorescent lights and, 247
  haze penetration and, 243–244
  infrared photography and, 249
  lenses and, 128
  light balance and, 245
  maintenance of, 254
  neutral density, 239–241
  partial filtering with, 249–251
  polarizing, 247–249
  position of, 254
  as protection for lens, 239
  quality of, 253–254
  special effects and, 252–253
Fine line focusing screen, 159
Fine matte screen, 159
Fish-eye lenses, 128, 143–144
Flash, 213–237
  as accent light, 236–237
  aperture with, 218
  automatic, 222–225
  batteries with, 216
  covering power of, 217
  daylight combined with, 230–231
  energy-saving circuits with, 225–226
  exposure with, 226–228
  fill-in with, 232, 233–234
  filters and, 219
  firing failures with, 215
  focal plane shutters and, 22, 70–71
  ghost images with, 221–222
  indirect and bounced flash, 228–229
  indirect light and, 229–230
  lens shutters and, 74–75
  lighting ratio and, 233
  light output and guide numbers with,
    216–217
  meters with, 226
  modeling lights with, 222

  portable units with, 214–215
  power ratio with, 218–219
  ready light with, 215–216
  shutter speed and, 219–221
  size of, 216
  slave units with, 214
  surrounding area and changes in,
    234–236
  synchronization of, 213–214
Floating lens element, 110–111
Fluorescent lights, 247
Fluorescent photography, 328–329
Fluoride elements, 117–118
Focal lengths, 102–103, 129
Focal plane shutters, 21–22, 69–73
  design of, 70
  distortion with, 71
  flash synchronization with, 70–71
  operating considerations with, 76
  single lens reflex camera, 43–44
  speed of, 72, 73
  vibration with, 72
Fog filters, 253
Foreshortening, 135
Format
  comparison of, 26–27
  importance of, 25
  points to consider, 25–28
  selecting, 25–38
  2¼ × 2¼ in. square, 28–34
45° finders, 167–168
Frame viewfinders, 173–174
Freezing action, 149–151
ƒ stops, 179–180
Fuji cameras, 62
Fungus, 337

Ghost images, 206, 221–222
Glass slide mounts, 307–309
Gray card, 195–196, 201–202
Grid patterns on screen, 162–163
Ground-glass screen, 17–18
  microprism with, 161
  plain, 159
  split image with, 160–161
  2¼ × 2¼ in. square camera with, 30
  using, 158–159
Guide numbers with flashes, 216–217

Hand-held photography, 264–266
Hasselblad cameras, 56, 62–64
Haze, and filters, 242–243

High magnification photography, 322–325
Historical overview, 1–11
Hyperfocal distance, 147

Identification of slides, 309
Image, 155–177
  camera steadiness and, 267–268
  composing, 175–179
  depth of field and, 172–173
  evaluation of, 15–17
  frame and sports viewfinders and, 173–174
  lenses and quality of, 116–117
  parallax and, 155
  quality of, 263–273
  seeing, as it appears on film, 171–172
  sharpness of, 13–15, 38–39
  what not seen with, 172
  zoom lenses and, 127
Indirect lighting, 229–230
Industrial photography, 330
Infrared photography, 249, 329
Instant film, 88–95
  care of, 91–92
  exposure for, 90–91
  shutter speeds and, 89–90
Instant photography, 21
Intervalometer, 259
Inverted telephoto lenses, 109

Leaf shutters, 22, 58
Lenses, 101–128
  aberrations with, 113–116
  angle of view with, 103–105
  area coverage with, 106–108
  backgrounds and, 135–136, 148
  cleaning, 336–337
  close-up photography with, 283–284
  color correction and, 117–118
  color rendition and, 122
  control of, 140
  cost of, 101
  covering power of, 108
  depth of field with, 144–147
  distortion with, 123–125
  filters with, 128, 239
  fish-eye, 128, 143–144
  floating lens element with, 110–111
  focal length and, 102–103

foreground sharpness and, 148–149
foreshortening with, 135
hyperfocal distance and, 147
image quality with, 116–117
image viewing through, 171–174
long telephoto, 108
maximum aperture with, 108
multicoating of, 118–119
names of, 111
partial close-up, 287–288
perspective control (PC), 124–125, 280–281
proxar, 285–287
rangefinders, 54
relative illuminance with, 122
retrofocus, 109–110
reversing, 284
shades for, 119–121
single lens reflex (SLR) camera, 48–49
teleextenders with, 111–112
true telephoto, 109
twin lens reflex (TLR), 52
using, 129–154
verticals and, 136–140
viewing distance with, 131–135
wide angle, 54–56
zoom, 126–128, 140–142
Lens shutters, 73–75
  design of, 73–74
  electronic, 75
  exposure accuracy of, 75
  flash synchronization with, 74–75
  prereleasing cameras with, 74
  single lens reflex (SLR) camera, 44, 73
Leveling the camera, 174–175
Light ratios, 202
Linhof cameras, 64
Loading film, 94–99
Long roll film, 85–87

Macrolenses, 283
Magazines
  loading with, 97–98
  rotatable, 98–99
Magnification, with close-up photography, 284–285, 322–325
Maintenance, *see* Cleaning and maintenance
Makroflash units, 228
Mamiya cameras, 64–65
Manufacturers, 59–68
Medical photography, 328

Meters
    exposure, *see* Exposure meters
    flash, 226
MFT diagrams, 116
Microprism, 161
Mirror lock-up, 268
Modeling lights, 222
Monopods, 272–273
Motor drive, 255–262
    AC operation of, 262
    batteries with, 260–262
    benefits and applications of, 256–259
    intervalometer and, 259
    multiple camera operation and, 259–
        260
    winders versus, 255–256
Multicoated filters, 254
Multicoated lenses, 118–119
Multiple camera operation, 259–260
Multiple exposures, *see* Double and
        multiple exposures
Multiprisms, 252–253

Nature photography, 321–322
Neutral density filters, 239–241
Newton rings, 308–309

Operating signals, and film, 99–100
Outdoor photography, 331–332

Palm readings, 197
Panoramic cameras, 40–41, 56–58
    Fuji models of, 62
    lenses on, 56–57
    Linhof models of, 64
    35 mm film with, 57–58
Parallax error, 51, 155
Partial close-up lenses, 287–288
Partial filters, 249–251
Pentax cameras, 65–66
Perspective, 130–131
Perspective control (PC) lenses, 124–125,
        147, 280–281
Photometric system, 246
Pincushion distortion, 123
Plaubel cameras, 66
Polarizing filters, 247–249
Polaroid film, 21, 91, 93–94, 336; *see
    also* Instant film

Portrait photography, 327
Prerelease, 268
Press cameras, 58, 59
    Calumet model of, 64
    Mamiya models of, 65
Press photography, 325–326
Proxar lenses, 285–287

Rangefinders, 53–54
    advantages of, 53, 54
    focusing with, 156
    Fuji models of, 62
    lenses on, 54
    Plaubel models of, 66
    shape of, 53
Remote operation, 256, 258–259
Retrofocus lenses, 109–110
Reversing lenses, 284
Ring lights, 227–228
Rolleiflex cameras, 67

Screens, 158–163
    cleaning, 163
    clear glass, 162
    combination focusing, 161–162
    fine line focusing, 159
    fine matte, 159
    grid patterns on, 162–163
    ground-glass, 158–159, 161
    microprism with, 161
    plain ground-glass, 159
    split image with, 160–161
Screws, tripod, 272
Self-timing shutters, 76
Shades, lens, 119–121, 128
Sharpness of image, 13–15, 38–39
Sheetfilm, 87–88
Shutters, 21–22, 69–76
    action and speed of, 149–154
    blurred motion effect with, 154
    flash use and, 219–221
    focal plane, 21–22, 69–73
    following moving subjects with, 151–
        154
    freezing action with, 149–151
    image seen with, 156–158
    instant film and, 89–90
    leaf, 22
    lens, 73–75
    operating considerations with, 75–76

self-timers with, 76
single lens reflex camera, 43–45
Sinar cameras, 67
Single lens reflex (SLR) cameras, 43–49
    Bronica models of, 61
    close-up photography and, 293–294
    convenience features of, 47
    design of, 49
    Exacta model of, 62
    film changing in, 20
    Hasselblad models, 62
    image seen in, 171–172
    lenses on, 48–49, 73
    Mamiya models of, 64–65
    Pentax models of, 65–66
    Rolleiflex models of, 67
    rotating film magazine in, 47
    shutters and mirrors with, 43–45
    size and shape of, 46–47
    2¼ × 2¼ in. square with, 29
    viewing on, 45–46
    35 mm in, 41
Sizes, 25–41
    comparing, 38
    image sharpness and, 38–39
    panoramic, 40–41
    2¼ × 2¼ in. square, 28–34
    2¼ × 2¾ in. (6 × 7 cm), 37–38, 39
    6 × 4.5 cm, 34–35
    6 × 9 cm, 39–40
    40 × 40 mm, 35–37
    35 mm, 13, 15, 21, 22–23, 41
    70 mm, 22, 85–87
Slave flash units, 214
Slide projectors, 310–314
Slides, 317–320
    close-up photography and, 294–297
    color transparency film and, 82–83
    legibility of artwork in, 314–315
    mounting, 307–309
    panoramic, 41
    sound combined with, 315–320
    storing, 340–341
    superslides (40 × 40 cm), 35–37
    2¼ × 2¼ in square, 32–34
    2¼ × 2¾ in (6 × 7), 37–38
    6 × 4.5 cm, 35
    6 × 9 cm, 40
SLR camera, *see* Single lens reflex (SLR)
        camera
Space photography, 330
Special effects accessories, 201, 252–253
Speed of the lens, 180
Spirit level, 55–56

Split image screen, 160–161
Split-screen effects, 207–208
Sports photography, 327–328
Sports viewfinders, 173–174
Spotmeters, 194–195
Square cameras (2¼ × 2¼ in), 28–34
    prints with, 31–32, 33
    slides with, 32–34
    using, 29–31
Starfilters, 253
Studio cameras, 59
Superimposed subjects, 205–206
Superimposed titles, 206–207
Superslides (40 × 40 mm), 35–37
    projecting, 35–36, 310
    shooting, 36–37

Table tripods, 272
Teleextenders, 111–112
Telephoto lens
    at close range, 108
    inverted, 109
    perspective with, 131
    true, 109
Toyo cameras, 67
TTL metering, 226–227
Tripod, 267, 269–272
    center post, 269–271
    coupling and, 271
    head of, 271
    screws with, 272
    selecting, 269
    table, 272
Twin lens reflex (TLR) cameras, 49–52
    advantages of, 49
    image seen with, 156–158
    lenses on, 52
    Mamiya models of, 65
    parallax with, 51, 155
    Rolleiflex models of, 67
    shape of, 51
    2¼ × 2¼ in. square with, 29
    viewing on, 50–51
    Yashica models of, 68

Ultraviolet (UV) filters, 242–243
Ultraviolet photography, 328
Underwater photography, 330

Verticals, and lenses, 136–140
Video displays, 329–330
View cameras, 58–59
    Linhof models of, 64
    medium format, 277–279
    Sinar models of, 67
    Toyo models of, 67
Viewfinders, 163–171
    accurate focusing and, 169
    camera steadiness and, 164–165
    cleaning, 171
    diopter correction eyepieces with,
        169–170
    diopter correction lenses with, 170–
        171
    film format and, 165
    45° finders, 167–168
    frame or sports, 173–174
    prism versus waist-level, 165–167
    top viewing with, 168
Viewing distance, 131–135
    chart for, 133
    formula for determining, 132

Waist-level finders, 18
    prism finders versus, 165–167
    2¼ × 2¼ in. square camera with, 31
Wedding photography, 32, 326
Wide angle cameras, 54–56
    distortion with, 125
    Hasselblad models, 56, 63–64
    lens with, 54–56
    perspective with, 131
    Plaubel models of, 66
    2¼ × 2¼ in. square with, 29
Wildlife photography, 321
Wireless remote operation, 258–259

X-rays, and film, 340

Yashica cameras, 68

Zoom lenses, 126–128, 140–142